NIALL STOKES

U2

THE STORIES BEHIND EVERY U2 SONG

CARLTON
BOOKS

Dedicated to Bill Graham, 1951-1996.

THIS IS A CARLTON BOOK

Text copyright © Niall Stokes 1997, 2001, 2005, 2009
Design copyright © Carlton Books Limited 1997, 2001, 2005, 2009

First published in 1997 by Carlton Books Limited
This edition published by Carlton Books Limited 2009

ISBN 978 1 84732 287 6

Managing Art Director: Lucy Coley
Design: Barbara Zuñiga
Executive editor: Rod Green
Editor: Ian Gittins
Picture research: Paul Langan
Production: Claire Hayward

Printed and bound in China

The publishers would like to thank the following sources for their kind permission to reproduce the pictures in this book.

All Action: /Tony Kelly; /Jim Steele
Camera Press
Anton Corbijn: © U2 Limited
Corbis: /Bettmann; /Everett; /Dave Hunt/epa: 165; /Justin Lane/epa: 176-177; /Reuters; /UPI
Caroline Forbes
Amy Garvey: /Hugo McGuinness
Getty Images: /Mark Allan/Wirelmage: 172; /Carlo Allegri; /Finn Costello/Redferns; /Pete Cronin/Redferns: 158; /Gems/Redferns: 156; /Dave Hogan: 152, 160; /Dave Hogan/distributed by Getty Images on behalf of the Band Aid Charitable Fund: 162; /Bob King/Redferns; /Hayley Madden/Redferns: 149; /Kevin Mazur/Wirelmage: 171; /David Redfern/Redferns; /Kerstin Rodgers/Redferns; /Ebet Roberts/Redferns; /John Shearer/WireImage: 169; /Barbara Steinwehe/Redferns; /Bob Willoughby/Redferns
Anja Grabert: © U2 Limited
Greg Evans International
Colm Henry
Hot Press
London Features International: /Adrian Boot; /Andy Catlin; / Kevin Cummins; /Nick Elgar; /Steve Granitz; /Gie Knaeps; / Colin Mason; /Kevin Mazur; /Andy Phillips; /Derek Ridgers; / Tom Sheehan; /Van Tine
Mansell Collection
Mary Evans Picture Library
Pacemaker Press
Pictorial Press: /Patrick Lyttle; /Jeffrey Mayer; /William Rutter
Barry Plummer
Popperfoto
Press Association Images: /Julien Behal: 166; /Jeffrey R. Staab
Landov: 174
Retna: /Stephen L Davis; /Steve Double; /Photofest; /Clemen Rikken; /Paul Slattery; /David Tonge; /Theodore Wood
Rex Features: /P. Bertini; /Andre Csillag; /Ilpo Musto: 154; / Kamenko Pajic; /PF/Keystone USA; /Simon Roberts; /Sipa Press: 150; /Jacques Witt
S.I.N.: /Peter Anderson; /David Corio; /Hayley Madden; / Kieron Murphy; /Ilpo Musto; /Katia Natola; /Ian Tilton; / Virginia Turbett
Stephane Sednaoui

Special thanks are due to Colm Henry

Every effort has been made to acknowledge correctly and contact the source and/or copyright holder of each picture and Carlton Books Limited apologises for any unintentional errors or omissions, which will be, corrected in future editio of this book.

CONTENTS

INTRODUCTION

A book is a mysterious object, I said, and once it floats around the world, anything can happen. All kinds of mischief can be caused, and there's not a damned thing you can do about it. For better or worse, it's completely out of your control."

Paul Auster, *Leviathan*, 1992

As with books, so with songs…

Writing a book about the stories behind U2's songs, it seemed necessary to live, sleep and eat the music. You keep looking for extra clues, something you might have missed. Some songs begin to grow, the more you listen. Others fade. But some just keep on growing till you know you're never going to get them out of your head. Ever. "*Take my hand,*" you sing, "*you know I'll be there if you can, I'll cross the sky for your love.*" And people look at you. You hadn't even realised you were singing.

It's one of the standard questions nearly every cub rock reporter asks, with all solemnity, as if it's never been asked before: how do you write your songs? Bono calls it songwriting by accident and it describes the process pretty well. But however the songs are written, more often than not over the past nearly 30 years, the end results have been glorious.

U2 have developed in every imaginable way. *Boy* was a brilliant, original, debut album, which had its share of insights, but no one could claim that the lyrics were its strongest suit. Travelling, within six years, from there to the maturity of *The Joshua Tree* was an extraordinary achievement.

But even then, in an industry where so many artists who consider themselves to have arrived are content to rest on their laurels, U2 refused to allow themselves to stagnate. *Achtung Baby*, released in 1991, was their second acknowledged masterpiece and also introduced a new phase for them aesthetically and intellectually. Broadly speaking, *The Joshua Tree* and *Rattle and Hum* had been direct, emotional and heartfelt. In contrast, Achtung Baby was oblique, coded and elusive, and the follow-up *Zooropa* continued in the same vein.

Would the remaining
passengers for
Zoo Airlines flight
U2 please board
immediately…

There were reasons for this shift other than the ever-present desire to make great records. It had to do with the fact that, with *The Joshua Tree*, U2 became one of the most successful rock groups of all time. And with that success came a whole lot of baggage. Suddenly U2 found that they were a target for the tabloids. *Rattle and Hum* was widely panned. And, in some quarters, their commitment in itself became a cause of ridicule. Against that backdrop, on the surface at least, *Achtung Baby* reflected a strategy to conceal rather than reveal. It was a deliberate attempt to step out of the mainstream, to challenge audiences and to confound critics.

With *Achtung Baby*, with the *Zoo TV* tour that followed it, and with *Zooropa*, U2 became more playful and experimental. The group's sense of humour was discernible in their music for the first time. Sometimes misunderstood, *Pop* continued in the same vein. But for *All That You Can't Leave Behind* and *How To Dismantle An Atomic Bomb*, the band released themselves again from the need to run everything through the hip-ometer – and made music that was no less hip at all as a result. This tendency continued with their last release to date, 2009's *No Line On The Horizon*.

They say that in love there are no rules. Nor should there be in rock 'n' roll. One of the great things about U2 is their attitude that nothing is sacred in the pursuit of excellence.

It's a fine theory until you attempt to put it into practice; that's where the sheer grinding hard work comes in. But since they first blazed a trail into our hearts towards the end of the '70s, U2 have put in more of that than almost any other band on planet Earth, and they have the songs to prove it.

And the scars.

Niall Stokes

BOY

It was always going to be called *Boy*. "The album cover has been in the back of my mind for two years," Bono explained, just after its release. "There is a feel to it. Holding the cover and listening to the album is perfect."

The title was decided on long before this band began to record. It wasn't a concept album, but there was a strong linking thread running through the songs. U2 were still in their teens when they signed to Island, and *Boy* reflected it unashamedly.

"The songs are autobiographical," Bono stated. In an explosive burst of adolescent energy, they embraced the teenage themes of confusion, longing, faith, anger, loss and burgeoning love in a nakedly emotional way. At the heart of the record was the frantic search for an identity in which all of the band were themselves still immersed.

Having played most of the songs for over two years, U2 probably believed that they knew them thoroughly. It still wasn't an easy album to make. A lot of tough, disciplined work went into getting the rhythm section tight, and Bono had to confront in earnest for the first time the need to finish definitively the band's songs.

Under Steve Lillywhite's sympathetic direction, Boy emerged bright and shiny, all glistening treble, shimmering guitar, exuberant drumming, breathless vocals and urgent bass. It was a lyrical, romantic, spiritual odyssey, which resonated with one particularly marvellous, distinctive quality. Above all, *Boy* was an honest record.

I WILL FOLLOW

I WILL FOLLOW
Written: U2
Length: 3' 36"
Album: *Boy*,
October 1980
**US singles chart
position:** 81

Iris Hewson died on 10 September, 1974, following a brain haemorrhage. It was a terrible twist of fate, coming as it did just after her own father's funeral at the Military Cemetery in Blackhorse Avenue, Dublin. Bono was 14 at the time, and the experience devastated him. Even now, he admits that he finds it difficult to remember what his mother looked like. It is impossible to imagine what he might have become if she had lived.

What we can say is that he was plunged into a period of emotional turmoil, that he began running in 1974 and that he has scarcely stopped since – and that this restlessness has been a powerful motivating force in his work. Bono remembers his adolescence as a time of psychological violence and 'I Will Follow' captures some of the drama of that era, the four walls coming down on top of the song's narrator in an image that captures well the suburban claustrophobia that was returned to, almost obsessively, throughout the first album. But there is something else going on here: a sense of terror and confusion which runs deeper than the common crises of identity from which teenagers suffer.

His friends on Cedarwood Road remember Bono as a kind of stray after his mother died. He'd turn up at Gavin Friday's house one night, and Derek Rowen's the next, just in time for tea. "He was calling around as much to be with my mother as he was to be with me, I have no doubt about that," Gavin recalls now. They fed him and minded him, but he had to return all the same, as twilight fell, to a house inhabited only by men – his father Bob, his brother Norman and himself.

7

Bono felt his mother's death deeply.

In the past, Bono has talked about the song being a sketch about the unconditional love a mother has for a child, but it is clearly more than that. There is a palpable yearning in the lyrics that has much more to do with what a child feels when his mother walks – or is taken – away from him, and the suicidal urge to follow. "A boy tries hard to be a man/His mother takes him by the hand," Bono sings and immediately you know that this is not the stuff of which teenage pop is normally wrought. Opening *Boy*, 'I Will Follow' was a perfectly appropriate statement of intent, signalling that this was an album about teenage confusion and rites of passage, but also – and perhaps more crucially – that there was a restless spirit at work which could never be satisfied with conventional or clichéd answers. Looking back now, with the benefit of both hindsight and experience, it's a song of which Bono clearly remains proud.

"I think it's coming from a very dark place," he says. "Pop music at its best seems to have a duality. Whenever it's one thing or the other it's flat, but if it has two opposing ideas, pulling in different directions, it achieves a different kind of power. 'I Will Follow' has both anger, real anger, and an enormous sense of yearning."

The band's performance was suitably urgent, marking the track down as one that would inevitably be released as a single to coincide with the launch of the album. In particular, The Edge careens in on the kind of treble high that became his trademark. At the time a limited guitar player in conventional terms, he was an original stylist even then. "I knew more what I didn't want to sound like than what I wanted to sound like early on," he said later. "In some ways that's why my playing is so minimal. Play as few notes as you can, but find those notes that do the most work. If I could play one note for a whole song I would. 'I Will Follow' is almost that."

It is, as a result, concentrated and hugely powerful. "Most of the early rehearsals were just rows," Bono recalls. "It was just one long argument. I remember picking up Edge's guitar and playing the two-stringed chord for 'I Will Follow' to show the others the aggression I wanted. It was his riff but I wanted it to have an edge to it."

There is a hallucinogenic quality to the lyrics – "Your eyes make a circle/I see you when I go in there," Bono sings in the bridge, desperately trying to make sense out of feelings of separation and loss. 'I Will Follow', finally, is the love song it set out to be. But it is as much about a boy's confused love for his mother as it is about a mother's unconditional love for her child.

The journey had begun. U2 were going in two different directions at once.

TWILIGHT

TWILIGHT
Written: U2
Length: 4' 22"
Album: *Boy*,
October 1980

"The subtext," Bono says, looking at the lyric sheet, "is everything. Isn't it?" He can't resist a wry chuckle, looking at the rough type from the inner sleeve of *Boy*. "Those lyrics are wrong," he says looking at the text of one track. "That's wrong," he repeats, scrawling the correct lyric to another. 'Twilight', he leaves untouched.

The song first surfaced on the B-side of their second single 'Another Day', released through CBS in Ireland. Legend has it that it was recorded in just five minutes and suffered as a consequence. But on *Boy* it comes through strongly, a small epic that's loaded with sexual ambiguities. No one in Ireland thought of the song as dealing with homosexuality, or the confusion of sexual identity that so many adolescents feel to one degree or another. And yet it's there in the lyrics, once you come at them from a certain angle. In Dublin, "the old man" was the common term for your father. But in Britain and the US, where gays expressed their identity in more overt ways, this song seemed to be for them. Bono sings: "The old man tried to walk me home, I thought he should have known." Who he was and what he should have known is never explicitly stated.

"It was curious," Adam Clayton reflects. "But we picked up a strong network of gay fans on the strength of *Boy*. We didn't have a clue what was going on."

"Then we did an interview with this guy, Adam Block," Bono continues, "who was gay, and he was saying that he'd always thought of us as a gay band. And I was like, 'Wow! you must be joking!' He made the point that within the gay community, people were excited about the fact that we were the first band to deal with sex outside machismo. Rock 'n' roll was always written from the point of view of men – or at least of boys pretending to be men – but we were doing something different."

9

he boy can't help
: Peter Rowen
ops Larry.

AN CAT DUBH / INTO THE HEART

When U2 formed in Mount Temple Comprehensive School on the north side of Dublin, Bono had already started the relationship with Ali Stewart that would result in marriage. But the path of true love didn't always run smoothly.

They split for a short time and Bono – as ever, restless and hungry for experience – had a short fling with another schoolmate.

"That one's about sex, definitely about sex," Gavin Friday says, without the slightest hesitation. "But I think you should ask him why 'An Cat Dubh'? Irish wasn't his thing. If that had been me, fine, because I was Fionán and that Irish thing was there in the background, but not in Bono's case. So why not just call it 'The Black Cat'? Where sex was concerned, Bono was very precocious as a teenager. He was a lot more knowledgeable than the rest of us in Lypton Village."

"It's definitely about sex, that," Bono agrees. "I think the title is in Irish because the girl it was about was a sort of 'as Gaeilge' type of person. What happened was that Ali and myself had split up for a minute and I just ran off with somebody and felt guilty about it.

"The image is of a cat and a bird. The cat kills the bird and shakes it – you know the way they do, they play with the dead prey – and then sleeps beside it. That's where the image comes from. It's like someone has taken you, thrown you around the place and then you sleep beside them. I think for the sake of the song I switched things around, but in reality I think I was

History records that at least a million people attended this gig: U2 at one of their legendary Dandelion Market shows in Dublin, 1978.

the cat. I was the one who did the dirty. That lyric should read 'and when she is done/she sleeps beside the one'."

In fact, 'An Cat Dubh' was as important for its muted, evocative instrumental passages as for its – again – sexually ambiguous text. The lyrics may have been improvised, as Bono told Neil McCormick of *Hot Press* during 1981, but the music felt as if it had been thought through. The restraint in the instrumental passage leading from 'An Cat Dubh' into 'Into the Heart' is especially impressive, a performance from The Edge that anticipated the unique genius he would bring to contemporary rock guitar-playing.

"We spent all our time on the music," Bono reflects now, "and on working out improvisations. We got hooked on guitar sounds, on bass lines, on drums. And then when we were doing that, we'd maybe seize a few minutes and I'd write the song down. Even though a lot of these songs were played live before we recorded them, I never learned the lyrics. Playing the Dandelion Market – or wherever – the lyrics would be changed. I think we can blame Iggy Pop for that. We'd read that he improvised his lyrics on the microphone and if it was good enough for Iggy, it was good enough for us. So it wasn't like I had worked out the lyrics and then had time to think about them. They were always changing."

The segue from 'An Cat Dubh' into 'Into the Heart' had more to do with the exigencies of performance than with theme. The sequence worked on stage, and therefore it made sense to do it that way on record. It remains a piece of shimmering, quiet beauty. The dynamics are beautifully controlled by producer Steve Lillywhite and the clear, ringing guitar has a haunting, ethereal quality. The lyrics of 'Into the Heart' beset the weakness that could inhabit songs that were being made up as the band went along. No doubt the intention is to mourn lost innocence and what the late Bill Graham of *Hot Press* called the destruction of the secret garden of youth – and that effect is evoked musically with great tenderness and feeling. But it wouldn't have taken much in the way of craft to hone lyrics that seem curiously self-contradictory on paper to a stage where they had a level of internal coherence. Craft would come later.

"It's really a non-lyric period, in one sense," Bono reflects now. "Nobody talked about lyrics back then. It wasn't really on the agenda. I think it was only really after *Unforgettable Fire* that we started saying – or that I started saying – hold on a second, give me a bit of space here, to think about these things, to thrash these things out."

For now, to a very large extent, it was down to where the group's collective instinct would take them. On balance, they weren't doing badly.

**AN CAT DUBH/
INTO THE HEART**
Written: U2
Length:
6' 21"/1' 53"
Album: *Boy*,
October 1980

OUT OF CONTROL

U23 was U2's debut recording salvo. Released on CBS Ireland, it came in 7" and – almost unique in Ireland at that time – 12" formats. Jackie Hayden, then marketing manager of CBS, enlisted the assistance of Ian Wilson, the producer of the Dave Fanning Rock Show on 2FM, the pop channel attached to the State broadcaster, RTE. Listeners to Dave's show were invited to help pick the record's A-side from 'Out of Control', 'Stories for Boys' and 'Boy Girl', by voting for their favourite. They opted for the first, which went on to become one of U2's best-known anthems.

Compared to the original version, the *Boy* re-interpretation had an even greater power and clarity. In the neo-punk era "oh-oh-ohs" and "oh-e-oh-e-ohs" were commonplace and the band indulged themselves here, but it scarcely diminished the energy and sense of compulsion which marked this song as something special from the start. It had been written on Bono's 18th birthday.

"'Out of Control' is about waking up on your 18th birthday and realising you're 18 years old and that the two most important decisions in your life have nothing to do with you – being born and dying," Bono told me in 1979, before the release of *Boy*. "The song is written from the child's point of view and it's about a vicious circle. He becomes a delinquent but the psychologist says, 'It's in his childhood'. No matter what he does, it can't be because he wants to – it's always because of what went before, and there's no decision in anything. Then again, that's [a] slightly spiritual [theme] – the question, what is happening if you've no freedom?"

Remembering now in tranquillity, Bono places the song in the context of his own psychological traumas at the time. He recalls flipping out in school at the age of 16, turning over chairs and tables, and not knowing himself what switch had gone on – or off – to cause the explosion. It was a feeling that recurred: he was haunted by the sense that the whole crazy business of human life, and human reproduction in particular, was out of control. The song was an attempt to come to grips in an adolescent but nonetheless urgent way with the reality of existential angst as it gnaws away at the heart's core.

Nowadays he isn't inclined to take it too seriously. "That one was translated by the Japanese," he says. "It went out with the album and the Japanese version of the opening lines translated back into English as 'Monday morning/Knitting years of gold,' which is a hell of a lot better than 'Monday morning/Eighteen years of dawning'" [laughs].

OUT OF CONTROL
Written: U2
Length: 4' 13"
Album: *Boy*,
October 1980

"Is this a record?" – The Edge and Bono examine their first waxing.

But for an 18-year-old those feelings were utterly real, and the sense of impending disaster which accompanied any notion that you might simply replay the same old suburban dramas enacted by your parents was impossible to shake off.

"My father had lived through the '50s depression," Bono reflects, "and as a result he taught us not to expect too much in case we might feel let down. His attitude was: don't do anything that seems like you're aiming higher than your allotted station. All my mates were intent on going to college and on doing things. I'd always been bright in school – I never did a tap but I'd done well and the last thing I wanted was to stay stuck in any kind of rut.

"Joining the band was my emancipation from all this. At that age, it was my ticket to freedom. It was my way of attempting to change the circumstances of the world I was living in."

Again, the musical arrangement is significant. From Larry Mullen's thumping drum entry, the song powers along with the expected urgency. But where other bands of the era might have gone for overkill in a tortured guitar solo, U2 instead dissolve the focus to let Adam Clayton's quietly insistent bass line through. There's a languor to the instrumental break which suggests that U2 will refuse to go for the obvious.

"We knew what sort of material we wanted," The Edge told *Hot Press* at the time, "so if you want a particular idea, you start picking instruments and amps and effects and what have you. When you start doing that, you start to develop a sound. Then, when you have a sound, you find certain things work better on that and you get into a certain vocabulary of music. And before you know what's happening, you're on the way to a style, a sound and to musicianship."

'Out of Control' was an important stepping stone along the way.

STORIES FOR BOYS

'Stories for Boys' was one of the band's earliest songs. A highlight of their live set, it was chosen for *U23*. At the time, Bono explained it in relatively conventional terms. "All the songs point to one thing – getting people to think for themselves," he told *Hot Press*. "There's also a reaction against heavy advertising and television images. I remember seeing heroes on TV – people like James Bond – and thinking, 'I'm not very good looking – I'm not going to get things like that,' and being unhappy about it."

But there were other things that they might have been qualified to comment on, too. The band's manager, Paul McGuinness, was always convinced that it was a song about masturbation. Gays too identified with it, reading a homo-erotic slant into the lines: "Sometimes when a hero takes me/Sometimes I don't let go/Oh oh oh/Stories for boys."

"This was it. For the gays in our audience, this was definitely a love song to a man," Bono smiles. "I thought of 'Stories for Boys' as just simple escapism. And it's not really. We were very conscious on one level but there was a whole subconscious thing going on too."

Bono has often spoken about the feeling that he is merely a conduit, the vehicle by which ideas, emotions and feelings, are delivered into the public realm. Now, he wonders if he and the band really knew what they were saying. "I never write lyrics until the last minute because they're constantly building as we work out the song. They build subconsciously, because I found that I can write exactly what I want to write subconsciously, better than sitting down and trying."

It's a very particular approach to the aesthetics of songwriting and sometimes it works. But at this early stage there was often a feeling that, in fact, the words to U2's songs were themselves out of control.

Or maybe that was appropriate, after all.

STORIES FOR BOYS
Written: U2
Length: 3' 02"
Album: *Boy*, October 1980

Adam flanked by Larry and Paul McGuinness.

THE OCEAN

THE OCEAN
Written: U2
Length: 1' 34"
Album: *Boy*,
October 1980

U2 grew up on Dublin's north side. Along the complicated shoreline of the county, a series of beaches run from Dollymount strand out to Sutton beach, on to Howth and then back into the Portmarnock inlet.

Out further there's Portrane, Skerries and Rush – they were small towns, their economies built around the summer holidays, weekend breaks and day-trips that people from the north of the city used to take there. Bono's family, on his mother's side, had bought a former train carriage, located on a farmer's land, close to the sea in Rush. All of the family would go there at weekends and revel in the lure of the sea.

The farmer who owned the field died and his son took over. He told the family that there was no contract entitling them to keep their holiday home on his land and that he wanted the carriage removed. When it didn't happen, he had the site levelled, destroying the carriage in the process. They took him to court and won, but Rush didn't hold the same appeal any more and they moved their holidaying to a caravan in Skerries. The Irish sea was common to both places.

Dubliners are familiar with the sea, so there was no giant leap of the imagination required for Bono to picture himself wandering at its edge. "'The Ocean' is just a complete teenage thought," Bono said in 1981. "It is the thought of everybody in a band who thinks he can change the world. There is another verse which got left out on the record: 'When I looked around/The world couldn't be found/Just me by the sea', which is the resignation that no matter what, people are going to go their own way."

The most crucial line, however, is in the first verse:

"A picture in grey, Dorian Gray/Just me by the sea/And I felt like a star." On one level, this is just teenage narcissism and self-indulgence. Musically, it achieves an appropriately lyrical and poetic quality – but Bono's response now is one of amusement. "That takes some fucking neck," he says. "We used to open the show with that. In a way it was so audacious. And it's nicely ironic. It's quite smart and a great opening gambit for a show. 'I thought the world could go far/If they listened to what I said.' So many people feel that, but so few say it. That's great."

The Dorian Gray reference is to Oscar Wilde's character. Gavin Friday remembers it as being on the Leaving Certificate syllabus. "I'd certainly read Wilde," Bono recalls. "I'd read Joyce. I'd read other Irish writers, as well as people like Baudelaire, because I thought they were arty or whatever."

There was a poet on the premises. He was searching for a voice.

A DAY WITHOUT ME

The Edge had already begun to fashion a distinctive guitar style. There was very little of the blues in his playing. You'd never hear him plucking out a 12-bar walking rhythm on the bass strings. He seldom played solos. And he didn't torture his young musician's fingers by attempting to b-e-n-d the notes. Instead he used open strings to create a drone-like effect.

There was a lot of treble in his playing, arpeggios and harmonics touched and left to hang. And against that cushion he'd play melody lines, often of crystalline purity. If he was already advancing along this alternative track, there's no doubt that getting hold of an echo unit confirmed his direction as a guitarist.

Bono remembers a developing interest in atmospherics within the band, referring to David Bowie's *Low* and to Joy Division among the influences that were coming on-stream at the time. From Tom Verlaine of Television, The Edge had learned that less is more, and had begun to develop an awareness of the architecture of sound: songs could be built. It was, as he later told John Waters, about judgement and your brain rather than your fingers. It was about ideas. Gavin Friday identifies the Jam, the Associates and the Skids as having made a huge impact on the way U2 saw themselves.

Bono claims that he acquired the Memory Man echo unit for the Edge, believing that it would take the band into another musical realm. The guitarist admits that it was Bono's idea. He remembers borrowing money from a friend and getting a really cheap unit. With it as inspiration, they wrote '11 O'Clock Tick Tock' and 'A Day Without Me'. Originally intended as an enhancement, it became an integral part of The Edge's guitar sound. 'A Day Without Me' resonates with its cheap but highly effective technological magic.

It was the first track that U2 recorded with Steve Lillywhite as producer. Released as a single in advance of *Boy*, it confirmed for both Lillywhite and the band that they could work together. As singles go, this was a song with a big theme – or series of themes – which were only sketchily executed. A guy Bono knew – "He was an acquaintance of a friend of mine, Sean d'Angelo" – had tried to commit suicide. "In fact I went up to the hospital with Sean to see this guy and they tried to keep Sean in! He went to find a bathroom and he was gone for half an hour. When he came back he had this strange look in his eye. He'd been walking around the pharmacy, looking for a toilet, when they stopped him. They thought he looked like an inmate. They were asking: 'Where are you going?' And he was telling

A DAY WITHOUT ME
Written: U2
Length: 3′ 14″
Album: *Boy*, October 1980

The late Ian Curtis of Joy Division.

them that he was just visiting. And they were taking him by the arm and saying 'Everything is going to be alright. Just come this way.' It was very funny. He had a hard job trying to convince them that he was just in to see his mate."

The suicide attempt played on Bono's imagination and emerged in 'A Day Without Me', with the protagonist looking back at the world he has "left behind" from the perspective of the grave – or more likely a vantage point somewhere above the graveyard, as he watches the funeral and takes note of those who haven't shown up. "I was fascinated by the thought: would it make any difference if you did commit suicide?" Bono recalls.

Typically, that is just an undercurrent. The song also touches on the theme of insanity, and on the collapse of the self, reflecting another common teenage insecurity. But Bono also sees in it continuity from 'The Ocean'.

17

Most teenagers wallow in the feeling that the world has reserved a special kind of misery for them. They want to run, and to keep on running. But in the midst of all that self-pity, the feeling that they are special inspires some with a belief that, given half a chance, they can do almost anything. This was true of Bono. But it was also true of the whole band, who never had any doubt about the fact that they were going to become huge. As early as 1981, Bono was comparing U2 to the Beatles and the Stones, as if they – rather than Echo & the Bunnymen – were U2's true peers. He's inclined to view 'A Day Without Me' against that kind of backdrop.

"'I started a landslide in my ego'," he quotes. "That's a great opening line. A lot of this stuff is awful but that's really ballsy. I think this is about our own megalomania, actually [laughs]. There was never any doubt in our minds, certainly in my mind, that the band had something special, and that we were going to go all the way. That was it. And so this is – this was writing about the future success of the band. It's so embarrassing [laughs]. It's actually writing about this as a given. And saying 'good luck' to everyone else! Against the background of what was going on in and around Ballymun, I think the band gave me a sense of 'we're off'. That's how it felt."

And that's how it was.

ANOTHER TIME
ANOTHER PLACE

Happiness is always somewhere else. The tragic hero of teenage artifice is frequently forlorn and disillusioned. There was very little in the way of joy on *Boy*, if you looked at the lyrics. And yet in many ways it was a very "up" record: the joy was in the making, in the musicianship, in the mission. It was in Larry Mullen pounding the drums.

It was in Adam finding the confidence to launch into a melodic bass run to fill the space between The Edge's angular, ringing guitar slashes. It was in Bono unleashing the demons inside, posing and pogoing around the stage, leaping into the crowd and being – sometimes literally – carried away. The joy was in the group's sense of abandonment – of the conventions and restrictions implicit in being four suburban Dublin boys in the bleak '70s.

'Another Time, Another Place' is one of those wistful, evocative titles which sounds like it came first, though Bono has no memory of the Bryan Ferry album of that name. "At that stage, because so little attention was paid to lyrics, most of the songs did begin with the titles. Usually, we'd work on the music first, in fact we still do. And then, as the music begins to feel a certain way, the first thing we do is to find a title that captures the feel of the music, and then you work back from that."

You can argue that 'Another Time, Another Place' is merely self-indulgent, romantic stuff. It sounds seriously under-worked. But there is in it – as there is throughout *Boy* – an admirable sensitivity to the plight of children, lost in the suburban jungle. Here, simply, because they're here, because they're here, because they're here…

"I actually think it's about sex in Dublin as a teenager," another acquaintance from the era suggests. "It's about finding a place where you can be with your girlfriend, which was a real problem at that time."

'Another Time, Another Place' certainly prefigures a theme that would dominate U2's later music. "In my sleep I discover the one," Bono asserts, but it is never clear whether he means the Loved One or the Supreme Being – or both. Possibly he didn't know, although the promise "I'll be with you now/We lie on a cloud" certainly suggests some sort of romantic intent, Ali working her muse on him already.

Bono: "That's me by the sea."

ANOTHER TIME
ANOTHER PLACE
Written: U2
Length: 4' 34"
Album: *Boy*,
October 1980

THE ELECTRIC CO.

A quick glance at the lyrics and you'd scarcely get any sense of what 'The Electric Co.' was about. Within Lypton Village, a defining emphasis was on developing a private language that only insiders could understand. There was a desperate desire to communicate – but only to those you thought would be capable of understanding.

Within the village set, people may have known that 'The Electric Co.' was a reference to Electro Convulsive Therapy, but the lyrics only hint at the deep sense of disturbance that the song in its entirety explores.

Gavin Friday remembers it as a common feature of the neighbourhood. He pictures women walking the suburban streets in mid-afternoon in their nightdresses. "It'd be a case of 'Oh, there goes Mrs So-and-so again.' And a couple of days later you'd hear that she was back in hospital. And everyone would be whispering that she'd got 'the treatment'. They'd whack her with an electric shock and she'd be back a few weeks later and she'd be stable for a while. There were a few women like that. Today they'd give them Valium or Prozac but they were big into ECT at the time."

When Sean de Angelo's friend tried to kill himself, he went about it in a spectacular way, with a chainsaw. He ended up in St Brendan's psychiatric hospital, notorious in Dublin lore simply as Grangegorman, or "the 'Gorman". It was a foul institution in which those with long-term psychiatric problems were effectively incarcerated. Electric shock treatment was frequently used and so the prospects for de Angelo's friend were bleak.

It was as a musical set-piece, however, that 'The Electric Co.' exploded with the power of its concealed intent. 'The Electric Co.' burned with anger at the injustice of it all – beginning with the reality of mental disturbance and insanity itself, but more particularly raging against the hubris of doctors who took on themselves the power to mess with people's brains. "ECT is nothing more than witchcraft," Bono commented bitterly at the time.

"'The Electric Co.' was about anger," he says now. "It used to be an incredible release on stage. This idea that rock 'n' roll is a kind of revenge – on society, and on the people you perceive as having done you down – is really true. When you're on stage, and going all out, certain songs do become vehicles or vectors for that. For me 'The Electric Co.' was a licence to get in touch with that desire. I've jumped off balconies, I've whacked people, I've been whacked doing that song live. There's a bit of an Alex, the main character from *A Clockwork Orange*, in there. But essentially it was an angry, cathartic experience every time we performed it."

THE ELECTRIC CO.
Written: U2
Length: 4' 48"
Album: *Boy*,
October 1980

SHADOWS AND
TALL TREES

William Golding's *Lord of the Flies* was an important text around Lypton Village. Part of the driving force behind that community within a community involved the rejection of adulthood and the mind-numbing convention that seemed to accompany it. The purity and innocence of childhood seemed far more attractive than a life of never-ending compromise.

And so Bono, Gavin, Guggi and the other inhabitants of this imaginary place resolved to live like children, and to behave with a child-like honesty. "We got into this *Lord of the Flies* idea of not growing up," Bono told John Waters, later. "We said, 'we won't grow up. We'll stay as we are . . . nine!' Ahem, I guess we succeeded there! It was a little bit gauche and a little bit all over the place, but that's where it was coming from."

Amazing pictorial confirmation that The Edge actually has two heads!

**SHADOWS AND
TALL TREES**
Written: U2
Length: 4' 36"
Album: *Boy*,
October 1980

That belief in the purity of a child's-eye view of the world is important in understanding the entire ethos of *Boy*. It underscored the band's reliance on instinct in the way the lyrics were written. And it explains, in part at least, the nakedness of some of U2's emotional pleading.

The title 'Shadows and Tall Trees' was taken from the fourth chapter of *Lord of the Flies*. "When I came up with the title, I remember thinking, 'Wow! I can do this!' Again it was like a moment of realisation," Bono recalls. It was an early U2 song, the only one from their original demo session, recorded with Barry Devlin of Horslips as producer, which made it onto *Boy*. A ballad, it feels as if more attention was paid to the lyrics than on most of the tracks on the album. "Yeah," Bono laughs. "Look at that: 'Is life like a tightrope/Hanging on my ceiling?'. Ouch! I guess I would have considered that to be quite writerly at the time. But then there are other parts of it that are quite beautiful. 'Do you feel in me, anything redeeming/ Any worthwhile feeling?' – which I guess if you were listening to it as a song or at a concert would have to bring something out. It would have to hit you on an emotional level."

The shadows and tall trees of the title were a reference to the atmosphere around the pylons that towered over Cedarwood Road and environs. "I remember thinking about that comparison between *Lord of the Flies* and where we were in Cedarwood, between Ballymun and Finglas. It was a quiet little street in one sense but my memory of it, growing up, is of being stuck between cowboys and indians, rumbles between the top end of the street and the bottom end of the street, between bootboys and skinheads, and so on. That's the way it was. And I remember thinking the shadows and tall trees are different here – but it's the same story, isn't it? It's all about war. We're all stuck on this island of suburbia and we're turning on each other."

The Mrs Brown, whose washing turns up in the third verse, was in fact Mrs Byrne, Iris Hewson's best friend and near neighbour on Cedarwood Road. Inevitably, the Byrne kids recognized the fact that their dirty laundry was being washed – or watched! – by Bono in public. "They were happy enough about that," he laughs.

And why wouldn't they be, with immortality? Of a sort.

21

OCTOBER

Portland, Oregon. 22 March, 1981. Four Irish boys, wide-eyed and trusting. Three girls sashay backstage. Hey, these must be groupies. The Irish boys are happy just to talk. And they do for half-an-hour. "Oops," the girls say, "time to go." And they're gone. They seemed pretty cool, didn't they? Very cool. "Has anyone seen my case?" Bono asks. Shit. His case is gone.

Three smart Portland girls opening the door to their apartment, carrying a case. Inside are $300 and a bunch of hand-written scrawls. Lyrics. Bono's lyrics. For the new record. All gone.

Four Irish boys searching high and low. For the lyrics. Gone. Three years to write *Boy*. Now, 12 months' worth of hard labour stolen – with only 12 weeks left to write the follow-up. Nervous breakdown time.

Things were fraught. Bono, Larry, The Edge heavily into Shalom Christianity. Adam, isolated. Touring taking its toll. The band almost falling apart. Steve Lillywhite driving Bono: "You can write a song in five minutes. Do your job."

Thought of calling the album *Scarlet* (the colour of Bono's face when he discovered the lyrics had been nicked?) Decided instead on *October*. A big theme hinting at our own insignificance?

Or it was the month the album would be released in?   The Tyne is now...

GLORIA

Paul McGuinness may privately have raged about the possibility that the involvement of Bono, Edge and Larry in the Shalom group might derail a band which he instinctively knew could become enormously successful. But he always respected the fundamental impulse behind the trio's action.

'His attitude was always very cool," Bono recalls. "He'd say: 'Look I don't share your views but I do believe it's the most important question, and I do respect the fact that you're trying to come to terms with it.' The only thing that he found in his own religion that he could relate to was the music, so he gave us an album of Gregorian chants."

The opening lines of 'Gloria' crystallise the central dilemma with which the band were forced to grapple throughout the album: "I try to sing this song/I, I try to stand up but I can't find my feet/I try, I try to speak up/But only in you I'm complete." The song reflects a desire to find a voice, a way of expressing at once the faith that was at the heart of their conversion, and the terrible confusion it had plunged them into. Bono feels now that he may have been too embarrassed about the ideas that were beginning to flood his work as a lyricist to write them down. Instead he improvised, with the result that he is stuttering, barely achieving any kind of coherence.

On 'Gloria' he succeeds. From listening to the Gregorian chant album, the idea emerged of doing the chorus in Latin. Gavin Friday remembers Bono asking a mutual friend to do the initial translation. The final draft was completed by Albert Bradshaw, a teacher in Mount Temple.

Whether Mr Bradshaw would have been aware of the song's more heathen antecedents is uncertain. As an Irish band, U2 were certainly conscious of Van Morrison and his sexual paean to 'Gloria'. However, on *Horses*, an album which hugely influenced U2, Patti Smith had done a magnificently potent, erotic, lesbian version of Them's garage band classic. "It is a love song," Bono says. "In a sense it's an attempt to write about a woman in a spiritual sense and about God in a sexual sense. But there certainly is a strong sexual pulse in there."

"You could hear the desperation and confusion in some of the lyrics," The Edge told Bill Flanagan. "'Gloria' is really a lyric about not being able to express what's going on, not being able to put it down, not knowing where we are."

Not being able to express what's going on? Perhaps. But – in this instance at least – doing it very well, all the same.

23

GLORIA
Written: U2
Length: 4' 12"
Album: *October*,
October 1981
UK singles chart
position: 55

I FALL DOWN

"A really funny thing happened during the *October* tour," Bono recalls. "We were playing the Ritz in New York and this girl slipped onto the stage. I used to do this thing even then of dancing with someone from the audience. She said, 'I'm Julie.' I met her afterwards. She's a daughter of a wealthy lawyer in New York, who kind of spun out and ended up coming back here to Ireland and getting involved in the Shalom group. She ended up in a relationship with Pod, who was in our road crew at the time."

"I think that John in 'I Fall Down' was actually Pod, who was originally the drummer with the Virgin Prunes," Gavin Friday recalls. "He was one of the staunchest Christians going. It got to the stage where Pod couldn't talk to me because I was a heathen. An atheist. There was a period of about a year and a half when myself, Guggi and Bono didn't see eye to eye over various things. People used to run when they saw me and I was saying, 'I'm not going to sacrifice animals on stage.' And so Pod left the Prunes and went to work with U2 on their American tour, as their main roadie."

Gavin himself had been involved in the Shalom group. "That didn't last long," he laughs. "I was pushed into a corner. It was a case of 'Let's change the name to The Deuteronomy Prunes, Gavin. Let's stop wearing eyeliner,' and so on. So I just said no, no, no. I knew I didn't want to buy into all this. But after he'd left the Prunes, Pod fell in love with Julie, who is also mentioned in the song. I think Pod was almost like a religious prayer-master in the group at the time. And so when he got together with Julie, she became another ringleader of the Shalom group, along with Pod."

The song is experimental in a number of ways. Whether the influence of Elvis Costello, Joe Jackson and Squeeze was seeping through is a matter for conjecture, but the introduction of the Julie and John characters frees the band from the tyranny of the direct declarations of emotional intensity that Bono was prone to. The Edge's shimmering piano, tightly worked backing vocals and a superbly judged Steve Lillywhite production mark this as one of the band's most fully realised early cuts.

Bono wouldn't go so far as to suggest that 'I Fall Down' was written about Julie before he met her. "I don't really know," he says. "That's what she thinks. And who's to say?" It could, of course, merely be a case of life imitating art. But if so, surely Bono would know who he originally had in mind when he created the Julie character in the song. "There was really no one that I can think of," he admits. "I have no recollection about where the idea for the song came from."

I FALL DOWN
Written: U2
Length: 3' 39"
Album: *October*, October 1981

I THREW A BRICK THROUGH A WINDOW

I THREW A BRICK THROUGH A WINDOW
Written: U2
Length: 4' 54"
Album: *October*, October 1981

Punk rock was crucial to U2's formation. "Bono was the first punk in school," a former classmate recalls. "He turned up one day with a new haircut, tight purple straights, a '60s jacket and a chain leading from his nose to his ear. He wanted to freak everyone out and he succeeded."

Bono acknowledges the anger that gripped him as a teenager. But he never felt easy with the emotion. "The old cliché of rock 'n' roll rebellion is a joke," he said around the release of *Boy*. "I think rebellion starts within your heart. I think going out and getting pissed and dying your hair red is not necessarily any indication of menace at all."

Thematically, 'I Threw a Brick Through a Window' would have sat comfortably on *Boy*. Musically it was more spacious than most tracks on the band's debut with a hint that they had been listening to some of Island's huge reggae catalogue. Lyrically, it returns to suburban claustrophobia.

"Bono was always crashing, bikes, cars – everything broke down on him, he'd always be losing things," Gavin Friday recalls. "We were walking around the neighbourhood and suddenly it was like: 'They're on drugs', and 'Paul Hewson's gone mad on a motorbike.' Suddenly we were weirdos. Now we were in bands, we were no longer lovely boys. We were brats.

"Once Bono was going to a party and decided to splash out on a bottle of wine. There was this couple up the road called Mr and Mrs Curley, and Bono was driving this crock of a car and crashed into their gate. The wine spilt all over the car and the Gardaí thought he'd been drinking. And there were all these fucking neighbours standing in judgement. And it was, like, 'I have to get out of this fucking kip.'"

There is anger and confusion here but it is as much about the senseless violence that erupts between men confined together in a small space. "There was a row in the house," Bono recalls. "My father, my brother and myself didn't get along at the time. I remember throwing a carving knife at my brother and it sticking in the door. I missed – but that's what 'I Threw a Brick Through a Window' was about."

25

John Lydon: punk up the volume!

REJOICE

Bono talks about an extraordinary renewal that took place in 1976. Amazing things happened in Mount Temple, with nearly half the school undergoing some kind of religious experience. One of the teachers had quite an effect on a lot of people. She was always on about the Scriptures, the thing took hold, and during a period of about two months there was an eruption of spiritual fervour.

One of the girls eventually blew it by going to the headmaster's office and asking him to announce over the intercom that the school now belonged to Jesus. It was a measure of how intense the collective feeling had become.

Look what Bono's got up his sleeve – his arm!

"That was the first wave," Bono says, "and there was a kind of an echo of it around about 1981 or '82. Charismatic things started happening. That was when we became involved in the Shalom group. We were studying the Scriptures. When everyone else was figuring out how to get served and how to score, we were all completely wrapped up in this."

'Rejoice' is a celebration of that spiritual involvement. It is also quite explicitly a rejection of the pretentions of bands like The Clash who were coming on at the time as if punk rock were the key to the revolution.

The Edge has commented that some of Bono's best lyric writing is done under pressure, on the mic, but that theory isn't borne out here. You can sense the bluster, feel the desperation. "And what am I to do?" he asks. "Just tell me what am I supposed to say." Improvised on the spot, the line almost certainly sparked a silent cynical rejoinder from Steve Lillywhite, who was finding Bono's apparent lack of preparation enormously trying. But the singer succeeded in coming up with some memorable lines even under pressure.

"Only last week I had some American come up to me and say, 'I can't change the world/But I can change the world in me.' So naive!" he reflects. "But there was something real happening all the same. At that point we were so removed from the culture. Rock 'n' roll – that was just the day job. We used to get together every single night, meeting in people's houses, reading, studying Scriptures. The band was what we did during the day."

The Edge remembers *October* as an album that suffered because of the lack of time U2 had to prepare it. He has a point, especially given that it was his superb, propulsive guitar-playing that rescued 'Rejoice'. But, overall, there was less to celebrate here than Bono felt at the time.

REJOICE
Written: U2
Length: 3' 38"
Album: *October*,
October 1981

FIRE

I remember Bono taking me out to his car, parked outside Windmill Lane studios in Dublin, and playing me the band's new single. The implicit distinction was important in itself. At that stage, U2 were still thinking about putting stuff together that would crack the charts, and during a break in their American tour, they'd stopped off at Chris Blackwell's studios in Nassau, in the Bahamas, to increase their chances.

On an initial listen I was struck by the glistening guitar power, the suggestion of sabres rattling and the sun glinting off them. It was a small triumph at least: released in June 1981, in advance of October, it provided the band with their first British chart success.

With its roots in the Book of Revelations and the circumstances of the second coming, it is apocalyptic in tone. But if you weren't already aware of the band's interest in religion, there was nothing that explicitly signalled the underlying biblical frame of reference. At a push, 'Fire' could have been about some imagined nuclear-fuelled Armageddon. However it was read at the time, Bono dismisses it now as nonsense.

"As I recall, 'Fire' was our attempt at a single. God knows where our heads were at," he laughs. "There was something good about it – I just can't remember what it was."

He isn't entirely serious when he attributes the song's failure to the fact that they were recording, for the first time, in the lap of luxury. "That was an amazing trip," he says. "It was our first time going to the Caribbean and it just blew us all away. There is that thing when you're in a baby band, where you feel that you're on holidays all the time, and you can't believe that you haven't been found out. So when you're in a place like Nassau, you don't really want to go in and work, do you? And you realise why all these great groups make crap records when they go to record there! It's because they just don't feel like working when they're in the Bahamas."

The whole debacle had its lighter side – in retrospect. "You know the story about *Top of the Pops* and 'Fire'?" asks Bono. "It was our first time on *Top of the Pops* and the record company were really thrilled because we were going to have a hit single. We went on and the single went down because we were so bad. The miming was all over the shop and it was operatic in a way that TV will never understand. I was dressed in this black military kind of sleeping bag shirt, with a bad haircut."

Calling, calling…

FIRE
Written: U2
Length: 3' 52"
Album: *October*,
October 1981
UK singles chart
position: 35

27

TOMORROW

When Bono went to see Ridley Scott's chilling futuristic thriller *Bladerunner*, he was impressed. But there was a flaw. At first he couldn't figure out what it was. Then it dawned on him. It was the music. "I am a fan of Vangelis," he said, "but in the '90s, people won't be listening to electronic music. Who wants electronic music in an electronic age?"

A scene from Ridley Scott's *Bladerunner*.

Bono felt that modernism was about to be rejected, because in the era that *Bladerunner* represented, it was not technology that would be needed most in art and in music but those instruments that restored people's humanity. On Bruce Springsteen's magnificent, low-fi *Nebraska*, he identified a fragile quality to the music that had to do with the tones and textures of the acoustic guitar and the harmonica. Released a year earlier, 'Tomorrow' had explored the same terrain, utilising the timelessness and the power of Vinnie Kilduff's uileann pipes as its signature.

The choice of an instrument that was intimately associated with Irish traditional music was undoubtedly a reaction to touring and the band's initial experience of the rigours of American roadwork. Bono talked about waking up suddenly and realizing that he was Irish. The more attention you pay to the lyrics, the more poignant they become. There was a time when Bono used to talk about 'Tomorrow' as a song about what was happening in Northern Ireland at the beginning of the '80s. In an atmosphere of deepening sectarian conflict, a knock on the door increasingly became an invitation to accept a bullet in the head. No one knew for certain what was waiting for them when they opened the door, opened the door . . .

But Bono has been revisiting the song recently, and is in no doubt now about what had really been troubling him so deeply back then. 'Tomorrow' is a song about the death of his mother – no more and no less. "Won't you come back tomorrow/Won't you be back tomorrow/Can I sleep tonight?" he pleads, and the sense of desolation and loss is palpable.

"There are things that have to be worked out, that are going to come out," he says. "They'll find holes. It's still amazing to me that I could have convinced myself that this was about anything else. It's amazing that you can be so completely out of touch with yourself and with feelings you're trying to express."

TOMORROW
Written: U2
Length: 4' 39"
Album: *October*,
October 1981

OCTOBER

Bono was always ready with a theory. "U2 music is not urban music," he said in 1980. "It's more to do with hills, rivers and mountains." He might have been talking about the context that gave rise to the immensely troubled and still deeply moving 'October'.

The Edge remembers it as a song that could have gone places, but Bono was bereft of further lyrical inspiration and they didn't have the time to squeeze out whatever sparks might have been flickering. They decided to put it out as it was.

'October' is suffused with an other-worldly sadness that taps into the tangled emotions that were driving the band just then, and that risked driving them apart. On the run-up to recording 'October', Bono, The Edge and Larry were living out in Portrane, beside the beach on the north coast of Dublin, with the Shalom group. Bono was baptised in the sea and they were living in a caravan in a field. They were praying a lot and fasting.

The three Christian members of the band had been under a lot of pressure from other members of the Shalom group to quit. It was on the beach in Portrane that The Edge broke the news to Bono that he might be leaving the band. If The Edge was going, Bono decided that he would too – that they'd break up the band. The Edge asked for two weeks, to give him time to go away and consider his position. When he came back he had decided that being a Christian in a rock 'n' roll band involved a contradiction alright – but one he could live with.

"'October' . . . it's an image," Bono said in 1981. "We've been through the '60s, a time when things were in full bloom. We had fridges and cars, we sent people to the Moon and everybody thought how great mankind was. And now, as we go through the '70s and '80s, it's a colder time of the year. It's after the harvest. The trees are stripped bare. So 'October' is an ominous word, but it's also quite lyrical."

As extrapolations, go it makes some kind of sense. The title came first: it was what Bono wanted to call the album. The Edge hadn't played the piano in years but he had a real feel for it and he began to pick out this pure melody. 'October' was the result, and its nakedness said much about the crises the band had been going through, both personal and creative.

'October' captures U2 in a moment of supreme vulnerability, and is all the more compelling as a result. There may indeed have been a bigger, more complete song there to be written. But sometimes, as U2 would find again and again, these things are best left to find a life of their own.

OCTOBER
Written: U2
Length: 2' 21"
Album: *October*,
October 1981

WITH A SHOUT

There is an underlying tone of defiance that runs throughout *October*. U2's debut album had been made in a spirit of optimism. The culmination of almost four years of apprenticeship, *Boy* harboured a surfeit of bounce: you got the feeling that U2 were ready to take on the world.

But touring the album had been draining. The more they got to know about the music industry, the more U2 were repelled by the cynicism of it. Their idealism had taken a battering, hearing stories about how bands they'd respected and been inspired by, like the Clash and the Jam, treated their road crew, and seeing the inner workings of the record business for the first time. In a sense, they went into the recording of *October* with the attitude that if people didn't like it, it just might be better for everyone concerned. Rejection would make it easier to walk away.

It's hard to conceive of anything that could have been so terminally unhip as Bono exhorting the great unwashed to make tracks for Jerusalem, but that's precisely what he did on 'With a Shout'. "We don't want to be the band that talks about God," he had said during 1980, but the crucifixion imagery was unmistakable. You could interpret it as a logical conclusion of Bono, Larry and The Edge's belief in what they thought of as the spirit that moves all things. Equally, you might dismiss it as an effective abdication of the responsibility he had, both to the band and to their audiences. Whatever the cause, there is no mistaking the spirit of abandon with which Bono met the challenge of constructing the lyrics. On the one hand there was trust: I will rely on Him for inspiration. On the other there was doubt: No matter what I do, it is all meaningless. And finally, there was perhaps a core of self-belief: Fuck them. Why should we hide what we feel?

Bono had been reading the Psalms of David at the time.

"Yeah, there's triumphalism there," Bono reflects. "But in an odd way the walls of Jerusalem, or the walls of Jericho, were a great image for punk music, and the idea that went with it, that music could shake the foundations. The Psalms are amazing about music. They're all about bang that drum, whack that cymbal and, you know, dead bones rising up. Music as a wake-up call for the spirit – that was what we were driving at."

You could say that it was a brave failure. The imagery would be revisited, much more effectively, later.

Take one, take two... take three! U2 recording their video at Kilmainham Jail, Dublin.

WITH A SHOUT
Written: U2
Length: 4' 02"
Album: *October*,
October 1981

STRANGER IN A STRANGE LAND

In the early days, David Bowie had been a significant influence on the band. You could see it in some of Bono's stage moves: there was a self-conscious theatrical Bowie-esque side to the band in their pre-*Boy* days, that disappeared for a long time, resurfacing only with Zoo TV. It's curious then that Bono doesn't recall seeing Nicolas Roeg's *The Man Who Fell to Earth*, in which Bowie made his screen debut. That film was based on a Robert Heinlein novel; Heinlein also wrote *Stranger in a Strange Land*, which gave Bono the title for one of *October*'s most effective lyrics. Touring was a time for reading. Books were consumed on the tour bus and in hotel rooms. Some images, ideas, titles, lingered. The experience could also provide its own moments of inspiration.

"You have to remember that the only travel we did as kids was to go over to Wales on camping holidays," a friend recalls. "Bono used to go over to Wales to see some girl he knew from camping when he was ten.

"I remember we all went over and knocked on her hall door and she was going out with another guy and it was like 'Fuck off!' And we were left camping on this site and it was the middle of winter so we thought, 'Let's walk around town in our underpants.' And we had airguns and we were all arrested – they thought we were the IRA or something. That was a big adventure for us. We were very sheltered."

So when U2 began to tour, it was an eye-opener. Perhaps if Bono hadn't lost his lyrics, there'd have been more postcards from a tour bus on *October*. In the event, 'Stranger in a Strange Land' seems like an exception.

"We were going to Berlin," Bono recalls. "We were all in the back of the van in our sleeping bags and we had to travel through the corridor between East Germany and West Berlin. And we were stopped by this border guard. The song was just a little portrait of him. He was our own age, with short hair, in a uniform and his life was pretty grim and he was seeing these guys in a rock 'n' roll band passing through."

The song had a quality that was scarce on *October*: empathy: "We asked him to smile for a photograph/We waited around to see if we could make him laugh/The soldier asked for a cigarette/His smiling face I can't forget." "That's quite a good lyric," Bono says, looking at the song afresh. It's been speculated that the soldier could as easily have been a British Army squaddie in Northern Ireland but, at most, that's an undercurrent.

STRANGER IN A STRANGE LAND
Written: U2
Length: 3' 56"
Album: *October*, October 1981

SCARLET

An Edge power chord has unforesee consequences.

There had been a lot of pressure on the band to use their music in the cause of Christianity, of Jesus, of Shalom. People within the tightly knit group thought that U2 should use the platform they'd won to proselytise.

"I remember thinking: does God need salesmen?" Bono recalls. "Do we really have to reduce this to pulpit-thumping? By this stage I'd been to America and I'd seen the state of the evangelicals and the fundamentalists, and of religious broadcasting in America – the preachers with their hands reaching out of the television trying to steal your money. People would say, 'Are you embarrassed? Are you ashamed?' I'm not ashamed. I'm just not going to go around and flog it like a second-hand car salesman."

And so, 'Scarlet' takes a minimalist line. It may originally have been an instrumental piece for which Bono failed to come up with a lyric, but it stands the test of time all the better for its simplicity. The Edge is at the piano again, Adam Clayton contributes a resonant, melodic bass part and Larry plays the role of percussionist with admirable restraint.

The influence of Paul McGuinness' album of Gregorian chants is discernible in the straight choral lines of Bono's delivery. And there is something healing rather than triumphalist about the effect when he sings the one word over and over: "Rejoice".

A prelude to '40', it identified a vein that would yield further, greater riches later.

SCARLET
Written: U2
Length: 2' 53"
Album: *October*,
October 1981

IS THAT ALL?

IS THAT ALL?
Written: U2
Length: 3' 01"
Album: *October*,
October 1981

The album could have ended with 'Scarlet', but for some reason that no one can quite figure out now, they felt that it needed an end-piece. Patti Smith used to make her records by writing her titles first, sketching out the word-frame and then creating the music with those suggestions in mind. Or so U2 had read. An ambience was created, the music took shape and then the lyrics were written and improvised on the mc, coming together by a kind of process of trial and error. She may have had an end-piece on *Horses* and the band wanted to follow suit. Or it might just have been that someone had thought that it was a good title for a final track – and once the title had been invented, they had to deliver the "song".

A good title it may indeed have been, but the end result is a mess. The guitar riff is lifted from 'The Cry', an earlier song that was often incorporated into 'The Electric Co.' but never made it onto disc. Otherwise 'Is That All?' was written in the studio, and it shows. Larry's cracking snare and superb drumming notwithstanding, it is confused and incoherent, but unintentionally revealing nonetheless. "Is that all that you want from me?" Bono pleads, in a giveaway line that seems to acknowledge his own feelings of creative frustration and failure.

"I think after the album came out we thought, 'Uuh'," Bono shrugs. *October* has its moments of sheer beauty. For an album that was frequently dismissed, parts of it stand up surprisingly well. But even when it fails, it tells us much about the confused and perilous state of mind U2 were in at the time. Arguably, 'Is That All?' says more about that theme than any other track precisely because it says so little. They should have known better.

33

2: stars and bars.

WAR

For all its ringing assertions of faith, *October* had been conceived in an atmosphere of doubt. The involvement of Bono, Larry and The Edge in Shalom Christianity had temporarily undermined U2's conviction about their mission as a rock 'n' roll band. The album was recorded under a cloud, in a rush. It had moments of sweet inspiration but it felt unfinished.

The trio were under increasing pressure from within the Shalom group – about how they should dress, what they should look like, the way they should sound. They resented being crowded, dictated to. Looking around, they didn't like the nihilism into which punk had descended. The New Romantics were seen as irrelevant, peddling pop of the most self-regarding and vacuous variety. Everything was out of kilter.

As U2 toured *October* through '81 and '82 they became hardened by roadwork. They had regained their confidence as a rock 'n' roll band. Bono was driven by a need to bring all the pieces together. Now was the time to declare war on everything that was cynical, phoney, defeatist and limiting. Their third album would be a document of the times. There could be no shirking. Personally, politically and musically, U2 would declare their independence. Loud, angry and demanding, the *War* album and tour would see U2 triumph.

Constant touring toughened up U2.

SUNDAY BLOODY SUNDAY

The events which formed the backdrop to one of U2's most explicitly political songs are etched indelibly into the text of Ireland's troubled colonial history. The counter-intelligence unit of the original Irish Republican Army, under Michael Collins, identified 14 British undercover agents who had been responsible for the systematic killing of members of Sinn Féin over the previous months. On 21 November, 1921, they broke into their houses early in the morning and assassinated them in their beds.

In retaliation, armed forces – in the form of the Regular Royal Irish Constabulary and the notorious Black and Tans, a ruthless auxiliary police force used to crush nationalist opposition – went into the headquarters of the Gaelic Athletic Association in Croke Park. There they opened fire on the crowd attending a football match. In all, 12 people were shot dead and 60 others were wounded. That day became known as Bloody Sunday.

That horrific double incident was echoed in Derry in 1972. In an infamous attack, the elite Paratroop Regiment of the British Army opened fire during a civil rights demonstration and killed 14 unarmed people. Another 14 were badly wounded. The images of that day remain unforgettable. In particular, footage of the man who would become Catholic Bishop of Derry, Edward Daly, holding his handkerchief aloft as an improvised white flag, as he crawls on his hands and knees towards the lifeless silhouette of one of the victims of the slaughter, serves as an emblem of the innocence of those who had been slaughtered. Those two events formed the immediate political backdrop to the opening song on *War*…

"I can't believe the news today." It was an introductory line which crystallised the prevailing response to the series of outrages that devastated Northern Ireland throughout the '70s and early '80s. To a large extent those who lived in Dublin had been immune. But, in an increasingly politicised band, Bono had come around to the view that they could not simply wash their hands of the violence in the North, or of the injustices which had spawned it. "It was only when I realised that the troubles hadn't affected me that they began to affect me," he said at the time. "The bombs may not go off in Dublin but they're made here."

'Sunday Bloody Sunday' was not a partisan statement. Live, it was always prefaced with a disclaimer. "This is not a rebel song," Bono would declare. By that he meant that it was not to be taken as supporting the Republican cause. "What I was trying to say in the song is: there it is, in close-up," Bono explained. "I'm sick of it. How long must it go on? It's not

SUNDAY BLOODY SUNDAY
Written: U2
Length: 4' 39"
Album: *War*, March 1983

even saying there's an answer." The important thing was at least to ask the right questions. It was The Edge's idea to explore the theme, and to link what was happening in Northern Ireland back to the original Christian blood sacrifice and subsequent resurrection on Easter Sunday. "Bono was away on his honeymoon," The Edge recalls. "I wrote the music and hit on an idea for the lyrics and presented it to the band when they got back."

Edward Daly, then a priest, later Bishop of Derry, seeks a safe passage for the fallen. Bloody Sunday Derry, 1972.

The song would articulate the band's own sense of bewilderment at the Northern conflict, but an incident at a US gig provided an immediate context for Bono. "I walked out of the backstage door in San Francisco," Bono explained, "and there were 30 or 40 people waiting for a chat and for autographs, and I was scrawling my name on bits of paper as they were handed to me. I got this one piece of paper and it was folded and when I opened it, it was a big dogma thing looking for signatures – I was about to sign my name on a petition to support some guy I'd never heard of, an Irish guy with Republican connections. And I got worried at that stage.

"As much as I'm a Republican, I'm not a territorial person. The whole idea of U2 using a white flag on stage was to get away from the green, white and orange. To get away from the Stars and Stripes. To get away from the Union Jack… I mean, I'd love to see a united Ireland but I don't believe you can put a gun to someone's head to make him see your way."

In that sense 'Sunday Bloody Sunday' was a protest song – not against any one act of violence but against a cycle of violence into which all of the protagonists in the Northern conflict seemed to be locked. Adam remembers that it was originally much more vitriolic, with an opening line that would have hung like an albatross around U2's collective neck for years to come: "Don't talk to me about the rights of the IRA." But better judgement prevailed. "The viewpoint became very humane and non-sectarian," Adam reflects, "which is the only responsible position." The urgency of the emotion did not, however, make it an easy song to produce. During the writing of *War*, Bono suffered from writer's block and one of his abiding memories of making the album relates to how his wife, Ali, helped him through this traumatic period. "She was literally kicking me out of bed in the morning," Bono recalled. "She literally put the pen in my hand."

During recording, considerable time was spent on the drum part. Larry Mullen Jnr. was exiled from the studio and located under the front staircase in Windmill Lane, the open spaces above lending his sound the natural reverb that producer Steve Lillywhite was looking for.

By chance, The Edge had bumped into Steve Wickham on the way home from a writing session and the violinist was brought into play, his fiddle colourations effectively stirring up some old ethnic ghosts and lending the song deeper Irish resonances. "Actually it starts as a folk song and ends up as one of those Salvation Army songs," Bono says now. "That was a good idea, but I don't think it came off, really."

A powerful song, it became a live staple, its anthemic quality lending itself to the stadium treatment towards which the band were inevitably being drawn. It resurfaced on the mini-album *Under a Blood Red Sky*, also released in 1983, but its apotheosis came during the *Joshua Tree* tour, which was being recorded for the *Rattle and Hum* album and film.

The version in the film was recorded on the day of the Enniskillen massacre, 8 November, 1987. This, too, was a horrific military operation, in this instance carried out by the IRA. A bomb was placed at the war memorial in the centre of Enniskillen town in Fermanagh. As a crowd gathered there to mark Remembrance Day, the bomb was detonated, killing 13 people. It was an action which was impossible to defend, and the ensuing wave of condemnation and revulsion shook the Republican movement to its core. Many would remember the Enniskillen bombing as the most appalling atrocity committed in the cause of Irish unity.

"Fuck the revolution," Bono declared on stage in Denver after the news had come through from Ireland, and the band proceeded to unleash a cathartic, emotional version of the song which reflected their anger – and that of so many Irish men and women – at another senseless, brutal act of violence, in which innocent people had been butchered. "It was the ultimate performance of the song," Bono confided in 1988. "It was almost like the song was made real for the day, in a way that it was never going to be again. Anything else would be less than that."

SECONDS

The acoustic guitar that opens 'Seconds' and drives it was The Edge's idea. In fact, the song is a tour-de-force by the guitarist. For the first time, he sings lead vocals. It was The Edge's voice that U2 tended to double-track for harmonies. Bono figures his partner-in-crime's singing was under-rated: now that he was out in front, a lot of people failed to notice the difference and assumed it was Bono on vocals.

SECONDS
Written: U2
Length: 3' 11"
Album: *War*,
March 1983

The track offered ample evidence that U2's canvas was broadening. There was musical irony in the juxtaposition of The Edge's jaunty acoustic pop confection with lyrics about the imminence of nuclear catastrophe. There's humour in the reference to a track by sland labelmates Troublefunk: "They're doing the atomic bomb/Do they know where the dance comes from?" And in a move that in many ways was ahead of its time, they lifted a sample from a 1982 TV documentary entitled *Soldier Girls*.

"The whole spectacle of these girls going through this incredible routine of training seemed perfect to slip in here," The Edge said in 1983. "It's not obvious but if you listen close you can hear the refrain 'I want to be an airborne ranger/I want to live the life of danger.' It's very disturbing."

"I remember watching it in the Green Room in Windmill," Bono recalls. "It happened to be on and we made a recording of it. Sometimes things like that just fall into place." Overall, the track was curiously reminiscent of the Beatles – a positive recommendation at the worst of times. Not to be outdone, one close associate insists that the group were subconsciously influenced by the Human League, who had a track with the title 'Seconds' (about the assassination of John F. Kennedy) on their *Dare* album.

Meanwhile, in global political terms, during the early '80s, there was reason to believe that the lunatics had taken over the asylum. Under Margaret Thatcher's bellicose regime, American Pershing cruise missiles had been freshly installed in Britain. And in the USA, there was the scary picture of Ronald Reagan, a right-wing fundamentalist president who was quite clearly doddering and incompetent into the bargain. With his finger on the button, you got the impression that Armageddon might be unleashed at any time. Maybe even by accident.

"I've always felt physically ill at the concept of nuclear fall-out," Bono says. "We are the first generation of people to have to live with that possibility. It's all around us, it's in our heads. And it affects the way people feel about the world. I always saw it in apocalyptic terms. For the first time, it became possible – it is possible – to destroy everything."

NEW YEAR'S DAY

NEW YEAR'S DAY
Written: U2
Length: 5' 35"
Album: *War*,
March 1983
UK singles chart
position: 10

Adam had come up with the bass figure at a soundcheck. The Edge had developed the piece on the piano. Now, the band were five, maybe six tracks into recording *War* and Bono still hadn't got down the lyrics for 'New Year's Day'. "It was an unsettled time," Adam recalled later. "You looked around and there were conflicts everywhere. We saw a lot of unrest on TV and in the media. We focused on these."

In the end, Bono had to make up the lyrics on the spot. The singer had a set of images in his head that he felt would fit the mood of the piece. He began to describe them to the backdrop of the music. He was flying on a wing and a prayer and testing everyone's tolerance for the nth time in the process. But the opening line is beautifully arresting and what emerges is a haunting love song of considerable depth. It was the only real single on *War* and went straight into the UK Top 10 on release.

"I personally am bloody sick, every time I switch on the radio, of being blasted with this contrived crap," Bono said shortly afterwards. "It would be stupid to start drawing up battle lines but the fact that 'New Year's Day' made the Top 20 indicated a disillusionment among record buyers with the pop culture in the charts."

It does conform to the basic chart model in one respect at least, however. It is a love song, doubtless written by Bono with his new wife, Ali, in mind. But the impressionistic political backdrop connected with the mood of the time in an unexpected way. With the emergence of the

Solidarity leader and ter President of oland, Lech Walesa.

Solidarity movement, from 1980 onwards the communist regime in Poland was being challenged for the first time since the Iron Curtain had been erected. Following a series of strikes, martial law had been imposed, in December 1981. Solidarity became a proscribed organisation and its leaders were arrested, among them Lech Walesa. "Subconsciously I must have been thinking about Lech Walesa being interned and his wife not being allowed to see him," Bono commented. "Then, when we'd recorded the song, they announced that martial law would be lifted in Poland on New Year's Day. Incredible."

Nothing changes on New Year's Day? You knew what he meant all the same.

LIKE A SONG

Initially, U2 conceived of *War* as a knuckleduster in the face of the new pretty-boy pop that was flourishing in Britain in the early '80s. But it was also intended as a musical two-fingers to the self-styled cognoscenti who had been stepping up their attacks on U2 as being too worthy and sincere by far, not real rock 'n' rollers.

"I think 'Like a Song' was addressed to the critics who didn't get what we were about, who thought we weren't really punk enough," Bono recalls. "That's a subject that comes up again and again because people really do fall for this rebel thing. It's such a cliché."

"It made some kind of sense in the '50s and '60s. Against a conservative backdrop, that punk attitude had a real meaning. Now a lot of it is just dressing up."

Bono's anger isn't always well articulated in the song itself. "I don't think I got the tone of voice right," he observes. But he hits the bullseye once at least, in identifying the selfishness at the heart of most rock 'n' roll posturing. "When others need your time/You say it's time to go," he accuses. The band make a lot of thunderously impressive noise, but in the end 'Like a Song' remains just that. Like a song.

LIKE A SONG
Written: U2
Length: 4' 47"
Album: *War*,
March 1983

Bono observes the soundcheck.

DROWNING MAN

DROWNING MAN
Written: U2
Length: 4' 14"
Album: *War*,
March 1983

There aren't many songwriters who would attempt to get away with it. It remains inscrutable: there is no reference to a drowning man in there.

It's to do with the way U2 constructed their songs at the time. "It was the title of a Sam Beckett-style play I'd started about a drowning man," Bono recalls. "I had a few scenes written. There was to be a guy in a chair with a blindfold and there was to be a little ballet thing."

In the build-up to recording *War*, The Edge remembers that it was a song they took for granted. Although most of the work still had to be done on it, they knew that there was the root of a very strong piece in there.

When it came to putting it down, the song took flight, developing into one of the band's most sophisticated and successful artefacts. Rhythmically, Larry and Adam stitch it together beautifully, with more than a little help from The Edge on acoustic. Bono's singing is transcendant and there's a lovely eastern inflection to the counter-melody when Steve Wickham's violin lifts off towards the close.

"Whereas I know some of the songs on *War* could be re-recorded and improved," The Edge said in 1985, "with 'Drowning Man' it's perfection. It's one of the most successful pieces of recording we've ever done."

I have a hunch that the phrase "drowning man" may have featured in the first draft of the lyrics, to be replaced as the song developed by the altogether more musical "take my hand". Whatever the truth in that, 'Drowning Man' has been interpreted as a love song in which the subject and object are deliberately merged, with Bono surrendering himself to a higher love, embracing both the sexual and the spiritual.

Looking back now at the reflection of his younger self in the mirror of the lyric sheet, Bono hesitantly describes it as a psalm. Mostly these are written from the point of view of David railing at God – but occasionally the perspective switches and what we read instead are God's words. At the height of his involvement in charismatic Christianity, Bono had been experimenting with the experience of speaking in tongues within the Shalom group. Bono would search for that higher state, improvising lyrics on the mic, allowing the words, the feeling – at its best, the ecstasy – to take hold. He remembers being up there recording 'Drowning Man'.

It's a song written from the perspective of a loving God. It may, in its way, be entirely presumptuous – but, far more importantly, its cup is overflowing with tenderness.

And it is addressed to Adam Clayton.

THE REFUGEE

Steve Lillywhite had a rule that he would not do more than two albums with any one band or artist. It was time for U2, also, to move on to fresh alliances, and to use the opportunity to remodel their sound. They knew what they wanted: a harder, more urban, more rock 'n' roll feel than *October* had exhibited. Among those considered were Jimmy Destri, then of Blondie, Sandy Pearlman, who had worked with Blue Oyster Cult and The Clash, Roxy Music's Rhet Davies, and Jimmy Iovine, who had phoned repeatedly, insisting that he wanted to produce the band.

Along the way they'd considered the possibility of using an Irish producer. Bill Whelan had already formed a publishing alliance with the band's manager, Paul McGuinness, and they demoed one song at least with him. It turned up on *War*.

Mick Jones and Paul Simonon of the Clash

"I think when Bono went to America he became more politicised," one friend suggests. "He was hanging out with Cubans in San Francisco. In America, the blacks, the Italians and other immigrants have an *amour* for the Irish. Bono always got that kind of response, so he started to take an interest in what the Irish and the blacks and the Caribbeans had in common. I think that's where 'The Refugee' was coming from."

It was that, and more besides. The Irish film-maker Bob Quinn had been exploring the roots of Celtic culture. In an influential documentary, the *Atlantean* trilogy, he advanced the theory that the Celts had come to Ireland from Egypt and North Africa, taking their music and their art with them. Similarities had been detected between Irish traditional melodies and those of Middle Eastern folk and ethnic music. And in the same vein, art historians were beginning to identify unmistakable connections between Coptic art and the intricate and elaborate artwork hand-drawn by Irish monks in manuscripts like the *Book of Kells*.

That kind of discovery, and the debate it inspired, was hugely important in a country like Ireland, whose culture had been stultifyingly rigid and enclosed in the 50-plus years since independence had been declared in 1921. Among the younger post-'60s generation in particular, there was a

THE REFUGEE
Written: U2
Length: 3' 40"
Album: *War*,
March 1983

growing awareness of the need to look outwards, and to learn from other cultures and other societies. This was now given fresh impetus by the recognition that our own roots and origins were far more complex – and far more interesting – than we'd traditionally been led to believe. Bono saw the *Atlantean* trilogy and later met Bob Quinn. It was almost inevitable that the curiosity which had thus been aroused would find an outlet in a song.

"That was a passion at the time, that Irish music had to be re-invented or re-incarnated. At around the same time, I was trying to get in touch with John Lydon, to see if I could get him to record with The Chieftains. I had this idea that his voice sounded like bagpipes and I thought that they'd be amazing together. Then we met Steve Wickham, who came in and played on 'Sunday Bloody Sunday'. I had spoken with Steve, over many nights, about how Irish music could be re-appropriated, because it was terribly unhip at the time. That became his project. He went off with that in mind and joined In Tua Nua. [He also later hooked up with The Waterboys.] So a lot of good came of all that."

The Troublefunk reference on 'Seconds' wasn't the only reason to suspect that someone had been doing some serious listening to black music. When *War* was being pieced together, Steve Lillywhite – who'd agreed to become involved one more time when all else had failed – took the Bill Whelan track and put the finishing touches to it. Larry Mullen's thumping tribal drums were mixed right up front and the band engaged in some suitably primitive chanting. The noise was impressive enough: it just didn't sound entirely as if U2 were wearing their own clothes, playing their own riffs, using their own voices.

"I haven't listened to that song in 10 years," Bono confesses, "but I think it's probably in the wrong key and is trying to be exciting and not quite pulling it off."

Curiously, Bill Whelan, who was credited with producing the track, found his own angle on the theme later in *Riverdance*. If reinvigorating Irish music, and in particular Irish dancing, was the objective, then Whelan achieved it spectacularly, with a successful musical that explored again the connections between Irish, American and – to a lesser extent – African music.

In doing so, along with the show's producer Moya Doherty, Whelan succeeded in re-introducing an erotic, sexual dimension to an ethnic dance culture that had become sterile and antiseptic.

43

TWO HEARTS BEAT AS ONE

Bono tied the knot with Ali Stewart on 21 August, 1982. The band were hugely in debt to Island Records at the time and the singer didn't have a whole lot of money to lavish on the occasion. Still, the Island connection had one distinct advantage: the owner of the label, Chris Blackwell, had extensive properties in Jamaica and the Bahamas. He loaned one of them, a house called Goldeneye which had once belonged to Ian Fleming, to Bono and Ali for their honeymoon. 'Two Hearts Beat as One' was one of two songs that Bono wrote there.

The second single to be released from *War* – and the band's second hit in Britain – it was another stab at fusing rock and funk and it was at least a partial success. Lyrically, Bono is still struggling to find a voice. "I don't know how to say what's got to be said," he confesses. But even more revealing, perhaps, is the undercurrent of desperation which the song announces.

You can imagine Bono unable to bask in the comfort of his honeymoon house, his restless spirit inevitably contemplating with mounting horror the prospect of entering the studio again with a bunch of under-worked lyrical ideas and half-completed choruses scrawled on the back of cigarette papers and Air India sickbags. "I can't stop to dance/This is my last chance," he says, as if to excuse himself to Ali. And of course he may have been right: if U2 had not taken off with *War*, then it might well have been their last album, on Island at least. And if Island had dropped them, who knows what might have happened then?

"I didn't really write that many love songs in the straight sense because I think – does the world really need any more silly love songs?" Bono asserts. "But this is one. And in many ways I do think that it's beautiful. We're trying to make it groovy and we ain't quite pulled it off. I think if we'd tried it in a different key, we might have discovered a sexier groove and it might have worked better. But we never did that. Whatever the jam was in, I'd sing the song in that key. That's why there was a tightness in the vocals, which I find it hard to listen to now. I was screeching a lot of the time. But I think if a song like that had been delivered differently it would have more appeal to me now 'cos it's a good song."

TWO HEARTS
BEAT AS ONE
Written: U2
Length: 4' 03"
Album: *War*,
March 1983
UK singles chart
position: 18

Two hearts: Bono and wife Ali.

RED LIGHT

An outsider visiting Ireland in the late '70s and early '80s might have been forgiven for concluding that the locals knew nothing about carnal delights, and had little interest in the pleasures of the flesh. The dominant ethos was still extremely conservative on sexual issues. The underlying reality was that the people had begun to move on, and the seeds of a more tolerant and liberal society were beginning to take root. But officially, it was a culture where condoms were still available from chemists only on prescription, homosexuality was illegal, and highly restrictive censorship laws ensured that erotic or pornographic books and magazines were almost completely unavailable.

It couldn't have been more different to New York, Hamburg or Amsterdam. Inevitably these somewhat exotic destinations held a particular allure for four young Irishmen in a rock 'n' roll band, enjoying the freedom of the cities they were visiting for the first time.

"I certainly remember a fascination with prostitution," Bono recalls. "We played Amsterdam and I remember seeing the girls for sale in the windows, lit in red. Thinking about it. Trying to figure out the reality of it, whether there was any or not. I was never judgmental about it."

'Red Light' is decidedly ambiguous. It's a love song, which could be addressed to one of the girls Bono had observed in the windows. Equally, it might be another somewhat parental, albeit affectionate homily directed at saving Adam's immortal soul. Or it could be written from the point of view of a prostitute, watching her clients come and go. Probably, in a way that was typical of U2's songs then, it is any or all of these things at once.

Musically, the band make a stab at evoking an appropriately steamy cityscape. Kid Creole and the Coconuts, who were knocking on the door of stardom at the time, passed through town while U2 were recording the album, and the ensemble's trumpeter Kenny Fradley was hauled in to add a brassy bit. And then there were The Coconuts themselves.

"They came in," Bono recalls. "They wanted the lights turned down to do the recording and I think we had the studio lit in red, for effect.One of them started to take her top off. She wasn't undressing. She just took her top off, but we weren't used to that kind of thing. I remember the temperature in the studio was at an all-time high. Everyone was running around looking for cold water. We were that naive!"

Lyrically, the song is reasonably strong, but 'Red Light' is widely regarded as one of U2's most unsatisfactory cuts. At least we now know who to blame.

RED LIGHT
Written: U2
Length: 3' 46"
Album: *War*,
March 1983

SURRENDER

Bono was beginning to write songs. You can tell by the way he was getting into using characters. And then there were the small poetic flourishes, lines that had a more finished feel to them. He was beginning to know his own strengths, to understand how to channel his creative energies more effectively. He was becoming a songwriter.

He'd met Sadie – not her real name – in New York. She was living on the street, hustling and doing whatever was necessary to keep body and soul together. Over 10 years on, she's still at the same game, only by now she's got a smack habit to feed. Back then, he was attracted to her and to the way in which she'd been able to let go of all the trappings of domesticity and respectability. He probably still is.

There's an ambivalence here that involves a huge leap forward from the biblical certainties of *October* and hints at the more complex world of *Achtung Baby* and *Zooropa*. The concept of

Bono live: never about to throw in the towel.

surrender is a spiritual one, but it's rooted not in any conventional concept of virtue. It wasn't enough for Sadie to be a good wife, to raise a good family, to lead a good life. And so she took to the streets. "You've got to learn to let go in order to really live. That's what 'Surrender' is all about," Bono explains.

There's a reminder of the fascination with suicide on *Boy* when Sadie takes herself up to the 48th floor to find out, in the words of the song, what she's living for. "In one sense everyone's got to jump off. That's what it's all about – the idea that if I want to live, I've got to die to myself."

The rest of the band provide the atmospherics, with The Edge enjoying himself playing a free role on slide guitar. But this is primarily Bono's track as he himself lets go, blissfully surrendering, fading, fading into the background.

SURRENDER
Written: U2
Length: 5' 33"
Album: *War*,
March 1983

40

The recording of *War* had been exhilarating, tense and finally draining. There were times during the course of their incarceration in Windmill when Steve Lillywhite had had to push Bono to the limits, forcing him to sing until his throat bled. Now, here they were, a track short and with their allotted studio time almost up. The band had enjoyed themselves in the past improvising B-sides and starting and finishing songs in an hour. The results were usually throwaway, but what the hell? They wanted to get '40' done. Steve Lillywhite said to go for it.

Adam was out of the studio and The Edge stood in, supplying a sweet, resonant melodic bass line that worked beautifully over the simple guitar strum. No point in changing it. At 6 o'clock in the morning, a belligerent bunch of musos in a local Dublin band arrived to begin the session they'd booked. They wanted U2 out. The band had to lock the door and mix the track while Bono was doing his final vocal take. His voice sounds ragged, 6 o'clock in the morning ragged. But whatever chemistry was at work as dawn crept in from the east over Dublin Bay, the band achieve a remarkable serenity. If this was what they'd been looking for throughout *War*, they'd found it in that final hour.

Partly it may be that they knew that their ordeal was over, that there was no point in trying too hard. Keep it simple. Get it down. It'll work out. '40' emerges as a lullaby, a hymn that's suffused with a deep feeling of peace and resignation. For the most part, the lyrics are lifted from Psalm 40, in the Psalms of David. But the desperate plea in the opening track, 'Sunday Bloody Sunday' – "How long must we sing this song?" – is revisited here as an incantation, a prayer.

'40' would become one of U2's best known tracks, chosen by the band to close their live shows throughout most of the '80s. The Edge called it a monument to U2, created in an instant.

"I really love that song," Bono says simply now. "I've seen some incredible scenes, I've seen some extraordinary sights, through it. I really love it."

Amen.

40
Written: U2
Length: 2' 39"
Album: *War*,
March 1983

THE UNFORGETTABLE FIRE

For their next studio album, it would help to find a new producer. They thought of Conny Plank. It didn't happen. And then in a flash of inspiration The Edge thought of Brian Eno. It is impossible to speculate what might have happened if Eno had said no. Instead he brought Daniel Lanois with him.

They began the album in Slane Castle with the mobile. The sessions were open-ended, spacious, free. The band did a day's recording naked. "We got into gaffer art," Bono commented. Lanois, for one, lost some pubic hairs as a result.

But Danny was good on rhythms. Larry's playing became looser, funkier, more subtle. Adam's gained in confidence and poise. Gradually Bono learned to sing again. The relaxed, experimental feel of those initial sessions gave the record its fresh, exploratory tone. Not everything worked and, as the deadline approached, they opted to go back into Windmill. Bono was still agonising over lyrics. Less than two weeks before the band were due to go on tour, he announced that he couldn't do it.

He was given an ultimatum. Do it. The final ten days' recording were a nightmare. One or two tracks sound seriously undercooked. But on balance the exercise was thoroughly successful, producing U2's first album with a cohesive sound.

With *The Unforgettable Fire*, U2 were reborn.

Bono, suffering "gaffer art".

A SORT OF HOMECOMING

Bono had become a voracious reader. He was still interested in the Bible and in opening up its myriad secrets, but he was casting his net more widely now than ever before. He was immersing himself in fiction, philosophy, poetry. And the more poetry he read, the more he began to understand his songwriting mission as a poetic one.

He could occasionally be self-conscious about it. "I am a writer of words," he reflected in 'Dreams in a Box', a poem written during 1987. But there is no doubt that by the making of *The Unforgettable Fire*, he had begun to find his poetic voice.

Bono had been reading the work of Paul Celan, a Jewish poet of mixed German and Romanian origin. Celan was an intensely spiritual writer, a mystic whose life and death were shrouded in ambiguities. His work posed a set of questions that were highly problematic for anyone of fixed religious convictions. Gradually, Bono, Larry and The Edge were leaving those certainties behind. But Celan opened up new avenues of spiritual doubt.

"Poetry is a sort of homecoming," Celan had written, and it rang true for Bono. The phrase inspired a meditation that seemed to encompass in one impressionistic reverie many of Bono's familiar obsessions. It is written in a dreamy, cinematic style, the camera briefly capturing vivid images which then dissolve one into the next, a constant sense of movement propelling the song along. "She will die and live again, tonight," Bono sings, and sex and spirituality intermingle, in an unmistakable allusion to the little death and the (little) resurrection.

But while there is a sense in the lyrics that things are falling apart and the centre cannot hold, the extent to which the narrator seems in control of the words, of the ideas, of the poetry, is in itself reassuring.

It's as if Bono is re-affirming his commitment to a life devoted to the search for poetic truth. While it might seem like a veiled reference to 'I Will Follow', the chant "O come away/O come away/O come away/O come away say I" is more likely an unconscious allusion to WB Yeats' 'The Human Child', and it was towards influences of that ilk that he was now drawn.

"A lot of rock 'n' roll is banal ideas well executed," Bono reflects. "Whereas I think a lot of what we do is really very interesting ideas, badly executed." 'A Sort of Homecoming' involved a lot of very interesting ideas well executed. It was a powerful opening to the album.

49

A SORT OF
HOMECOMING
Written: U2
Length: 5' 28"
Album: *The
Unforgettable Fire*,
October 1984

PRIDE (IN THE NAME OF LOVE)

On the road, U2 are constantly working informally on new ideas. Rehearsals and sound-checks are recorded. From a musical point of view, this is how a substantial number of songs began.

The band played Hawaii during the *War* tour, in November 1983. Live engineer Joe O'Herlihy was recording the sound-check. The Edge led the way into a series of chord changes. There was a mistake, and the band picked up on it: someone's slip had given a new twist to the piece. Joe recorded the incident in his mind: by now he'd learned to recognise these special moments. When the time came to record *The Unforgettable Fire*, he remembered precisely where the roots of 'Pride' were to be found.

Gonna use her voice: Chrissie Hynde of The Pretenders.

Bono was working on something about Ronald Reagan. He had the title 'Pride' in mind for it, thinking about the kind that comes before a fall, thinking of the hubris which was the dominant characteristic of America's foreign policy during the Reagan era. But it wasn't working, and he began to get the feeling he was going to have to switch tack. The band had been to the Chicago Peace Museum and were impressed by the exhibit there dedicated to the black civil rights leader Martin Luther King. Shifting emphasis to the kind of pride that King had inspired in black people, Bono sensed that there was an entirely different song to be written.

At the centre of the song is a series of images that have the grainy feel of wire photos sent back from the front-line of resistance: "One man caught on a barbed wire fence/One man he resist/One man washed up on an empty beach/One man betrayed by a kiss." There is no sense that Bono had abandoned his religious beliefs, but the references are more subtle.

Recording 'Pride (In the Name of Love)' was extraordinarily difficult. U2 had done a backing track in Slane, but when they moved across to Windmill Lane it didn't feel right. With time ticking away, they decided to ditch what they'd done in Slane and re-record the track from scratch. It worked. Almost immediately they knew that 'Pride' was a killer. Chrissie Hynde of The Pretenders was in town and she dropped into the studio to assist with the backing vocals, though the sleeve credits refer to Mrs Christine Kerr. Not surprisingly, it became the first single from *The Unforgettable Fire*.

PRIDE (IN THE NAME OF LOVE)
Written: U2
Length: 3' 49"
Album: *The Unforgettable Fire*, October 1984
UK singles chart position: 3
US singles chart position: 33

WIRE

"When I started writing I didn't even know what a couplet was," Bono recalls. But by *The Unforgettable Fire* he had developed a much stronger sense of what the conventions were. When he got it right, then a song lifted and soared: 'A Sort of Homecoming' was a case in point, a tremendously visual, poetic, emotional word-festival. Things didn't always work out so well, however.

Whereas Steve Lillywhite had been highly rigorous and exacting in his attitude to songs, Eno was far more indulgent. Bono tended to come at his themes obliquely. Eno let him get away with it even when he ended up saying very little.

Bono was aware of the heroin that had begun to flood Dublin. He knew a couple of friends who'd become involved. Now he wanted to write a song that captured his own ambivalence to the drug. "I'm probably an addictive kind of person myself," Bono admits. And so that was what he wanted to convey lyrically.

There's an openness and sparkle to the music on 'Wire', which skips along on a light funk groove courtesy of an in-form Larry Mullen. The hand of Eno and Lanois is in evidence here, as the band veer in a direction already sign-posted by Talking Heads, whom Eno had also produced. But while the noise is impressive, the lyrics never get beyond mere sketchwork. "There is the fascination of death and of flirting with death that's part of heroin use," Bono reflected later. But none of that is conveyed here. There are moments of sardonic rhetoric that almost work – "Such a nice day/To throw your life away" – and the song ends in a kind of a nagging rap. But 'Wire' is an example of how flat a song improvised on the mic can be. "Is this time, the time to win or lose?" he asks, "Is this the time, the time to choose?"

Bono knew what a couplet was now, alright. But that didn't mean he was William Shakespeare.

WIRE	
Written:	U2
Length:	4' 19"
Album:	*The Unforgettable Fire*, October 1984

THE UNFORGETTABLE FIRE

When the Americans dropped the atomic bomb on Hiroshima and Nagasaki, it was one of the final and most barbarous acts of World War Two. These two Japanese cities were utterly destroyed, and in human terms the toll was even more horrific.

A total of 67,000 people died immediately as a direct result, and thousands more were scarred, injured and maimed. But it was a catastrophe truly like no other in terms of its psychic impact: the effects of radiation from the bombs would last for generations, producing genetic mutations of the most chilling kind, and causing widespread leukaemia and cancer. The final death toll is almost impossible to calculate, though 200,000 is probably a conservative estimate. It was as close as we had ever come to Armageddon, a terrible spectacle of such frightening immensity that anyone who was close to it could never, ever forget – the whole world, it seemed, transformed into a gigantic charnel house.

Iwakichi Kobayashi was a survivor of the holocaust that had engulfed Hiroshima and Nagasaki. He drew a picture to illustrate his memory of what had happened. Japanese television picked up on the theme and invited other survivors to submit their own paintings. It became a kind of exorcism, a therapeutic outpouring of grief and horror at the atrocity which had been visited on innocent people.

The Japanese created an exhibition of the paintings and drawings from survivors of the holocaust, entitled *The Unforgettable Fire*, and it was housed within the Hiroshima Peace Memorial. During the early '80s, some 60 of the pictures had been taken on tour; they went on display at the Chicago Peace Museum, and U2 saw them there. "Painting was part of the therapy to help these people purge themselves of their internalised emotions," The Edge said at the time. "The image of that purging quality, coupled with the insight it gave into the horror of nuclear holocaust, stuck in Bono's mind. Later we found the title fit the new record in many ways, especially in reflecting its multicoloured textures."

It was Bono's magpie instinct at work again. In a reversal of the norm that would be typical of the band, Bono thought of *The Unforgettable Fire* as the name of the album first. It was too good a title not to use it for a song as well – though what Bono produced by way of a lyric had little or no connection with the original source of the title.

"It was a soundtrack piece I'd been messing around with on the piano at home," The Edge reflected later. "It was a beautiful piece of music but I

THE UNFORGETTABLE FIRE
Written: U2
Length: 4' 55"
Album: *The Unforgettable Fire*, October 1984
UK singles chart position: 6

couldn't see how one could approach it lyrically or vocally. It was knocking around for quite a while, and myself and Bono were out in his house doing work on material for the record and I found this cassette of the piano piece and we decided to mess around with it. Within an hour, we'd written a verse section with Bono playing bass, and we virtually wrote the song there. Obviously it changed with drums and bass in the studio, but it was the first 20 minutes in Bono's house that counted."

Bono was still in a state of semi-permanent writer's block. "Writing songs scares the living daylights out of me," he said at the time. "It's been a huge problem and I just ran away." Even in a situation where they had the melody and the music, he was finding it hard to get a fix on the lyrics.

"I see the rhythm of words as being important," he reasoned afterwards. "They build up slowly and often I don't think it's ready yet – though everyone else may think it is, I can't let it go. That's why a lot of the songs tend to be sketches. 'The Unforgettable Fire', it's a sketch: 'Carnival/wheels fly and colours spin/face to face/in a dry and waterless place.' It builds up a picture, but it's only a sketch." Some sketches, however, work better than others. This is an emotional travelogue, images shuffled through the memory to underscore the song's sense of yearning. It is a love song that links thematically back to 'A Sort of Homecoming', but it's imbued with a sense of foreboding that seems to anticipate the end of a relationship.

"It's classical, almost," The Edge said in 1985. "I see it as a music piece rather than as a song. Bono, in a very unconventional way, explores numerous melodies over sections. Instead of repeating melodies – you know, verses and choruses, which is what everyone does – we've got three chorus melodies and two verse melodies. It has a certain symphonic feel for me because there are so many intertwining themes. We could have recorded it better but for all its flaws, I just see it as a great piece of music."

PROMENADE

Van Morrison's legend looms large in Irish music. From U2's perspective, he was crucial. Following a period in seclusion, he had re-emerged in the late '70s and, the man's reputation as an abrasive genius notwithstanding, his music reflected a renewed sense of inner contentment. His interest in language, and in squeezing out new meanings from it, was undiminished. Van Morrison stretched words, broke them down, created new ones, and – occasionally in despair at the limits which this discipline imposed – plunged into a kind of primal articulation, letting the inner self rise to the surface and express itself. But guiding this search for descriptive, expressive resources beyond language was a profound interest in spirituality.

U2 could never merely follow the Morrison model, but it was reassuring to them, nonetheless, that he had managed to infuse his work with such a powerful sense of spiritual mission. It was inevitable that Bono would listen to and be inspired by his music, and on 'Promenade' that influence is unmistakable. Words are used for their sound as much as their sense, which was not new for Bono – but here there is a poetic surefootedness in the writing that marks a significant step forward.

After the *War* tour, Bono had spoken about the need for U2 to re-invent themselves. "Today was the last U2 gig," Bono said on the evening the tour finished. "But I'm not talking about the end of U2. This is the end of a cycle. We must develop new areas now. U2 is just beginning."

"I find it very difficult to listen to *War* now," Bono admits. "There is so much anger and the effect of that is to tighten up the voice, so that it becomes higher and more shrill. But on *The Unforgettable Fire* I learned to relax again. I learned to sing again."

Bono and Ali had moved from one side of Dublin Bay, in Howth, across to Bray. He was living in the Martello Tower, which he'd had re-designed. A spiral staircase led from the living room up to the bedroom. Above the bed was a glass roof, opening up a spectacular view of the night sky. The tower overlooked the Carlisle Grounds, where Bray Wanderers played their League of Ireland football games. All along the promenade are amusement parlours, snooker halls, fast-food outlets, restaurants and guest houses. That background is evoked in impressionistic strokes, but 'Promenade' is unmistakably a love song that celebrates the spiritual dimensions of sexual desire. "Turn me around tonight/up through the spiral staircase/to the higher ground."

It's where we all want to go, if we know how to get there.

PROMENADE
Written: U2
Length: 2' 34"
Album: *The Unforgettable Fire*, October 1984

4TH OF JULY

4TH OF JULY
Written: U2
Length: 2' 14"
Album: *The Unforgettable Fire*, October 1984

One of Brian Eno's rules is that there are no rules. Sometimes, if you work too hard at something you kill it.

Occasionally when you're doodling, something emerges which is transcendent. Inspiration can strike in the most unexpected situations. You can frame the maxims in different ways. You can hone them till they're razor sharp. You can even develop them, as Eno did, into a set of Oblique Strategies. "The first I wrote was 'Honour thy error as a hidden intention', a reminder not to have too fixed a view about what was appropriate in a given piece," Eno explained to David Gan, "to accept the possibility that sometimes the things one doesn't intend are the seeds for a more interesting future than the one one had envisaged."

It is impossible to speculate about what Adam might have intended when he began to amuse himself with a sliding bass figure, in a break during recording, after U2 had put down a version of 'Bad' in Windmill Lane. Musicians do this kind of thing all the time and more often than not the germ of an idea is lost once somebody walks in with a cup of coffee.

"I started playing along with Adam, totally unaware that Brian was listening in the other room," The Edge recalled. "He happened to have some treatments set up for the vocal Bono had been doing and he applied those to the guitar. He thought it was really nice, so without bothering to put it on multi-track, which is the 24-track tape machine, he just recorded it straight down to stereo tape. It was very much a live performance. There was no way we could mix it or re-do any of the instruments." There was probably a temptation to get Bono to stick a vocal on top, but the singer must have been relieved when that option was dismissed. One less lyric to write. Whew!

The track is pensive and exploratory. In no way an attempt to celebrate Independence Day, it should be taken rather as a kind of musical diary-entry. Eno captured the moment for posterity. That was a vital part of his genius.

...o's hand was
...evidence.

BAD

For the second time on *The Unforgettable Fire*, we are given to understand that Bono is addressing a heroin addict. There is a sense throughout 'Bad' that he doesn't know what he wants to say, and that he doesn't know what he's saying either. But, in a way, he says it eloquently anyway.

To begin with there's an empathy in 'Bad' which gives the song resonance. "If I could," Bono sings, "Yes I would/If I could/I would let it go/ Surrender, dislocate." It's an honest admission of his own vulnerability to the temptation that drugs like heroin represent. "It relates to what I was trying to do, much more overtly on Zoo TV," he states. "With those characters, I wanted to admit to those things, those sides of yourself, that want to run away from responsibility, and that find people who have run away attractive. I've always had a real respect for responsible people but I also have a real respect for irresponsible people."

'Bad' begins on a kind of drone, but it's the light, shuffling rhythm track, with Adam throwing in a dub-influenced bass part, that gives the track its addictive propulsion. "I think the experience of working with Brian and Daniel Lanois was a revelation to Larry," The Edge says. "Instead of his goal being technique or drumming ability, he became aware of new approaches to rhythm. He became aware of percussion."

Bono, meanwhile, was engaging in his own inarticulate speech of the heart. Like 'Wire', there's nothing in the night-lit world of 'Bad' that makes it clear this song has to do with junk. But there is a restlessness that speaks volumes. You begin to imagine the narrator prowling his room in the darkest hour before dawn, wrestling with the temptation to take the plunge. There is a desire to go over the edge, to experience whatever the other side might throw at him. The feeling is so intense that he can't express it clearly. His thoughts emerge in disconnected fragments. He repeats himself. If you wanted to get tough about it, you'd argue that 'Bad' says nothing. But it's a trip – a tense, nervy, intoxicating, exhilarating trip.

"Comprehension had never been particularly important to me," says Adam. "It's much more important how the lyrics feel. If it doesn't sound right, then I'll consult Bono and try and figure out what's going on. But it's an instinctive thing. I find that it's only after six months of touring it and talking to different people that you get to the inner truths of the song."

Desperation, dislocation, separation, condemnation, revelation. All of those qualities are there in Bono's performance, except one. The time for condemnation was over. For now.

BAD
Written: U2
Length: 6' 08"
Album: *The Unforgettable Fire*, October 1984

INDIAN SUMMER SKY

Sometime in New York City – probably when the *War* tour hit Manhattan – Bono wrote the bones of 'Indian Summer Sky'. "Most of the writing was cinematic and very fast," Bono says. "It had a sense of wanting to break through a city to an open place."

A friend of Bono's had spent some time in Toronto. He felt troubled by a city that was "cool" and "shiny". "There had been a lot of massacres of Red Indian people in that area," Bono reports, "and he felt in some way as if there were troubled spirits still there. What I was trying to get across in 'Indian Summer Sky' was a sense of spirit trapped in a concrete jungle."

The song is imbued with an epic quality: on the one hand wind, ocean, sky and earth, on the other heart and soul. At one point, it anticipates 'With Or Without You' on *The Joshua Tree* as Bono sings, "You give yourself to this the longest day/You give yourself you give it all away." It's possible that the chorus – "So wind go through to my heart/So wind blow through my soul" – sounds as much like Talking Heads simply because of Brian Eno's involvement. He had, after all, produced *Remain In Light*. The influence seems unmistakable, but there's nothing forced or unnatural here.

"In many ways," Bono reflected later, "*The Unforgettable Fire* was a contrast between bricks and mortar and music with the sky over its head."

He was beginning to move to the rhythms of nature.

Now you could move your hips to U2. Now you could dance.

And it felt good.

INDIAN SUMMER SKY
Written: U2
Length: 4' 19"
Album: *The Unforgettable Fire*, October 1984

ELVIS PRESLEY AND AMERICA

The difference between the production styles of Steve Lillywhite and Brian Eno could not be more starkly expressed than by this track. Lillywhite was prepared to experiment, but Eno went much further.

He saw a piece that had been recorded as utterly malleable. You could open it up, slow it down, stand it on its head, reverse it – anything that might work was worth a shot. And so on an experimental day, when Daniel Lanois and he were fishing around for ideas, they slowed down the backing track from 'A Sort of Homecoming' and played it for Bono without telling him what it was. Eno encouraged the singer to improvise over it.

"It was partly a reaction to the Albert Goldman book, which tried to portray Elvis as the archetypal rock 'n' roll idiot," Bono explains. "But the way he held the mic, the way he sang into the mic – this was his genius. But his decline just tore at me, and when I picked up the mic it was a completely off the wall thing and I just began to sing." Bono approached the track like a jazzman, letting his voice take the song and following it, improvising the lyrics as he went along. Bono saw it as a dry run. The lyrical ideas could be sifted through and refined later. But Eno had other plans.

"He forced Bono to change his approach to recording," The Edge remembers. "Whereas previously with Steve, seven or eight different tracks would be collaged into a single vocal, Brian started insisting, whenever it was practical, on doing one take."

It still came as a shock to Bono when Eno told him that the cut was finished. It was one of Eno's oblique strategies in action: overtly resist change. And another: emphasize the flaws. "It was such an inspired performance," The Edge said flatteringly, "that we decided to leave it as it was." Not everyone would be so complimentary. Some of the band's most supportive critics hated the song. It wasn't what Bono was apparently trying to say about Elvis that rankled, it was the fact that 'Elvis Presley and America' so obviously sounded like a work-in-progress.

"I think that it does evoke that decline, the stupor, the period when he forgets his words and fumbles," Bono argued at the time. It wasn't a bad shot at post-rationalisation, but one thing's for sure: it may have been a useful harbinger for the journey to the heartland of rock 'n' roll that *Rattle and Hum* would involve, but 'Elvis Presley and America' would never be regarded as a U2 classic.

ELVIS PRESLEY AND AMERICA
Written: U2
Length: 6' 22"
Album: *The Unforgettable Fire*, October 1984

MLK

MLK
Written: U2
Length: 2' 32"
Album: *The Unforgettable Fire*, October 1984

The Unforgettable Fire had been coined as a phrase to describe the terror of the holocaust. However, U2 had seen another meaning in it. Just as 'Pride' could be conceived as a song about Ronald Reagan and written about Martin Luther King, it was possible to ascribe another sense to a phrase that played on Bono's imagination.

Fire, passion, belief – these were things that U2 had written about, things that they had dedicated their music to. Elvis Presley had lit a fire that was burning still. So too had Martin Luther King. With 'MLK', he became the hero of *The Unforgettable Fire*, the man whose memory was evoked in the end to soothe the anxieties which had riddled the album and which had crept up on U2 increasingly as the recording had progressed.

It was becoming a trademark. '40' had ended *War* – as 'Scarlet' should have ended *October* – on a healing note. Now that *The Unforgettable Fire* was done, it was time for a spiritual, and 'MLK' provided it. It was a lullaby, a song of reassurance and reconciliation. A song of hope. "Sleep, sleep tonight/And may your dreams/be realised," Bono sang, and it was made to be sung by thousands joined together in a gesture of communion. "Those people who were fighting for civil rights," Bono remarks, "they understood that music better than they understood 'Pride', which was rock 'n' roll music. They understood the tribute." Let it rain, rain on he.

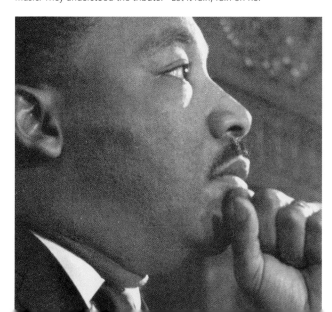

MLK:
Martin Luther King.

THE JOSHUA TREE

July 13, 1985. Live Aid. In front of the biggest television audience for a live music event ever, U2 stole the show. Sales of *The Unforgettable Fire* soared. Suddenly U2 were not just a big band. They were one of the biggest in the world.

It gave them some breathing space. The Edge wrote the soundtrack for Paul Mayerberg's film *Captive*. Bono went travelling, listened to the blues. Did 'Silver and Gold' for the *Sun City* album project with Keith Richards and Ronnie Wood, recorded with Clannad. The whole band did two tracks with Robbie Robertson.

In '86, they emerged in fits. For *TV Gaga*. The *Conspiracy of Hope* tour in the US. Self Aid in Ireland. A different band! They did dirty, loud, noisy cover versions of Eddie Cochran and Bob Dylan. They'd travelled a long, long way from the cultivated European atmospherics of *The Unforgettable Fire*.

Bono was listening to roots music, folk, the blues. He was thinking about songs, reading about the deep south. The Edge had looked east on *Captive*. The band moved west with *The Joshua Tree*, into the arms of America. Bono's songwriting had more focus now. Greater depth. He was dragging himself up there alongside Dylan, Morrison, Lou Reed. "It's our most literate record yet," he said. That was an understatement. It went straight to No.1 in the U.S. and the U.K. In America it became the fastest-selling album of all time. It also delivered the first platinum-selling CD.

In the arid wasteland of the Nevada desert, the Joshua Tree survives despite the dirt, bone-dry sand and stone in which it is embedded. Somewhere down there is water. Somewhere down there is the source of life. Somewhere down there is hope. The challenge is to find it.

Bono: on a journey back to rock's roots.

WHERE THE STREETS HAVE NO NAME

Sometimes you can hear it in your head first. A slow, dramatic, swelling keyboard drone.

A jangling rhythm part on guitar coming in over it. It sounds good – in your head. It feels like the start of something – an intro. But now you have to get it down on tape. Already there's some slippage. The first few steps you take never seem to capture the full glory of what you could hear, but if you come any way close, the momentum will carry you forward.

The Edge, in his house in Monkstown, fooling around on a four-track Tascam home recording studio. Sticking down the keyboard on his own. Listening back to it. It'll do. Rewind. Then the guitar. The rhythm holds good. Try some variations on the chord. Little flicks off the major. Now you can see the bigger picture again. Imagine a bass. The drums coming in. It does feel good. The beginning of a song…

'Where the Streets Have No Name' is one of those ones that seemed as if it didn't want to be born. "The way we write, we sometimes feel that the song is written," The Edge told John Waters, "the song is already there, if you could just put it into words, put it into notes. We have it, but it's not realised yet.

"If you saw us working in the studio sometimes, you'd be scratching your head trying to figure out what we were doing. Mostly, if we get the feeling that we're onto something good, we eventually do get there. And 'Where the Streets Have No Name' is a great example, because that took weeks of work to arrive at."

It nearly drove Brian Eno mad in the process. The more the band worked on the song, the more he resented it. At one stage he became so frustrated at the amount of time being devoted to 'Where the Streets Have No Name' that he wanted to erase the multi-track. "That's right," The Edge recalls. "We weren't in the studio at the time and he asked the assistant engineer to leave the room. He'd actually decided to do it. But the assistant engineer wouldn't go. He stood in front of the tape machine, saying, 'Brian, you can't do this'. And so he didn't. But it was close."

In the end it was Steve Lillywhite rather than Eno who mixed the finished product. "It took forever to get that track," Daniel Lanois told *Rolling Stone*. "We had this giant blackboard with the arrangement written on it. I felt like a science professor, conducting them. To get the rise and fall, the

WHERE THE
STREETS HAVE
NO NAME
Written: U2
Length: 5' 37"
Album:
The Joshua Tree,
March 1987
UK singles chart
position: 4
US singles chart
position: 13

song's dynamic, took a long time." Rise and fall? That makes it sound almost sexual – a thought that mightn't be too far from the truth.

Bono certainly sounds restless and agitated as he launches into a confession: "I want to run/I want to hide/I want to tear down the walls/that hold me inside/I want to reach out/And touch the flame/Where the streets have no name."

"It's been a theme all the way through the group's music," he says, "this sense of wanting to run, wanting to give in to the urge of the hunter. I always think there's two modes – hunter and protector. Or for me there is anyway. If I gave in to one I'd be an animal. And if I gave in to the other, I'd be completely domesticated. Somewhere between the two is where I live."

Bono and Ali in Ethiopia, 1985.

We all feel the crushing burden of domesticity to one degree or another at different times. 'Where The Streets Have No Name' expresses the corresponding desire to cut and run. But it also captures the desperate need for anonymity that someone in Bono's position frequently feels: where the streets have no name, neither do the stars.

The title undoubtedly draws on the time Bono and his wife Ali spent in Ethiopia during 1985. They'd gone there as volunteers, working with aid agencies on the ground, distributing food and assisting with health and educational initiatives. Bono came home to Ireland, to the Western world, with a profound sense of the vacuum at the heart of contemporary living. "The spirit of the people I met in Ethiopia was very strong," Bono says. "There's no doubt that, even in poverty, they had something that we didn't have. When I got back, I realized the extent to which people in the West were like spoiled children."

One of the strengths of the song is that it is never quite clear where the streets with no name are, or precisely what the phrase is intended to mean. He could be talking about Heaven. Maybe even offering us a glimpse into some kind of private hell.

"I can look at it now," Bono says, "and recognize that 'Where The Streets Have No Name' has one of the most banal couplets in the history of pop music. But it also contains some of the biggest ideas. In a curious way, that seems to work. If you get any way heavy about these things, you don't communicate. But if you're flip or throwaway about it, then you do. That's one of the paradoxes I've had to come to terms with."

I STILL HAVEN'T FOUND WHAT I'M LOOKING FOR

Some things stick in the memory. The Edge held a party in his newly reconstructed house in Monkstown on the south coast of Dublin, on New Year's Eve, 1986. By this stage the bulk of the work on *The Joshua Tree* was done and the band were relaxing. But Bono couldn't quite let go.

One of his most attractive qualities is the naked enthusiasm he shows for the band's own music. And so he explained to me that this was an album of songs, that U2 had finally learned what the word meant, and that he was convinced that they had just made by far their best album to date as a result. "There's one in particular," he explained, "that's amazing." And then he started to sing it to me. "It goes like this: 'I have climbed/the highest mountain/I have run/through the fields/only to be with you/only to be with you.' And it's got this refrain," he expanded and sang on till he came to it. "'But I still haven't found what I'm looking for'."

The bass drum of some thumping dance track was whacking away next door, and the hubbub of party voices reigned all around – and yet I'll swear that I could hum the song the next day. It was that catchy. A perfect piece of pop music, it went to No. 1 in the US when it was released there as a single, and no one could have been in the least bit surprised. From the start, Bono clearly knew that he was onto a winner.

The song had entered the world under another title, 'Under The Weather'. It also had a different melody. But once The Edge had come up with the title and the theme of spiritual doubt had crystallised in Bono's imagination, then the momentum became inescapable. Dermot Stokes, who was writing more extensively for *Hot Press* at the time, had given him a tape of blues and gospel music, including tracks by The Swan Silvertones, The Staple Singers and Blind Willie Johnson. Eno, who had listened to a lot of gospel, further stimulated his enthusiasm. Now Bono knew that 'I Still Haven't Found What I'm Looking For' had to have its roots in gospel. But he also sensed that the theme was big enough to allow him to go for broke, to write an anthem.

'I Still Haven't Found What I'm Looking For' is beautifully written and elegantly constructed. The band trip lightly along on a groove that's a model of restraint, with an acoustic rhythm guitar break from The Edge where others might have preferred an instrumental solo. Bono's singing is soulful and heartfelt. No one puts a foot wrong.

I STILL HAVEN'T FOUND WHAT I'M LOOKING FOR
Written: U2
Length: 4' 37"
Album:
The Joshua Tree, March 1987
UK singles chart position: 6
US singles chart position: 1

"I used to think that writing words was old-fashioned," Bono confessed. "So I sketched. I wrote words on the microphone. For *The Joshua Tree*, I felt that the time had come to write words that meant something, out of my own experience."

Shadows and tall trees.

You could sense it straightaway. 'I Still Haven't Found What I'm Looking For' was the real thing – though not everyone seemed to agree with that. In 1991, Negativland, an underground band based in San Francisco, released a record entitled 'U2'. It was a piece of attention-seeking pop larceny: they had re-mixed and re-modelled 'I Still Haven't Found What I'm Looking For', interspersing it with excerpts of an interview conversation between Bono and an American DJ, Casey Kasem. That it was a scam, both creatively and commercially, was underlined by the fact that U2's logo dominated the cover. One automatic reaction was that their fans might be conned into buying something under false pretences.

Island Records stepped in and took out an injunction to prevent further sale or distribution of the record. From the start it was a no-win situation for the U2 organisation. Negativland pleaded that there was no breach of copyright because 'U2' was a parody. And they argued that U2 were defining themselves as corporate rock animals by crushing what was essentially a subversive artistic statement. Which is all very well. But could U2 – or their record company – risk giving any and every scam merchant in the USA carte blanche to use and abuse their logo and their recordings on any pretence whatsoever?

"What was scary to me was that people who were criticising us weren't really listening to the records," Bono told David Fricke of *Rolling Stone*. "The records were not propagating any kind of 'men of stone' thing. *The Joshua Tree* is a very uncertain record. 'I Still Haven't Found What I'm Looking For' is an anthem of doubt more than faith."

WITH OR WITHOUT YOU

Before recording *The Joshua Tree*, the band rehearsed in Danesmote, a period house in Rathfarnham on the outskirts of Dublin. The room they occupied was beautiful, with high windows and natural light flooding in. The rehearsals went so well that they decided to do the album there.

"We had experimented a lot in the making of *The Unforgettable Fire*," The Edge recalls. "We had done quite revolutionary things like 'Elvis Presley and America' and '4th of July'. So we felt, going into *The Joshua Tree*, that maybe options were not a good thing, that limitations might be positive. And so we decided to work within the limitations of the song as a starting point. We thought: let's actually write songs. We wanted the record to be more straightforward, focused and concise."

There are few better examples than 'With or Without You'. It is that rare thing in the U2 canon – a love song – and it works, capturing an emotion that most people in serious relationships must have felt at one time or another when Bono sings, "I can't live/with or without you." But the more you delve, the more you become aware that beneath its surface restraint lies a tangled web of complex anxieties. There is a spiritual dimension to the song as erotic love and agape love converge again in Bono's personal mythology, and he returns to the theme of self-surrender and ego-loss. But what does he mean by "My hands are torn/my body bruised/She's got me with/nothing left to win/and nothing left to lose"? And who is "she"?

Bono doesn't like being specific about personal songs of this kind. Never did. "In 'With or Without You', when it says, 'And you give yourself away/ And you give yourself away', everybody in the group knows what it means," he said in 1987. "It's about how I feel in U2 at times – exposed. I know that the group feel that I give myself away. I think if I do any damage to U2 it's that I'm too open. For instance, in an interview, I don't hold the cards there, and play the right one because I either have to do it or not do it."

"The thing is to challenge radio," Adam told *Rolling Stone*. "To get 'With or Without You' on the radio is pretty good. You don't expect to hear it there. Maybe in a church."

What's more, U2 got it to No. 1 in the singles charts. "Paul McGuinness didn't want to release it as a single," Gavin Friday reveals. "But I told Bono that it was a certain No. 1. It was one of the biggest arguments I ever had with Paul, and in the end Bono sided with me. In fairness to Paul he did come up to me afterwards and apologise. He said 'You were right'. And of course I was."

65

WITH OR
WITHOUT YOU
Written: U2
Length: 4' 56"
Album:
The Joshua Tree,
March 1987
UK singles chart
position: 4
US singles chart
position: 1

BULLET THE BLUE SKY

In the sabbatical he took during 1985, Bono travelled extensively. With Ali, he went to Central America, under the auspices of Amnesty International, to observe and spent time in both El Salvador and Nicaragua. On the streets, Bono saw terrible poverty, a direct result of the American economic blockade and US support for the civil war being waged by the Contras.

Sandinista leader and, later, President of Nicaragua, Daniel Ortega.

"The spirit of the people in Nicaragua is being beaten down," he said at the time. "They've no food and no supplies. I was at a rally of Daniel Ortega's and you can tell from the look in people's eyes that they wanted so much to believe in their revolution. But people think with their pockets a lot of the time and you can't blame them for it. It's just very sad to see the stranglehold America has on Central America in practice."

The US had been good to U2. But the things that were being done by Americans in Central America, ostensibly in the name of freedom and justice, were appalling.

'Bullet the Blue Sky' howls with anger and with fear. In El Salvador, Bono had seen government fighter jets flying overhead in a mission. He had heard the bark of guns in the distance that followed. That's the reality someone else wakens up to every day.

"I still believe in Americans," Bono said. "I think they're a very open people. It's their openness which leads them to trust a man as dangerous as Ronald Reagan. They want to believe he's a good guy. They want to believe he's in the cavalry, coming to rescue America's reputation after the '70s. But he was only an actor. It was only a movie. I think the picture's ended now and Americans are leaving the cinema a little down in the mouth."

'Bullet the Blue Sky' made one other connection, linking the disastrous US foreign policy under Reagan to his own religious fundamentalism and that of the Christian tele-evangelists. The Edge talked of Jerry Falwell: "He preaches that God is white, speaks in a Southern accent and has a wife and children. How does that relate to a Chinese peasant? It doesn't at all."

Or to a Southern black? The song contrasts the burning crosses of the Ku Klux Klan with the liberating sound of John Coltrane's saxophone. America: everything that's great about the world, and everything that's repulsive about it.

BULLET THE BLUE SKY
Written: U2
Length: 4' 32"
Album:
The Joshua Tree,
March 1987

RUNNING TO STAND STILL

You couldn't escape the shadow of heroin in Dublin in the 1980. 'Wire' had dealt with this theme. So had 'Bad'. Now U2 returned to the theme, in a song clearly inspired by Lou Reed's towering 'Walk on the Wild Side'.

'Running to Stand Still' has an early lyrical reference to the seven imposing blocks of flats that scar the urban landscape of North Dublin and distinguish Ballymun, where Bono had grown up, from the rest of the city: "I see seven towers/but I see only one way out."

"I don't come from the viewpoint of someone who is completely unsympathetic to drug users," he said. Numerous friends, acquaintances and fellow musicians in Ireland had found themselves in thrall to heroin. Christy Dignam, lead singer with Aslan had endured a very public flirtation with the drug. And then in January 1986, Philip Lynott of Thin Lizzy had died of liver failure brought about by heroin addiction. When it comes that close to home, that there is no point in being judgemental.

"For two years, myself and Ali lived in Howth, on the same road as Phil," Bono confided, "and I would see him everywhere else but on that street. Every time I saw him he'd say, 'Why don't you come down for dinner? You know, you have to come down for a bite.' And I would say, 'You know, you have to come up for a bite. You have to drop up.' Every single time. And I never did call down and he never did call up."

The song is imbued with a real tenderness and compassion. But it isn't directed solely at those who are victims of heroin addiction. Bono goes further, empathsing with the central character.

"I heard about a couple," Bono explained, "and both were addicted, and such was their addiction that they had no money, so the guy risked everything on a run. He went and smuggled into Dublin a serious quantity of heroin, strapped to his body, so that on the one hand there was life imprisonment, on the other hand, riches. Apart from the morality of that, what interested me was what put him in that position."

Musically, 'Running to Stand Still' was improvised almost to tape using 'Walk on the WIld Side' and Elton John's 'Candle in the Wind' as a launching pad, but lyrically it was finely honed. It became one of the most important songs on *The Joshua Tree*. In its lack of moral certainty and its refusal to judge its subjects harshly, it looked ahead to the chaotic landscapes of *Achtung Baby* and *Zooropa*, in which the only certainty is uncertainty itself. That made it one of the band's most mature creations to date, a haunting, challenging piece of pop poetry that still resonates with lyrical truth.

67

RUNNING TO STAND STILL
Written: U2
Length: 4' 18"
Album:
The Joshua Tree, March 1987

RED HILL MINING TOWN

In '80s Britain, under the direction of Margaret Thatcher and its chairman Ian McGregor, the National Coal Board began to close what were deemed to be uneconomic mines. A miners' strike followed, with the National Union of Miners fighting the pit closures tooth and nail. It was one of the most bitter industrial disputes in recent history in Britain.

During the summer of 1984, Bob Dylan had played Slane Castle, just outside Dublin, and invited Bono on stage to join in an encore of 'Blowin' in the Wind'. Thrown a verse to sing by Dylan, Bono realised that while he recognised the song, he didn't know the words: he was forced to wing it. In some ways that unplanned live collaboration saw Bono cross the great divide in musical terms. It confirmed for him just how much he still had to learn about the great tradition of singing, songwriting and musicianship.

A friendship developed which saw him delving into Dylan's back catalogue and retracing the connections between the Irish and American folk traditions. This growing awareness of the power of the folk tradition was reflected in the band's participation in an Irish TV tribute to folk veterans the Dubliners. U2 chose a Peggy Seeger song and performed it with impressive authority. 'Springhill Mining Disaster' tells the story of how greed and exploitation in a coal mine in Nova Scotia ended in catastrophe. Bono delivered the song with passion and conviction.

All of these strands came together in 'Red Hill Mining Town'. It was criticised in some quarters for not being politically specific enough, but there is no doubt about where Bono's sympathies lie. "'Red Hill Mining Town' is a song about the miners' strike and the only reference to Ian McGregor is "Through hand of steel and heart of stone/Our labour day is come and gone",' he said. "People beat me with a stick for that but what I'm interested in is seeing in the newspapers or on television that another thousand people had lost their jobs.

"Now what you don't read about is that those people go home and they have families and they're trying to bring up children. And, in many instances, those relationships broke up under the pressure of the miners' strike. 'The glass is cut, the bottle runs dry/Our love runs cold in the caverns in the night/We're wounded by fear, injured in doubt/I can lose myself but I can't live without/'Cos you keep me holding on.' I feel other people are more qualified to comment on the miners' strike. That enraged me – but I feel more qualified to write about relationships because I understand them more than what it's like to work in a pit."

RED HILL MINING TOWN
Written: U2
Length: 4' 52"
Album:
The Joshua Tree,
March 1987

IN GOD'S COUNTRY

Bono was trying to find ways of communicating his increasing sense of unease about the USA. 'Bullet the Blue Sky' had come spitting out in a spirit of anger. 'In God's Country' was more measured; it had an air of resignation. The image of the desert was at the heart of *The Joshua Tree*. "It has a spiritual aspect," The Edge reasoned, "which the record has, and also a great deal of mystery, which I like."

Adam went further: "The desert was immensely inspirational to us as a mental image for this record. Most people would take the desert on face value and think it's some kind of barren place, which of course is true. But in the right frame of mind, it's also a very positive image, because you can actually do something with blank canvas, which is effectively what the desert is."

Symbol of America: the Statue of Liberty.

That's the kind of thinking that informs 'In God's Country'. It sounds a bit like U2 playing U2 until The Edge drops in an Ennio Morricone-style guitar figure in the break. Bono, meanwhile, is restrained. Coming to him in a dream, the USA is characterised as a desert rose, a siren whose dress is torn in ribbons and in bows. "We need new dreams tonight," Bono sings. He's thinking about the dearth of new political ideas. "Except in Nicaragua," he says looking back. "That's why the revolution there was so important."

69

"It's not your first reason for being on stage, to effect change in the political climate of a country," Bono said at the time. "I don't know what the first reason is, but that's not the first reason. But I like to think that U2 have already contributed to a turnaround in thinking."

Maybe 'In God's Country' would turn a few more heads around. Then again maybe not. You could argue that the chorus was too radio-friendly for that.

IN GOD'S COUNTRY

Written:	U2
Length:	2' 57"
Album:	*The Joshua Tree*, March 1987
UK singles chart position:	48 (as import)
US singles chart position:	44

TRIP THROUGH YOUR WIRES

U2 didn't need to rush a new album so they took some time out. Individually and sometimes collectively, they went in search of fresh stimuli. Bono was searching for new musical roots, listening to folk, blues and country. And that search was reflected in the way he was thinking and how he looked.

It also connected with the musical changes that Ireland was going through in the mid-'80s. Mike Scott had relocated to Dublin with The Waterboys and had become obsessed not just with Bob Dylan and Van Morrison but also with the Irish folk tradition. The Hothouse Flowers were also in the ascendant, and making similar links. Both tended to turn up for spontaneous sessions in the strangest of places, so that Dublin became a city of buskers. It was against that backdrop that 'Trip Through Your Wires' was conceived.

U2 were to appear on a new Irish television programme, *TV Gaga*. On the night, the band trooped on looking like extras from some B-movie remake of *Easy Rider*. They performed 'Womanfish' – a song which subsequently disappeared without a trace – and 'Trip Through Your Wires'. There wasn't an echo effect in sight. Instead, we witnessed The Edge getting down 'n' dirty in a bar room bluesy romp, a drinking song that featured Bono wailing away crudely on a Dylan-esque harp solo.

"It was a hootenanny, a big yahoo," Bono said. "We kind of made it up at the moment and I just blew into the harp. The thing about Lanois and Eno in the studio is they're very supportive of the idea of a session. They get carried away with it and we get carried away with them getting carried away with it. It's just a vicious cycle in the right sense of the word."

Lyrically it's relatively throwaway. It can be seen as another paean to the contradictory charms of America, personified as a woman. It could be about an unconventional sexual encounter and the attendant feelings of confusion and guilt. Or it can be read simply as an exercise in Dylan-esque personal myth-making: the singer broken down by the ravages of living the hard life being put back together by the love of a good woman.

Sex 'n' drink 'n' rock 'n' roll? It might have been Bono's own personal basement tape.

TRIP THROUGH YOUR WIRES
Written: U2
Length: 3' 32"
Album:
The Joshua Tree, March 1987

ONE TREE HILL

When U2 were on tour in New Zealand in 1985 they met Greg Carroll. A Maori, he worked doing front-of-house for the promoter on the band's Kiwi dates, beginning in Auckland. "There are five volcanic islands which make up Auckland," Bono explained, "and the tallest is One Tree Hill. Greg took me there on my first night in New Zealand."

Carroll was a bundle of energy, a live wire. "Paul McGuinness thought this guy's so smart we can't leave him here. Let's take him with us to Australia," Bono explained. Within a short time, Greg Carroll had become a valued member of the organisation.

Their world tour over, the band returned to Dublin. Greg Carroll came too. He worked as Bono's assistant and, in the few months he spent in Dublin, became like a brother to the singer. He was well loved and widely respected by those who knew him both within and outside the U2 camp.

What happened was horrific. On the run-up to recording *The Joshua Tree*, he took Bono's Harley Davidson on a courier run. It was a bleak, rainy night. A car pulled out in front of him and Greg, going full tilt, ploughed into it. He was killed instantly.

"It was a devastating blow," Bono reflected. "He was doing me a favour. He was taking my bike home. Greg used to look after Ali. They used to go out dancing together. He was a best friend. I've already had it once with my mother. Now I've had it twice."

Even six months later, Bono found it hard to talk about, choking back tears in an interview. "The emphasis," he reflected, "among family and friends when we had a No. 1 record and were a big band was on how much you'd got – and not how much you've lost. The sense of loss came home through losing Greg Carroll."

The imagery of 'One Tree Hill' superbly evoked the seafaring heritage of Carroll's Maori ancestors. A spiritual tour de force, it is a hymn of praise and celebration which describes the traditional Maori burial of their friend on One Tree Hill and links it poetically with themes of renewal and redemption, with the river running, running down to the sea.

"Greg Carroll's funeral was beyond belief," Bono said. "He was buried in his tribal homeland, as a Maori, by the chiefs and elders. And there was a three-day and three-night wake and your head would be completely turned around. And ours were, again and again."

71

ONE TREE HILL
Written: U2
Length: 5' 23"
Album:
The Joshua Tree,
March 1987

EXIT

Bono had gone west in his reading. He was interested in Flannery O'Connor, Raymond Carver, Norman Mailer. Looking for insights into the people of the vast place that had embraced them. Ways of understanding the ordinary stock first and then the outsiders, the driftwood – those on the fringes of the promised land, cut off from the American dream. He read *The Executioner's Song*, Norman Mailer's superb account of the life of Gary Gilmore. 'Exit' wasn't about Gilmore. It wasn't about Charles Manson either. But it trawls the area occupied by either or both, getting inside the head of a protagonist who's careening into psychosis.

Musically 'Exit' is like nothing U2 had ever done before. The antithesis of their bright, ringing, optimistic, inspirational selves, it was dirty, angry, loud, discordant, repetitive, noisy, black. If the intention was to invoke a sense of evil abroad, then it was effective, with Larry's blistering drum attack and Adam's low-down insistent muddy bass creating a powerful sense of being inside someone's skin, of feeling their palpitations en route to some unspeakable denouement.

"You could say that this is forbidden ground for U2 because we're the 'optimistic' group," Bono confided at the time. "But to be an optimist you mustn't be blind or deaf to the world around you. 'Exit' – I don't even know what the act is in that song. Some see it as a murder, others suicide – and I don't mind. But the rhythm of the words is nearly as important in conveying the state of mind."

That was the point of 'Exit': to convey the state of mind of someone driven, by whatever powerful urges, to the very brink of desperation. The undercurrent of religious imagery reflected a new awareness of the dangers of fanaticism implicit in faith. But there was no other message in 'Exit'. Except this is how it is out there: deal with it. And in a way, it was a method of purging the band's own demons, their own anger and fury at the vicissitudes fate had thrust upon them. It was a way of coming to terms with death and with grief. It was an exorcism.

As such, it was not without its own psychic cost. In the USA, a man accused of murdering Rebecca Shaeffer, a TV actress, claimed that he was inspired by listening to 'Exit'. It may have been no more than a smart defence lawyer coming up with a half-plausible plea of mitigation, but it wasn't the kind of accusation you wanted hanging over you, however spurious. But then, there was a whole list of positive lessons to be learned from *The Joshua Tree* too.

EXIT
Written: U2
Length: 4' 13"
Album:
The Joshua Tree,
March 1987

MOTHERS OF THE DISAPPEARED

During 1986, U2 had agreed to participate in the *Conspiracy of Hope* tour in the USA with Sting, Lou Reed, Bryan Adams, Peter Gabriel and Joan Baez, among others. The tour was both a money-raising and a consciousness-raising expedition, undertaken on behalf of Amnesty International.

The band had developed a close relationship with that organisation through Jack Healey, an Irish–American former priest, who put together the Conspiracy tour. He had helped in making connections for Bono in Nicaragua and El Salvador. Now, in a variety of shapes and guises, Amnesty concerns were resurfacing on *The Joshua Tree*.

Bono was struck by the accounts he'd heard of murder squads operating under the Argentinian military junta through the '70s and '80s. Those bleak decades precipitated a return to democracy during which hundreds of student opponents of the military regime had been arrested and were never seen again, dead or alive. In Argentina they became known as "the disappeared", and an organisation called Mothers of the Disappeared had been formed to campaign for full disclosure of what had happened to those who had been lifted.

MOTHERS OF THE DISAPPEARED
Written: U2
Length: 5' 14"
Album:
The Joshua Tree,
March 1987

'Mothers of the Disappeared' continues the tradition of '40' and 'MLK' – but it is less a celebration than a lament. It enters with disturbing sound effects and it never loses its ominous quality – The Edge's guitar is barbed wire, and Bono sounds like Dylan's man of constant sorrow, his yodel a high, lonesome sound. The song is an act of witness but there is no optimistic note of reassurance. Too much evil in the world. Some things just can't be explained. Even Bono was prepared to acknowledge that now.

RATTLE AND HUM

Having shot to No.1 on both sides of the Atlantic, *The Joshua Tree* went on to sell 12 million copies worldwide. It was the record of a radically different band to that which had set out on the *War* tour in 1983. And yet when TV stations wanted to show live footage of U2, all they had was the *Under a Blood Red Sky* video. It was time to consign that version of reality to history.

The movie was Paul McGuinness' idea. Whatever he had in mind, the band would inevitably screw it around. Conceptualise it. Complicate it. Make it as difficult as possible. And then make it more difficult again. So they did. Business as usual.

They wanted to explore American music. Travel back to the source. Hook up with some seminal figures. Take risks. Deflate the myth. Acknowledge that in the grand scheme of things they were only beginners. Right. And make the biggest, the best, the most dramatic, the most explosive rock movie ever.

Can I get back to you on that one, darling?

They could have done a straight concert film and a live double-album. "And made a lot of money for very little work," Bono argued. "That's what big rock bands do. They take the money and run."

Instead, U2's restless desire to keep moving got the better of them. Part documentary, part travelogue, part concert film, *Rattle and Hum*, the movie, is big, loud, sketchy, humorous, gauche, powerful, revealing. *Rattle and Hum*, the album, is sprawling, eclectic, eccentric, throwaway, inspiring, magnificent. Hammered in the press, it sold 14 million copies.

The myth wasn't going to be easily deflated.

HELTER SKELTER

ELTER SKELTER

Vritten: Lennon/
McCartney

ength: 3' 07"

lbum:

attle And Hum,

ctober 1988

There were people who ridiculed the choice of 'Helter Skelter' as the opening track on *Rattle and Hum*. In fact, it would be hard to pick anything more appropriate. *The Joshua Tree* had catapulted the band into the front line, right up there as contenders for the title that no one really wants: the biggest rock 'n' roll band on planet Earth. On a tour that was scheduled to run over 264 days and through 15 countries, they would do 110 shows at 72 venues in front of a paying audience of 3,160,998 fans. In addition, there was the San Francisco Save The Yuppie free concert, with an audience of at least another 20,000 people. And, meanwhile, chunks of all this mayhem were being filmed for a major rock 'n' roll film. It was a roller coaster ride all right, in which everything was capable of being turned upside down.

In one obvious sense, U2 were on top of the world. In another, they had been plunged into the vortex, where every aspect of their operation was under scrutiny, and every element of their increasingly hydra-headed organisation under severe strain. None more so than the band themselves.

"'Helter Skelter' was exactly what we were going through on *The Joshua Tree* tour," Bono said. "It was one of the worst times of our musical

Helter Skelter
n: Charles Manson.

life. First a falling light cut me up, and I had to have stitches in my chin. My voice failed for the first week because of dry heat – the press came to the opening show and I couldn't sing. We were on the run the whole time and I busted up my shoulder and was in a lot of pain. And I found that I was drinking a lot just to stop the pain."

Recorded at the McNichols Arena in Denver on 8 November, 1987, it featured in the black and white footage of the film *Rattle and Hum*. "The line about Charles Manson was just an off-the-cuff remark on the night," Bono recalls. "If I got up people's noses, that's fine. But I still think it was relevant. We were travelling around the United States and I had a few incidents coming up against the hard-core spontaneous combustion of violence that seems to happen there. I've always been fascinated with that and still am."

Look no further than the sign marked 'Exit'.

75

VAN DIEMAN'S LAND

In 1845, Ireland lost its potato crop. It was the signal for an economic and social catastrophe of ghastly proportions. Yet the worst ravages of what became known as the Great Famine could have been averted.

Enough food was being produced within the 32 counties of Ireland to feed the population. But the dictates of the market prevailed. Throughout 1845, '46 and what became known as Black '47, the food that was being produced in Irish fields on the back of Irish labour was being exported. Meanwhile, as successive potato crops failed as a result of blight, the death toll mounted. In the long run, two million were to die and as many emigrated to the USA in what became known as the coffin ships. Hundreds of thousands died en route, of starvation, typhoid and other diseases associated with malnutrition.

In Ireland, meanwhile, experience of the famine dovetailed with the nationalist sentiment burgeoning throughout Europe. In 1848, an uprising was planned but it petered out miserably and the leaders were arrested. Among them was a Fenian poet, John Boyle O'Reilly, who was deported to Australia for his role in orchestrating the rebellion. In Irish folk culture, the name given to Tasmania – where citizens who had fallen foul of the Crown and the courts were frequently transported – was Van Diemen's Land; it was already the title of a familiar rebel ballad. But U2's 'Van Diemen's Land' – like 'Sunday Bloody Sunday' – is not a rebel song. Written and sung by The Edge against the sparse backdrop of his own plucked electric guitar, it is a sad and moving reflection on the continuity of suffering, injustice and violence, with the scarlet coats of the Fenians now being replaced by the black berets of the IRA.

"It's an emigrant's song – or an immigrant's song," Bono comments. "That's what justifies its place on the album. But I have to be very focused in a record, and for me that record was set in only one place."

As it happens, The Edge's plaintive appeal for justice without violence, recorded in The Point Theatre where U2 were rehearsing, provides one of the most beautiful and striking moments in the film, with Phil Joanou's cameras sweeping kinetically down the River Liffey that runs through the heart of the city and out into Dublin Bay, a place from which at least some of the emigrants of the 19th century embarked.

John Boyle O'Reilly had been bound for Australia. U2 were travelling deep into the heart of the USA. All of us, to one degree or another, are on the run. Driven – but by what?

VAN DIEMEN'S LAND
Written: U2
Length: 3' 05"
Album:
Rattle And Hum,
October 1988

DESIRE

The first single off Rattle and Hum, 'Desire' confounded expectations. If anything on *The Joshua Tree* half-pointed in this direction it was 'Trip Through Your Wires' but that was sprawling and indulgent. By comparison, 'Desire' was loaded, cocked and ready to go off in the listener's hand.

The Edge claimed that they'd been listening to Iggy Pop's coruscating '1969', which may indeed have been the case, but this rhythm was sired by Bo Diddley and made its first global impact on the charts via the Rolling Stones, out of Buddy Holly's 'Not Fade Away'. On its release, 'Desire' went straight to No. 1 in the UK, and U2 were understandably pleased.

"We were going back to rhythm and blues as part of our wanting to understand America," Bono explains. "We'd been reading the beats and various travel writers. Then we started to get into the music. Travelling through America, you're listening to different radio stations, rhythm and blues, country, soul, jazz, and you realize that rhythm is the sex of the music. So I think we got into dealing with those subjects, including desire, when we were making that jump musically."

The Edge had never been an R'n'B fan. Now he'd begun to see the great emotional strength of the music. "At the time, I think I had begun to realise that music had become too scientific. Too often, listening to modern records, you'd hear a producer rather than musicians interacting. I liked about 'Desire' the fact that it was totally not what people were listening to. It was a rock 'n' roll record, not a pop song."

For Bono, however, it was also a reflection on the condition of being a rock star. "I wanted to admit to the religiosity of rock 'n' roll concerts and the fact that you get paid for them. On one level, I'm starting to criticise these lunatic fringe preachers, "stealing hearts at a travelling show" – but I'm also starting to realize that there's a real parallel there between what I'm doing and what they are."

'Desire' was the beginning of a process. Increasingly, Bono would consciously begin to own up to the contradictions in his own and the band's position. It was a reflection of the fact that U2 had come of age that they could produce with such enormous relish something that, on the surface at least, was so utterly basic.

77

Iggy Pop: he helped teach U2 how to rattle and hum.

HAWKMOON 269

The road can be a good place to write. The stimuli are all around – new sights, sounds, experiences that provide the base metal from which songs can be wrought. The Edge had the Walkman doing overtime during *The Joshua Tree* tour. 'Hawkmoon 269' was one of the structures he sketched on acoustic guitar, onto a cassette.

Bob Dylan: the dark side of Hawkmoon.

"Hawkmoon is a place in Rapid City, Dakota," he says. "We passed by it on the Amnesty *Conspiracy of Hope* tour and Bono, ever a man with a notebook handy, thought 'That sounds good'."

Bono remembers a crushing hangover that heightened the sense of dislocation that frequently infects musicians on the road, and the refrain comes straight out of that particular black pit: "When the night has no end/ and the day yet to begin/As the room spins around you/I need your love."

Maybe it was symptomatic that it became such a demon to record. Bob Dylan came along to play on the track and contributed a kind of inebriated hurdy gurdy effect. The band piled in but the battle to put a final shape on it continued. "It was mixed 269 times," Joe O'Herlihy laughs. "That's where the title came from." Bono looks unhappy even discussing it now. "That was my favourite song on the record," he says, "but we actually physically wore down the tape doing that number of mixes."

Not that anyone outside the camp would notice. Beginning as a love song, it transforms into a howl of lust, a molten volcano of a piece that climaxes in an intense gospel chant: "Meet all your love in the heartland", the backing trio of Edna Wright, Carolyn Willis and Billie Barnum repeat.

"I'm sure there was enormous sexual frustration in the performance of that song," Bono admits. "I don't know how long we'd been away but at this point we were fully grown men of 26, 27, 28. We were recording in Sunset Sound. Sunset Strip. Hookers. Every neon sign advertising sex in some way. You could feel all that coming through in 'Hawkmoon'."

It's there in the rhythms, in Larry Bunker's thunderous timpani explosions and Larry Mullen's crashing cymbals. It's there in Bono's tortured metaphors and his yowling vocals. It's there in The Edge's blistering, dirty guitar. It's there in Adam's palpitating bass.

'Hawkmoon 269' may feel less than perfect to the band but perfection is hardly what it's about. Robert Palmer may have sung about being addicted to love but this was the real thing. Even better than the real thing.

HAWKMOON 269
Written: U2
Length: 6' 22"
Album:
Rattle And Hum,
October 1988

ALL ALONG THE WATCHTOWER

It is 11 November, 1987. In between dates, the band decide to do a free gig on the back of a truck in an open space in San Francisco city centre, by the Embarcadero. Their own equipment is already on its way to Vancouver for the band's next show, so they borrow a sound system from – who else? – The Grateful Dead. Given the proximity of the location to the city's financial district – and in honour of the stock market crash of the week before – Bono dubs it the "Save the Yuppie" benefit.

The opening number they perform is a rough, improvised version of Bob Dylan's 'All Along the Watchtower'. In contrast to his first attempt at a Dylan cover, when Bono joined the maestro on stage at Slane for 'Blowin' in the Wind', on this occasion he clearly knows the words. Not that he's unduly constrained by that small detail.

The red guitar, on fire in 'Desire', reappears here, as Bono improvises: "All I've got is a red guitar/three chords and the truth/All I've got is a red guitar/the rest is up to you."

The band don't seem to know the chords quite as well as Bono does the lyrics, however, and there are some startlingly odd moments of musical disjointedness. The first 30 seconds of the guitar intro are missed by the recording engineer and The Edge has to dub it in later. "Otherwise, everything else is as it was performed live," The Edge confirms.

As it happens, the occasion becomes more memorable for its off-stage antics. Aware of the fact that the mayor of San Francisco, Diane Feinstein, has offered $500 as a bounty for bringing any of the city's numerous graffiti artists into custody, Bono climbs to the top of the adjacent fountain sculpture and sprays "Stop the traffic – rock 'n' roll" on it.

A warrant is issued for his arrest but, the graffiti having been cleaned off by the following day, the attempt to bring the singer to justice eventually peters out. In the long run, Bono puts it all down to mid-tour madness, but there's no mistaking the satisfaction U2 feel when Diane Feinstein is replaced as mayor soon after the gig and her successor, Art Agnos, abolishes the bounty and, instead, sets up a fund to sponsor the work of graffiti artists in the city.

ALL ALONG THE
WATCHTOWER
Written: Dylan
Length: 4' 24"
Album:
Rattle And Hum,
October 1988

I STILL HAVEN'T FOUND WHAT I'M LOOKING FOR

One criticism levelled at U2 during the squalls that surrounded their Self-Aid performance in Dublin was that, in the USA, they were still playing to predominantly white audiences. The implication was that they had failed to cross the class and racial divide, despite their overt celebration of Martin Luther King in 'Pride (In the Name of Love)' and 'MLK'.

My own impression at the time was that Bono had been stung by these accusations, angered at the suggestion that any artist or band could somehow be held accountable for the audience that chose – or chose not – to acknowledge them.

It may, however, have been a critical catalyst, inspiring the band to begin their odyssey in search of the roots of rock 'n' roll in black music, and in particular through rhythm and blues, gospel and soul. It must have felt like a remarkable vindication, then, when they first got wind of the fact that 'I Still Haven't Found What I'm Looking For' was being covered by a gospel group, trading under the name of The New Voices of Freedom, in Harlem. The choir had sent a tape of their version of the song to Island Records, who passed it on to U2. Bono, Adam, Larry, The Edge and Gavin Friday went to check out the choir in their Harlem church and were impressed. As *The Joshua Tree* tour wound up to hit New York, a collaboration seemed like an attractive option.

The band suggested some rehearsals, to see if the different versions of the song could be integrated. The result provides one of the outstanding moments in the movie *Rattle and Hum*, a gloriously exuberant, thrilling musical encounter in which the common spirituality of the different participants is celebrated, tentatively at first and then with a rare and infectious abandon. Later, the choir joined the band for their date at Madison Square Garden and, although more formal, the performance is hardly less compelling. Bono's vocals are superb, as he trades licks with the two soloists George Pendergrass and Dorothy Tennell, creating the atmosphere of a Pentecostalist gospel service at its most transcendent.

The New Voices of Freedom's own version of 'I Still Haven't Found What I'm Looking For' was released as a single on the New Jersey label Doc Records. The song was later recorded by The Chimes, who had a hit with it in the USA and the UK. You could say that it's on its way to becoming a standard.

I STILL HAVEN'T
FOUND WHAT I'M
LOOKING FOR
Written: U2
Length: 5' 53"
Album:
Rattle And Hum,
October 1988

FREEDOM FOR MY PEOPLE

FREEDOM FOR THE PEOPLE
Written: Magee/
Mabins/Robinson
Length: 0' 38"
Album:
Rattle And Hum,
October 1988

In the film, it was the kind of moment that inspired scepticism. U2 go for a stroll in downtown Harlem, to meet The New Voices of Harlem, followed by the cameras. There, they happen on a busker, one Mr Sterling Magee, with his harmonica sidekick, Adam Gussow, performing 'Freedom For My People'. The band hang about and observe, under the watchful artificial eye of the camera.

It's easy to see the point that's being made: a bunch of rock 'n' roll superstars still have something to learn from a rough 'n' ready street performer. In *Rattle and Hum*, U2 undertook their musical odyssey as both fans and pupils. But the presence of the camera made the value of that gesture a little harder to take at face intent: inevitably, it introduced an element of self-consciousness that a cinema audience would find it difficult to overcome.

k 'n' roll superstar
a bluesman?

On record, however, 'Freedom For My People' – written by Sterling Magee, Bobby Robinson and Macie Mabins – drifts in and out, a found piece of street noise that acts as an appropriate prelude to what follows.

81

SILVER AND GOLD

It was backstage at Slane, interviewing Bob Dylan for *Hot Press*, that Bono was given his first lesson in the importance of tradition. Dylan, who was almost as familiar with Irish ballads as he was with the work of Woody Guthrie, Leadbelly and Robert Johnson, mentioned the McPeakes from the north of Ireland. Bono looked at him blankly. "There's no particular musical roots or heritage for us," he explained about U2. "In Ireland there is a tradition, but we've never plugged into it."

"Well," Dylan insisted, "you have to reach back into the music."Bono was struck by an inadequacy at the core of U2's schtick, and he resolved to go about rectifying it. Part of the answer was to begin to move in different musical circles. Taking a break in New York late in 1989, he hooked up with Peter Wolf of the J. Geils Band. They visited a Rolling Stones session and became involved in a jam. With Keith Richards playing the piano, Wolf and Jagger traded vocals and harmonica licks. Bono was forced merely to watch – he didn't know any of the R'n'B standards that they were familiar with. They listened to some John Lee Hooker and Bono was hooked on the raw power of the voice, the rhythm and the stinging guitar.

To some extent the experience was humiliating, but Bono was spurred into action. Back in his hotel room, in a fever he wrote his own take on the blues. He had just been in Ethiopia with Ali. He had seen first-hand the impact of Western economic policies on the African continent and his sense of outrage is palpable in 'Silver and Gold', a song about imperialism, greed, exploitation and repression.

Bono borrowed the line "I am someone" from black civil rights leader Jesse Jackson. And he plundered the Irish literary landscape for a couplet deriving from Brendan Behan: "I have seen the coming and going/The captains and the kings." But in writing the song from the perspective of a black political prisoner, he made a crucial leap of the imagination.

The original acoustic version was recorded with Keith Richards and Ronnie Wood for the album. On *Rattle and Hum*, the whole band are on board and the result is inevitably heavier, Bono entering into the spirit of the performance with an improvised anti-apartheid rap, ending in a pre-emptive strike against the inevitable accusations of political posturing. "Am I buggin' you?" he asked sardonically. "Don't mean to bug you."

Curiously the throwaway line "OK Edge, play the blues", introducing the guitar break, generated the most flak. But the solo is quintessential Edge, and underlines just how far from the blues he'd been reared.

SILVER AND GOLD
Written: U2
Length: 5' 49"
Album:
Rattle And Hum,
October 1988

ANGEL OF HARLEM

ANGEL OF
HARLEM
Written: U2
Length: 3' 49"
Album:
Rattle And Hum,
October 1988
UK singles chart
position: 9
US singles chart
position: 14

The improvisations that had kick-started so many U2 songs weren't coming quite so easily. The Edge realized that they needed new ways of writing, and his response was characteristically sensible. He decided that he would learn. He had come up with the basis for 'Desire' and 'Hawkmoon 269' on the acoustic guitar. Now add to that list 'Angel of Harlem'. From a musical perspective, something curious happened.

Because he was at the centre of things on acoustic, The Edge found it more difficult to identify a space for himself on electric lead guitar. He was going to have to master some Steve Cropper-style licks to slot in and around the Stax-like horns on a sweet soul ballad of this kind.

Bono had been thinking about Billie Holiday. A friend of his, a girl called Alexis whom he'd met in San Francisco when she was 15 or 16, had moved to London and kept in touch. She'd given him a biography of the singer they called Lady Day. His fascination had been primed, and as U2 travelled around the States, picking up on gospel, jazz and R'n'B stations, it was intensified. 'Angel of Harlem' was written on the road but it's got the pulse of New York in its veins, with John Coltrane, Charlie Parker and Miles Davis making cameo appearances alongside the star of the scenario.

83

The lyrics have a strong visual, cinematic feel, but it was the Memphis Horns that completed the picture. Anyone familiar with Southside Johnny and the Asbury Jukes will know where this one is coming from. "Funny, I can hear Dylan in it more than Stax," Bono smiles now, and the reference makes sense. What's important, however, is the sheer mastery of it all.

The angel herself:
Billie Holiday.

On their musical odyssey through the American heartland, the band had decided to swing by Sun Studios in Memphis and to line up a session there. With the Memphis Horns in attendance and Cowboy Jack Clement at the desk, they recorded what became a tribute not just to Billie Holiday but to the vast legacy of great music that America had bequeathed to the world. Upful and celebratory, it remains one of U2's finest moments.

"It's a jukebox song," Bono says. "We don't have many jukebox songs, maybe six or seven, but that's one that people play in bars."

And anywhere else they need to get that rush.

LOVE RESCUE ME

The Joshua Tree tour was half-done. The idea for *Rattle and Hum* had been worked out, and it was clear that the band were going to have to do some serious recording. Rather than de-camping, returning to Dublin – where it was winter – and attempting to re-focus there, someone suggested heading for the West Coast and working in LA. If the album was going to be about America, then it made sense to hang out there.

The Edge took a house out in Beverly Hills with his wife Aislinn and their kids. It was the house where the Menendez brothers later murdered their parents. "We were the last guys there before them," Bono says. "I was staying in the mews and that was where I wrote 'Love Rescue Me'."

If "wrote" is the right word. After a night of debauchery, Bono was sleeping fitfully and had a bizarre dream about Bob Dylan. He woke up and, under the cloud of a massive hangover, began to write the lyrics of the song he thought he remembered Dylan singing in his dream, about a man people keep turning to as a saviour, but whose own life is increasingly shattered, and who could do with a shot of salvation himself.

Shortly afterwards, Bono got a call, asking him if he wanted to pay a visit to Dylan – and thus, with a weird synchronicity, he ended up finishing the song later that day with the man in his dream. "I thought it was a Dylan song," Bono recalls. "So when I met him I said, 'Is this one of yours?' and he said, 'No, but maybe it could be'. So we worked on it together."

How much of the finished product is Bono and how much Dylan remains unclear. "Listen, I'd polish his shoes, I really would," Bono says. "A lot of people want their heroes to not let them down. I think it's a duty of heroes to let you down in some ways." Dylan recorded a lead vocal for the track but it was withdrawn, apparently at Dylan's request, because of a potential clash with his Traveling Wilbury commitments.

The lyric that is powerful, poetic and unremitting in its harsh, tormented glare. "In the cold mirror of a glass/I see my reflection pass/I see the dark shades of what I used to be/I see the purple of her eyes/The scarlet of my lies/Love rescue me." Beginning as a country ballad, the song is transformed by the entry of the Memphis Horns, lifting it into the realms of country-soul à la Otis Redding. "I don't think I fully pull it off in the singing stakes," Bono admits. "At that point, I was still allowing black influences into my voice, whereas now I am fully content to be white. Pink even [laughs]. I like it as a musical influence but in the voice it's dangerous for me."

LOVE RESCUE ME
Written: U2/Dylan
Length: 6′ 24″
Album:
Rattle And Hum,
October 1988

WHEN LOVE COMES TO TOWN

WHEN LOVE
COMES TO TOWN
Written: U2
Length: 4' 15"
Album:
Rattle And Hum,
October 1988
UK singles chart
position: 6
US singles chart
position: 68

Early in 1986, B.B. King landed in Ireland. After his Dublin date, he hooked up with U2. B.B. asked for a song and Bono came up with the basis of it pretty quickly. "Writing songs for other people can be so easy," Bono reflects. "You're out of your own head and into someone else's." The challenge is to finish the job – typically, Bono completed the lyric in the bath in his hotel room just before he was due to present it to B.B.

It seems Bono had always envisaged sharing the vocals in the context of *Rattle and Hum*. Legend has it that when King met Bono after reading the lyrics he asked, "How old are you? They're heavy lyrics. Heavy lyrics." The album version was recorded in Sun Studios, where so much seminal rock 'n' roll had been produced by its original owner, Sam Phillips.

"You go into the Sun room, and it's a modest room," Adam recalled later. "It's got the old acoustic titles on the wall and the pictures of Elvis and Roy Orbison and Jerry Lee and Carl Perkins – it's just history."

'When Love Comes to Town' brilliantly fuses gospel and blues influences. With the redemptive power of love as its theme, it goes back even further for its clinching biblical metaphor as the two singers trade verses: "I was there when they crucified my Lord," B.B. sings, "I held the scabbard when the soldier drew his sword/I threw the dice when they pierced his side/But I've seen love conquer the great divide."

Bono is freewheeling. "It's like that line from Brendan Kennelly's *Book of Judas*: 'The best way to serve the age is to betray it'," he says.

at's entertainment!
no with B.B. King.

HEARTLAND

"We don't write many straight love songs," Bono says. But U2 do write about love all the time. In fact love in its many facets and guises is the terrain their music most frequently occupies. 'Heartland' is a love song.

It was written during 1986 for *The Joshua Tree* and was one of the five or six tracks that remained unfinished from those marathon sessions. When it came to the cut, the band went for 'Trip Through Your Wires' in preference; it was a question of flow and balance.

It gelled with the theme of *Rattle and Hum* perfectly. If *The Joshua Tree* had attacked the duplicity and deceit at the heart of US political machinations, its follow-up was a much more affectionate document, in its new songs celebrating popular culture and the country that had provided the breeding ground for the blues and rock 'n' roll. 'Heartland' emerges as a love song to the nation. Ireland had frequently been characterised as a woman by poets like James Clarence Mangan in 'My Dark Rosaleen' and William Butler Yeats, who cast the country as Caitlín Ní Houlihán in a variety of works. Now Bono was applying for the same kind of poetic licence. He passed the test with honours.

"America both fascinates and frightens me," Bono said. "I can't get it out of my system. Wim Wenders has said that America has colonised our unconscious. He's right. You don't have to go there – it comes to you. No matter where we live it's pumped into our homes in *Dallas*, *Dynasty* and *Hill Street Blues*. It's Hollywood, it's Coca-Cola, it's Levis. There's good and bad in all of these, but either way you've got to deal with it."

HEARTLAND
Written: U2
Length: 5' 03"
Album:
Rattle And Hum,
October 1988

"Let's see, have I forgotten anything Oh yes, a bottle of milk!"

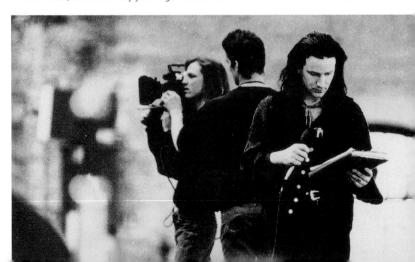

GOD PART II

You're trying to make sense of the madness around you. Album sales are going through the roof. The tour is like a military operation. There are hundreds of people on board now and they all want a piece of you. The record company wants a piece of you. The media wants a piece of you. The fans want a piece of you. And your family – they're entitled to a piece of you that you can't give them.

And on top of all that – the usual mayhem, only worse – someone had the bright idea of making a fucking film of the tour. Something inside keeps telling you that it could be a catastrophe.

There's so much money at stake and so little control you can exert. They get in the way, shove cameras up your nose, follow you around – as if you didn't feel that you were in a goldfish bowl already. You remember Washington DC. Falling on the stage. Dislocating your shoulder. Being wheeled into an ambulance. Looking up and seeing Phil Joanou – you'd nicknamed him ET – and his cameras. You said: "ET," you said, "what the fuck are you doing in my ambulance?" And he said: "Hey, you wanted me to make a documentary!" Madness. Complete fucking madness.

And if you whinge about this kind of thing, if you complain – it's like, "You ungrateful bastard, you. You've got money, success, hit records, hot and cold running groupies, stretch limos, champagne on ice everywhere you go – and you're complaining?" As if that was what it was all about. It makes you think about what it must have been like for Elvis. Why he hid himself away in Graceland and ate a mountain of cheeseburgers. It makes you think about what it must have been like for the Beatles, for John Lennon.

That was why you decided to open the set with 'Helter Skelter'. Now the word was out that Albert Goldman was about to do a hatchet job on Lennon. Goldman. His Elvis book stank. Made Presley out to be a rock 'n' roll idiot. Now the same asshole was going to do John Lennon over, and portray him as a rock 'n' roll fool. As a bully. As a reptile. Albert Goldman. What the fuck would he know?

There's a song in all this. Make it a tribute to Lennon. Jimmy Iovine knew him. Worked with the Plastic Ono Band. 'God Part II', you could call it. Send up all that Hollywood sequel stuff. That's a new twist. Give Goldman a going over himself. Get some of that pent-up bile out of your system. Say some things about Lennon. Own up to some things about yourself. Have some fun doing the whole thing in the Plastic Ono mould. Only re-vamped. Upgraded. Look for a new dynamic. A good excuse to check out how this

GOD PART II
Written: U2
Length: 3' 15"
Album:
Rattle And Hum,
October 1988

The God couple: John Lennon and Yoko Ono.

grunge thing feels. Nice and quiet and then WHAM! IN YOUR FACE! Keep it tight, restrained and then USE the SLEDGEHAMMER. Bam! Jimmy should be able to handle that.

'God Part II', you call it. It's hard alright, a sort of a half-way house between *The Joshua Tree* and the future. It's got Lennon written all over it. It's got drum loops for Larry to kick against, which is interesting. It's got you being all nice and reasonable and then WAH! Throwing a bit of a tantrum. You get a chance to quote Bruce Cockburn: a good line of his, that one about kicking the darkness till it bleeds daylight. You use the opportunity to show your own darker side. To be a bit irresponsible. To reveal your anger. And to do a Lennon yourself, trying to wrap up the truth in a single phrase. "I believe in love." Because it's true. You do. Not that it cut much ice with Yoko. "That was a nice cover version you did of John's song," she'd said when you met her. Cover version! At least she didn't look for royalties.

Looking back on it later, with a bit of distance and detachment, it's not a track you'll make a passionate case for. The thing that stops it coming off is the singing: it does sound like a bit of a tantrum. You can laugh at that now yourself, but there's not a lot of humour in the song or on the record. Vitriol is at its best with wit.

What the hell. 'God Part II' may not be the best thing you've done by a long shot but it was necessary. It helped. Sometimes that's the point. Whatever gets you through the night, it's alright. It's alright.

ALL I WANT IS YOU

One of U2's writing strategies was for Bono and The Edge to head off into the country somewhere, to isolate themselves, the better to let the muse speak through them. When *The Joshua Tree* tour finished, they took a short break, and then began the process of writing new material for *Rattle and Hum*. They retreated to a house in Connemara owned by John Heather.

The Edge was working on the basics of 'Desire' – the Bo Diddley rhythm, the main riff. He also had this beautiful chord sequence and melody that Bono immediately saw potential in. "It became a meditation on commitment and what that means," Bono says. It became 'All I Want Is You'.

If *Rattle and Hum* had begun with the Beatles via 'Helter Skelter', it would end with them too, in a string coda that was reminiscent of 'A Day in the Life'. Ironically, it was the wayward genius Van Dyke Parks who contributed an arrangement that leaned back in the direction of Europe, bringing the whole album to a haunting, ethereal finale.

'All I Want Is You' is a love song and Bono doesn't usually talk about these things – but on this occasion he does. "That's clearly about a younger version of myself and my relationship with Ali," he reflects. "It takes a huge generosity of spirit to be around somebody who's in the position I'm in, and who can expose you. If you're a very private person, as she is, that's something you have to be very careful about.

"That's a song about commitment, really. I don't think being married to someone is so easy. But I'm interested in the idea of marriage. I think it's madness but it's a grand madness. If people think it's normal, they're out of their minds. I think that's why a lot of people fall apart, because they're not prepared for what it is. Once they've made that commitment, they think that's the end of it, now they can rest easy.

"I'm very restless. I am not the kind of guy who would normally settle down with a family and one person. I'm a tinker. I like to travel. The only reason I'm here is because I met someone so extraordinary that I just couldn't let that go. So a lot of the sense you get from the work is that some of the characters want to run, to get to the airport and just fly away. And other characters could never be away from this."

He looks around at his living room. "I think that's a great dynamic for songs."

Onwards to *Achtung Baby*!

ALL I WANT
IS YOU
Written: U2
Length: 6' 30"
Album:
Rattle And Hum,
October 1988
UK singles chart
position: 4
US singles chart
position: 83

89

ACHTUNG BABY

Selina Scott in Central Park, New York. A mic stuck in Bono's face. She is flattering Bono, talking about his interest in social justice, his trip to Ethiopia, his involvement in the Sun City anti-apartheid project.

The Giants' stadium, later that evening. Selina is there again. So is Lou Reed. Lou can be curt. When he doesn't like Selina's questions he tells her where to get off. "Man, you got a lot of shit to deal with," he says to Bono.

Maybe Lou misunderstood, but Selina seemed to be casting aspersions on U2 being interested in social justice. Bono's face flushed. Then the anger hit. She had seemed so – sweet.

He saw a line about U2 marketing idealism. And he thought, We've got to get rid of this baggage. It doesn't matter how sincere you are. Perceptions are more important than truth. You're a rock 'n' roll star. Your job is riddled with contradictions. Time to put them on the agenda. Enter *Achtung Baby*. Enter Zoo TV. And then U2's whole world started to fall apart.

This is where it start getting weird...

ZOO STATION

Wartime Germany. The Allies are wreaking havoc. Cities being bombed. In the midst of chaos, surreal humour. The walls of Berlin Zoo are knocked down and the animals escape. The citizens emerge from their bunkers in the morning. There are rhinos, pelicans, flamingos in the streets

Achtung Baby was a nightmare to record. It nearly killed everyone in the band. There was a lot of tension in the air. On one of the darker days, Bono decided that a trip to the zoo would be in order. U2 bought ice-creams and walked round the zoo like school kids.

Bono was interested in the zoo. He'd read a novel about setting free the animals, a kind of introduction to Dadaism. Going right back to Lypton Village and the Virgin Prunes, that was his world. He began to feel that things were coming full circle, that maybe it was time to re-introduce characters like the Fool. They'd been moving in the direction of the literal. Now, they needed to become Dadaist again.

He was interested in the zoo as a metaphor. So there was a certain surge of recognition when they landed in Berlin to record the album. This place was like a fucking zoo alright. Even the train station was called Zoo Bahnhof. Zoo Station. The point was that the song would open the album with a statement of intent. Forget the previous reference points. You are about to embark on a journey into the unknown. So are we.

The first verse reads as if it could have been written from the point of view of a child about to be born: "(I'm) ready to say I'm glad to be alive/I'm ready, ready for the push." And that suspicion lingers throughout, as if Bono is drawing inspiration from having watched his own first child struggling to find her bearings in an unfamiliar and sometimes hostile world. "In the cool of the night/in the warmth of the breeze," he sings, "I'll be crawling around/on my hands and knees."

Bono was unhappy with his vocal performances when the band began to record *Achtung Baby*. He and engineer Flood distorted his voice. It gave Bono a different sound, and also a new persona to play with.

The band sounded different too. The drums were hard, insistent, industrial. There were moments of sunlight, as the train emerged from the underground, flashes of openness captured on The Edge's guitar. But this was the beginning of a journey into the dark underbelly of human experience and the suggestion of a child's-eye view only made it more poignant.

Achtung, baby, was right.

ZOO STATION
Written: U2
Length: 4' 36"
Album:
Achtung Baby,
November 1991
US singles chart
position: 10

91

EVEN BETTER THAN
THE REAL THING

It had been bugging Bono for a long, long time. You switch on the radio and hear a soulful voice bellowing out something that sounds almost spiritual. It turns out to be a promo for a bank. You flick on the television. There's this incredible piece of footage that could be straight out of *Vanishing Point*, only it looks richer, denser, more expensive. It's a car ad.

It was around the time of the release of *Rattle and Hum*. "You can't tell the difference between the ads and the records any more," Bono said to me, clearly rattled by the way in which music was being co-opted and manipulated to serve the needs of commerce. And yet wasn't rock 'n' roll itself about commerce, about selling records? That thought was there as an undercurrent in 'Desire', a song about turning people on, that had Bono stuttering about "Money, money, money, money, money, money".

'Desire' had been recorded with Paul Barrett and Robbie Adams handling engineering duties in STS studios in Dublin. Another song, started in the same session and then put to one side, had been called 'The Real Thing'. They took the multi-track of that to Germany and tried to work on it in Hansa Studios. But the atmosphere was so overloaded with melancholy that nothing happened. They couldn't crack it.

Back in Dublin, they set up in Elsinore, a mansion on the Dalkey coastline, near where Bono and The Edge live, to which the band give the name Dog Town.. It was there that *Achtung Baby* began to come together. The Berlin session had been racked by a mixture of creative divisions, personal tensions and an abiding sense of dislocation. Gradually these were overcome in the more relaxed, informal atmosphere of the new surroundings. The spirit of Berlin hung over the record, but now the darkness and claustrophobia could be turned to creative effect. By the time it came to finishing 'Even Better than the Real Thing', the band had rediscovered their sense of fun, tarting it up *à la* Marc Bolan in a tribute to the kind of glam rock that was on *Top of the Pops* when they were hitting their own teens.

"It had been called 'The Real Thing', which is a really dumb title for a song," Bono reflects. "So with these new eyes that we had, we thought 'Even Better Than the Real Thing' is actually where people live right now. People are no longer after experiences of truth. They are looking for true experiences, for the moment. People are no longer obsessed with the

**EVEN BETTER
THAN THE
REAL THING
Written:** U2
Length: 3' 41"
Album:
Achtung Baby,
November 1991
**UK singles chart
position:** 8
**US singles chart
position:** 32

Marc Bolan:
the real thing.

question 'What is the truth?' They want to know 'What is the point?' And the point is the moment. That's where we live right now, in this rave culture. Interesting things come out of that because living in the present, in the now – and not looking to what's around the corner – is very dangerous politically, ecologically, in relationships, to the family. But that's where people are at right now."

U2's interest in dance had been stimulated by their own plans to open a club, The Kitchen in the Clarence Hotel. Besides, there was an imperative always to be at the cutting edge of youth culture, to know what was going on, to absorb whatever lessons might need to be learned and to apply them smartly to the evolving band gestalt. 'Even Better Than the Real Thing' was evidence enough that Larry and Adam could mix it with the best of the new Manchester dance groups in the rhythm department but there was more than a hint of irony in U2's appropriation of the old Sly Stone gospel routine, the backing vocals pleading "Take me higher", before Bono delivers the chorus with what amounts to serene detachment.

The intention was to indulge the voyeuristic emphasis on appearance, to slide knowingly down the surface of things. The infatuation with the moment is superbly captured in the clubbers' heroic self-projection: "We're free to fly the crimson sky/The sun won't melt our wings tonight." But underlying these erotic chimerae is something tragic. What else but the sound of a relationship cracking up could explain the lines "Well, my heart is where it's always been/My head is somewhere in between/Give me one more chance/Let me be your lover tonight"?

Meanwhile, the joke was on Coca-Cola, who had been using "The real thing" as their advertising slogan for years. It almost came full circle when Richard Branson approached the band, seeking permission to use 'Even Better Than the Real Thing' for his campaign to launch Virgin Cola.

But that would have been one irony too far. The band refused.

ONE

Sometimes it can seem as if you're digging a hole. Another day, another recording session. Nothing seems to be coming right. You flounder around for six hours, and at the end of it you know that inspiration has gone on an extended holiday. But now that you're into the process there's no option but to keep going. And so you flounder some more. And then suddenly: BANG!

U2 were in Berlin for three months and they delivered two songs. And one of them happened by accident. They were in the throes of working on 'Mysterious Ways' and looking for a middle eight. The Edge came up with two alternatives. Bono heard one of them and he thought "Massive new song!" He improvised a melody over the chords and it sounded good.

"The Edge put the other middle eight on at the end of it and that just became the song. The melody, the structure – the whole thing was done in 15 minutes," Bono recalls.

Naturally, the band were excited. It was one of those happy accidents, those moments when the log-jam of ideas breaks and a song comes flooding through. Tapes of the work-in-progress were being delivered to Eno, who was coming back with comments and responses; in due course, he got this first, inspired draft of 'One'. The next time he showed up in Hansa Studios he was in buoyant mood.

"Brian arrived and he said that he liked all the material we had," Bono recalls. "We were surprised because everyone was freaked out about it. Then he said 'There's just one song I really despise, and that's 'One'.'"

Bono laughs. "He felt it needed some serious deconstruction. So we went about that, and that's why it works. Because you can play it on acoustic guitar now and it works, but if you had heard it on acoustic guitar first, it wouldn't have had the same feeling."

Flood remembers the session well. It was one of those special occasions alright. "It was very, very quick," he says. "Bono sang 90 per cent of the melody and a lot of the lyrical ideas off the top of his head. It just came together. There was a moment and we caught it."

It is extraordinary to think just how close 'One' came to not happening. Given the shambolic way in which U2 operate in the studio, there's always a sense that songs are written by accident, but this was a particularly extreme case. And yet it emerges as one of their finest creations, a ballad of great depth and beauty that's open to a multiplicity of interpretations.

"I think it was based loosely on the position I was in regarding my last girlfriend and my wife," Bono's old Lypton Village associate, Guggi, reflects,

ONE
Written: U2
Length: 4' 36"
Album:
Achtung Baby,
November 1991
UK singles chart
position: 7

offering one interpretation. "I was with my last girlfriend, Linda, for 14 years. And then I got a little studio down in the City Arts Centre. I was working there and then I heard that this German painter was coming over for six months, to work, and it turned out to be Sybil. We started painting together and it sort of went from there. And I was very close, physically close, to Bono at the time because he was around and we were spending a lot of time together. And I think a lot of that is captured in the song."

'One' is a song about relationships. The implication of guilt, felt by someone who has just walked out on a long-term love, is there alright when Bono asks, "Have you come here for forgiveness/Have you come to raise the dead/Have you come here to play Jesus/To the lepers in your head?" But the song is also a meditation on the extent to which their Berlin sojourn was testing the band's own sense of unity. "That's an extraordinary thing about songwriting," Bono relates. "What something is in essence, you don't have to play to it. In fact if you play against it, you often get much more.

"'One', of course, is about the band," he adds. "It was after Adam flipped out in Sydney, and we'd had to do a show without him. We had just two nights to film, and the first was gone because he wasn't there. So we had one night to get it. But he looks amazing in the film and there's a real boldness to his playing. I don't know how he kept it together.

"We thought that was going to be the end, to be honest with you. We didn't know if we wanted to go on if somebody was that unhappy. And that performance of 'One' suddenly becomes what it is about that night. It does have that quality as a song. Going around Europe, when the stuff was going on in Bosnia, sometimes 200 miles from where we were playing, you'd get a similar kind of feeling – that that was what it was about."

Three videos were made for 'One', each drawing on a different

o *TV*: the medium
the message.

interpretation of the song. One, directed by Mark Pellington and built around an image of buffalo being herded over the side of a cliff, was based on the work of the artist David Wojnarowicz, who died of an AIDS-related illness in 1992. It led to speculation that 'One' was a song about AIDS and that the lyric was a conversation between a father and his HIV-positive gay son. It always seemed like a somewhat liberal interpretation to me.

"It was part of one of the layers of the story," Bono argues. "If a song deals with any kind of sexual or erotic subject matter, then the spectre of AIDS has to be present. But it's not the only threat to relationships. Everything out there is against the idea of couples. The concept of fidelity is constantly undermined in every ad, every TV programme, every film, every novel you read. Sex is used to sell commodities. It has become a commodity itself. In fact, it's always been a commodity.

"If sex is even close to the centre of our lives, how come we've relegated the subject to where it's the property of the dullest of minds, to pornographers and the like? I still think it's virgin territory because you're prone to juvenalia in it, the 23 positions in a one-night stand type of boast, but there's much more out there than that."

With the Berlin session in the bag, the tape of 'One' was taken back to Dublin. What they had was a good foundation but it still needed what The Edge calls "foreground". That was when Eno came in and, with razor-sharp instinct, did a mix based on his personal prejudices, ruthlessly throwing out what he didn't like. It was the breakthrough they needed. They got a picture of an arrangement that would work.

Flood remained unconvinced. "I was the nagging doubter," he recalls. "I always felt it was a bit straight, until we did the final mix. It was all hands on deck. Bono didn't like a line in the vocal and we basically spent the whole day re-doing it. From that, we went into mix mode and it was me, Eno, Lanois and Bono sitting at the back, all doing different moves, getting the mix to be quite emotional.

"There's a point in the process when the technology gets lost and you can actually use the desk as an instrument. It started to happen on that mix. We got to just after the 'Love is a temple' section at the end and The Edge said, 'I've got this great idea for a guitar riff'. So on the mix, there were three of us on the desk, the rest of the band vibing around and The Edge at the back of the studio, playing the guitar part live to the half-inch.

"Personally, I feel that the song has such a strong emotional content – and we managed to completely honour and improve on that, the way we mixed it."

UNTIL THE END OF THE WORLD

UNTIL THE END
OF THE WORLD
Written: U2
Length: 4' 39"
Album:
Achtung Baby,
November 1991

What are the themes of *Achtung Baby*? You could put the same question to ten people and get ten different answers. The Edge said: betrayal, love, morality, spirituality and faith. Betrayal came first.

It was in the air. The Edge's marriage was falling apart. So was Guggi's. There was tension in the band. Now that they were working with rhythm loops, Larry wasn't even sure what his place was anymore. There was that morning where the others had succeeded in leaving him stranded. Larry had spent hours languishing in his East German hotel. When he got in to Hansa, in the end, he was furious and he let everyone know it. Betrayal.

Bono had been reading Brendan Kennelly's *Book of Judas*. Judas Iscariot was a remarkable character. The more you thought about him the more enigmatic he became. The redemption couldn't have happened without him. So was he the ultimate insider? It was interesting how he betrayed Jesus: with a kiss! What had been going on between them anyway?

Written for Wim Wenders, 'Until the End of the World' is about an encounter in which sex is high on the agenda. There's a hint that only men were involved. There's also a strong suggestion of prostitution. And there is an unmistakable reference to oral sex: "Surrounding me, going down on me/spilling over the brim." But it doesn't stop there. "In waves of regret, waves of joy," Bono sings, "I reached out for the one I tried to destroy."

And you know that he must be thinking of an orgasm that's drenched in feelings of guilt.

All of these elements are in there, of course, but the song is about betrayal and it's written from the point of view of Judas Iscariot. The line "In the garden I was playing the tart/I kissed your lips and broke your heart" refers to the scene in the Garden of Gethsemane, and there's no mistaking the implication of a homoerotic bond between Jesus and Judas.

On the other hand, there's a sense that Bono is writing about himself and his own capacity for betrayal. Or could it be about someone Bono felt had betrayed him? In truth it is about all the betrayals that were so central to U2 at the time.

...s in his kiss: Judas
...d Jesus in
...e Garden of
...thsemane.

SO CRUEL

You could listen to *Achtung Baby* every which way. You could turn it upside-down. You could look at it from a dozen different angles. It doesn't matter. No matter what way you come at it, there is blood on the tracks. And nowhere is this more evident than in the ballad 'So Cruel'.

To describe it as bittersweet would be an understatement. 'So Cruel' is the desolate complaint of a lover who has been spurned but who remains in love with his tormentor. As a statement about marital infidelity, the sense of betrayal that accompanies it and the rage that almost inevitably follows, it would be hard to surpass. Bono is clearly drawing on the experiences of those close to him, and particularly on the emotional turmoil that The Edge and Aislinn had been going through.

"That's in there, but it's unfair to lump it all on The Edge and Aislinn splitting up," he explains. "That was one of the saddest things. I was their best man, and we all went through that. But that was only one part of it. There were lots of other things going on internally within the band and outside it. People are desperately trying to hold onto each other in a time when that's very difficult. Looking around, you see how unprepared for it all people are, and the deals they make."

Looked at from another angle, 'So Cruel' deals with possessiveness, jealousy and obsession – that part of the brain where sex and power are connected in a heady and addictive cocktail. Scott Walker was an acknowledged influence on the song. So, too, was Roy Orbison, for whom Bono and The Edge had written 'Mystery Girl'. The arrangement is something Flood takes credit for, highlighting a subtle piece of studio chicanery that transforms the song.

"If you haven't got a song there in the first place, none of this would make a blind bit of difference," he says, "but I think the way we shifted around the rhythm was very important. It was put down as a very straight-feeling backing track. The bass is played, but in the studio we doctored it to change the emphasis of where the bass line lay. That turned it into something that had a more unique feel about it, meshed against the song. That was one track where the technology available to us was crucial to the end product."

But in the end it is the poetry that makes it memorable. "Her skin is pale like God's only dove/Screams like an angel for your love/Then she makes you watch her from above/And you need her like a drug."

SO CRUEL
Written: U2
Length: 5' 49"
Album:
Achtung Baby,
November 1991

THE FLY

THE FLY
Written: U2
Length: 4' 29"
Album:
Achtung Baby,
November 1991
UK singles chart
position: 1
US singles chart
position: 61

Blame it on the wardrobe man. Fintan Fitzgerald, who handles that end of the U2 operation, bought Bono the mad goggles. In the dark days in Berlin, Bono would stick on the fly shades and look at the world through the eyes of a character who was only barely forming in his imagination. It was childish, playful. Slowly but surely 'The Fly' was born.

The band had been hammering away at a piece with the working title of 'Ultraviolet'. Back in Dublin, the piece schismed into two parts. One became 'Light My Way'. The other was 'The Fly'. Fintan Fitzgerald also gave Bono a book of Jenny Holger's truisms. "I became very interested in these single-line aphorisms," Bono states. "So I got this character who could say them all, from 'A liar won't believe anybody else' to 'A friend is somebody who lets you down'. And that's where 'The Fly' was coming from."

Flood contributed the distortion in the voice, creating the distance that Bono needed to get fully into the part. Daniel Lanois helped with the lyric.

"I thought it was a fascinating character," Bono recalls. "Because there had been rumours of megalomania circulating and I thought – well, let's give them a megalomaniac! The faces of the people when that character walked on stage, was a sight to be seen. I couldn't see it as clearly as everyone else because I had the goggles and the boil-in-the-bag Elvis suit on. But it was a sense of 'Oh no, it's true'. And that was a great feeling."

Undercurrents had come together. 'The Fly' was about subversion. With

Bono: come Fly with me.

99

its hip-hop beats, distorted vocals and industrial edge, Bono called it the sound of four men chopping down *The Joshua Tree*. It is packed with little explosions of truth, some of them universal, others personal. "It's no secret ambition bites the nail of success," 'The Fly' announces, and it's a powerful image that's rooted in Bono's own gnawed fingernails.

With the Gulf War erupting in the middle of recording, there was a sense in which 'The Fly' represented everyman on the run from the sheer craziness of the world around him. And then there was Bono playing the Fat Lady, crooning in a gospel falsetto: "Love we shine like a burning star/We're falling from the sky." We should have known it was all over when she began to sing.

MYSTERIOUS WAYS

There is a feeling throughout *Achtung Baby* that man is but an awe-struck observer at the banquet of love. That woman is the superior being. That all she has to do is click her fingers – or crack her whip – and he will obey.

Images of submission abound. They're there in 'Zoo Station', 'One', 'Who's Gonna Ride Your Wild Horses?', 'So Cruel' and 'The Fly', with the narrator abasing himself in front of the woman, crawling around on his hands and knees. 'Mysterious Ways' continues in the same vein, with the celebrated couplet "If you want to kiss the sky/better learn how to kneel… (on your knees boy!)".

"It's a song about a man living on little or no romance," Bono says. "It's a song about women – or about woman – but it's addressed to him."

'Mysterious Ways' is not about a particular woman. It is about women in general, and the way they entrance men. "Ali often says, 'For God's sake will you let me down off this pedestal?'" Bono laughs. "At times I do tend to idealise women. It's easy to fall into the trap of separating them into angels and devils for the sake of the drama."

'Mysterious Ways' is one of the album's most upful, optimistic tracks. It had begun with a bass riff, Adam kick-starting the musical framework and Larry laying down a suitably funky dance, rhythm groove. Then they hit a wall. "A load of different ideas were tried," says Flood. They accidentally side-tracked into 'One', and then came back to 'Mysterious Ways'.

Daniel Lanois went into the studio in Berlin early one morning to try out a few ideas before the band got in. He didn't like what he was hearing. Then when Bono came in and started to sing, he seemed to be pushing the song in the opposite direction entirely. In a dark, tense period for the band, this was the nadir. Lanois and Bono argued solidly for over two hours – a bitter, intense argument during which no holds were barred.

"That's why I love Danny so much," Bono says. "He cares about the record he's making as much and more than any band or artist he's working with." But it wasn't funny at the time. Joe O'Herlihy remembers it as a brutal and bruising showdown.

"I really thought they were going to have a fight," Flood adds. "But I think it was just a product of the fact that this was such a hard record to make. Going into it everyone knew what we didn't want. It was like, you know what you want to throw out – but you're not quite sure of the place you want to go. It takes a series of mistakes, errors, learning, two steps forward, three steps sideways to actually get there."

MYSTERIOUS WAYS
Written: U2
Length: 4' 04"
Album:
Achtung Baby,
November 1991
UK singles chart position: 13
US singles chart position: 9

WHO'S GONNA RIDE YOUR WILD HORSES

WHO'S GONNA
RIDE YOUR
WILD HORSES?
Written: U2
Length: 5' 16"
Album:
Achtung Baby,
November 1991
UK singles chart
position: 14
US singles chart
position: 35

'Who's Gonna Ride Your Wild Horses?' had so many different incarnations. It was mixed a dozen different ways, and the pros and cons of each of them were debated in detail. Should Larry lighten up on the drums? Should he push them harder? What about that first rhythm track that The Edge put down? Where has the acoustic gone? The discussions went round in circles. And then it was time to be decisive.

Daniel Lanois was producing *Achtung Baby* but at times he seemed uncomfortable with what was going down. Eno was afforded the luxury of being a dilettante. Flood was there all the way through, at the desk, keeping track of everything. And when things were getting really hairy, there was always the option of calling in Steve Lillywhite as a fresh pair of ears. And when it came to the crunch, when decisions had to be made about 'Who's Gonna Ride Your Wild Horses?', they brought him in again.

"Steve mixed it and he went for the sonic blast of it," Bono says. "It started out as one of those Scott Walker things but we felt it was too rich. Daniel probably felt that the way we went in the end was too FM."

It had been more of a love song. Now it was about sexual jealousy. The lyrics may have been hurried but it has its share of telling psychological insights into the battlefield of love, all the same. "Well, you lied to me/'cos I asked you to," Bono sings, and you don't need to be told what the context is. And it comes back, in the final chorus, to oral sex: "Who's gonna taste your salt water kisses?/Who's gonna take the place of me?"

"It's been said to me, alright", Bono concedes, "that there's a lot of references to oral sex on the record. It's a very equal position. But I hadn't thought about the cumulative effect. I guess there's something for everybody. Don't try this at home! [laughs]."

trio of axe-grinders.

TRYING TO THROW YOUR ARMS AROUND THE WORLD

Sometimes it could get too intense in Dublin. Everyone watching your every move. The stupidest things being reported on, often inaccurately.

That was one of the reasons for deciding to stay in Los Angeles through the winter of '86. There was a sense of freedom there that Dublin didn't allow. When they began searching for a place to stay, the estate agents showed them a dozen fancy pads. "You don't want to see this place," they told The Edge. "It's more like a military compound. There's no air conditioning. No carpets. No en-suite toilets." The Edge said they'd take it.

It was a massive place. They could do anything they wanted to it, because it was up for demolition in the not-too-distant future. So they put down roots and went through the full LA experience. "We started to live at night a lot more," Bono says.

Downtown LA is an extraordinary scene: people stepping over bodies on the way into banks in the morning. Bobby Fischer was rumoured to be living downtown in a box. At night the place was full of illegal drinking joints and other nefarious clubs. There was a small community of lost souls inhabiting this twilight zone, and U2 embraced it.

"It was really important for me," Bono says. "Things that other people were going through at 18 or 19, I was going through then. You know, getting loaded and being a bit of a tinker. Not caring where you woke up. Ali was really good about it. She was coming over, but she recognized that this was a stage I might need to go through.

On the lyrics sheet of *Achtung Baby*, 'Trying to Throw Your Arms Around the World' is followed by a thanks to The Flaming Colossus, the infamous Hollywood celebrity late-nite bar. It revives 'The Fly', presenting him this time from a somewhat more sympathetic guy who goes on the town and finds himself staggering home in the early hours like a lost soul.

"That's a song about drunk ambition," Bono says. "As in 'I'll be home soon'. There's just warmth in that image." And great insight. "Nothing much to say I guess/Just the same as all the rest/Been tryin' to throw your arms around the world." Bono knew the character he was writing about very well.

TRYING TO THROW YOUR ARMS AROUND THE WORLD
Written: U2
Length: 3' 53"
Album:
Achtung Baby,
November 1991

ULTRAVIOLET (LIGHT MY WAY)

On most occasions it would pass unremarked. A bit of a chuckle, back to the top of the take and away we go again.

It was about half-way through when Larry dropped one of his drumsticks. You could hear it on the track, as clear as daylight. Everyone carried on. Larry got going again and they finished the take. Then someone threw a curve-ball. Maybe we should leave it in. That bit where Larry dropped the drumstick. He wasn't being funny.

"Given the choice," Eno would ask later, "how much do you allow a record to exhibit warts-and-all spontaneity and how much do you repair?" Put like that, it sounds like a reasonable question. But when you're the drummer and it was you who dropped the stick – at first, you think maybe they're winding you up. Then you realize they aren't, that they're for real about leaving this stupid little cock-up on the record. What are they trying to do? Make a record that, finally, ruins the band? That insults its fans? That exposes us all as incompetent? The debate lasts for three hours. At times it feels like people are trying to sabotage the record with dissent. When Bono first produces the chorus, it inspires a degree of mirth. "Baby, baby, baby," he sings, "light my way." What's so funny?

People hadn't heard Bono use the word "baby" like that before. He'd often scat things one way and then change them later, but it became obvious that this was the lyric of the song. It didn't feel right. And besides something was niggling about the smartness of it: was it not condescending to use the term for a woman anyway? "There was a lot of debate, and a good deal of laughter, about Bono actually coming out and going 'Baby'," Flood recalls. "It was less to do with the political correctness of it than whether he could actually get away with singing "Baby, baby, baby/Baby, baby, baby" and so on. That was very funny for a long time. But he got away with it alright."

Larry lays down funky groove.

103

**ULTRAVIOLET
(LIGHT MY WAY)**
Written: U2
Length: 5' 31"
Album:
Achtung Baby,
November 1991

ACROBAT

During the run up to *Achtung Baby*, U2 had been listening to KMFDM, Sonic Youth, Young Gods, My Bloody Valentine. As far as rock 'n' roll was concerned, the emphasis was on a hard-edged industrial kind of sound. The Edge was particularly into some of the speedy metal stuff that was in vogue. At the time, they'd also developed an interest in Roy Orbison, Scott Walker, Jacques Brel – in torch songs.

In terms of lyrics, that was the way The Edge wanted to go, towards a more personal kind of writing. The challenge that U2 had set themselves for the album was to do justice to both impulses.

Everything was in flux. *Rattle and Hum* had been so successful it was embarrassing. It had also been savaged by the press. Having started out as a band in the slipstream of punk, U2 remembered what they had felt about the supergroups of the late '70s. Were they now about to become what they had despised?

Their strategy had been radical. Take everything you know and throw it out. Work with the music you don't know, in a place you don't know, in a way you haven't worked before. Disorientate yourself.

Well, they succeeded in that – but they succeeded in disorientating Daniel Lanois even further. 'Acrobat' was a case in point. "Daniel had such a hard time on that," Bono says. "He did so well, but he was trying to get us to play to our strengths and I didn't want to. I wanted to play to our weaknesses. I wanted to experiment. With hindsight, some of the experiments didn't come off so well, to be honest."

The Edge cranks up the guitar and does a part that's half 'Where the Streets Have No Name', half 'Bullet the Blue Sky'. Larry's drumming adds to the sense of urgency, whipped along by Adam's driving bass.

But it is the lyrics that make 'Acrobat'. Not for the first time on the record, Bono acknowledges his own weakness and inadequacy. He is more conscious now than ever before of the contradictions in his own position. "And I must be an acrobat/to talk like this/and act like that," he sings. It was as far from the righteousness that U2 had so often been accused of as you could get. Or was it? "I think he was taking a swipe back at the press with that line 'Don't let the bastards grind you down'," suggests Gavin Friday.

ACROBAT
Written: U2
Length: 4' 30"
Album:
Achtung Baby,
November 1991

Super: Sonic Youth.

LOVE IS BLINDNESS

It was Gavin Friday who interested Bono in Jacques Brel. Gavin had run the Blue Jaysus club in Dublin's Waterfront cafe and for a few glorious months, it became one of the city's most celebrated nights-out with Agnes Bernelle, Maria McKee and Bono, among many musicians and comedians, likely to show up with something new to perform, in the spirit of the cabaret. Despite its distinctly European flavour, 'Love Is Blindness' had been written during the *Rattle and Hum* period. It was Blue Jaysus material, a song that could have been performed with the accompaniment of a lone piano. In Bono's head, it might have been sung by Nina Simone, one of his all-time favourite singers.

It takes us back – again – to the shadowy world of deceit, infidelity and betrayal. It depicts love at the end, the very end, of its tether. It is as bleak and as despairing a view of the world as you're likely to get, reflecting the emotional climate in which the entire album had been made. "All one's relationships, with your family, with your friends, with the members of the band – everything started to disintegrate with that record," Adam Clayton told John Waters. In terms of its mood, 'Love is Blindness' had the dark, sensual and decadent feel of pre-war Berlin. But its sentiments made it the perfect conclusion to *Achtung Baby*. "Love is blindness/I don't want to see," Bono sang – a desolate acknowledgement of the terrible reality that it is sometimes better not to know. The Edge plays a mournful, ejaculatory guitar solo, stabbing out thick emotional blues notes that linger and then fall away like tears. "A more eloquent prayer than anything I could say," Bono reflects.

And then darkness falls.

LOVE IS BLINDNESS

Written:	U2
Length:	4' 23"
Album:	*Achtung Baby*, November 1991

ZOOROPA

Achtung Baby had a message. You thought you had us pigeon-holed: now try sticking all this in that little box. You want to see the real U2? Well, here we are. Even better than the real thing!

Zoo TV developed out of the same impulse. It began with the proposition "Everything you know is wrong". It concerned media distortion. The truth behind the lies – and the difficulty in ever being able to dig deep enough to find it. The Fly and MacPhisto came alive during the *Zoo TV* tour. It was U2 in disguise. But it was also U2.

Bono was enjoying himself. He discovered that he likes putting on masks. It was fun being MacPhisto, arriving in St Peter's Square to get the Pope's blessing, pushing children out of the way. Method acting!

The whole band were enjoying themselves in this crazy hall of distorting mirrors. The energy being generated was phenomenal. A break in the tour was coming up. They didn't want to come down. Better to turn this energy into noise. Better to make a record. *Zooropa* here we come!

Well, would you Adam 'n' Eve it?

ZOOROPA

One of the most important things is to find a location. Then you get a sense of who's actually singing the songs. What they're really about. The emotional as well as the physical terrain. The Edge and Bono had been reading William Gibson's cyberpunk futuristic novels. "He has this location," Bono explains, "the sprawl, he calls it, the city in the future where a lot of stuff is set." Bono wanted to paint a similar kind of picture with noise.

During the *Zoo TV* tour, the band had been working with Roger Trilling, and part of the deal was to create the sense of a future that would be attractive, as opposed to the typical sci-fi scenario where what's in store is a wasteland. But other undercurrents were at work too. With the collapse of communism and the expansion of the European Union, borders were coming down all over Europe. Not always to the good. Civil war was breaking out in the former Yugoslavia and the horrors that would befall Bosnia were beginning to take nightmarish shape. Nazism was on the rise in the newly re-unified Germany. "Looking at all that," Bono says *Zooropa* seemed like a great image of a European location that was surreal."

During the *Zoo TV* tour, The Fly had taken on a life of his own. He had insisted on having his own dressing room. He began to crowd Bono's space, successfully replacing the singer as the band's frontman for a significant part of the set. He brought his friend MacPhisto on board. And between them they got to the designers who were putting the show together. They filled the gigantic screens with every conceivable kind of bizarre imagery. Some atrocity from the Gulf War? No problem. Bang it on. A clip from a blue movie? Go ahead, sweethearts. Do your stuff.

More of those mad aphorisms that had been premiered on 'The Fly'. TV ads. Copylines. Scenes from a Nazi movie. Members of the audience enjoying their 15 seconds of fame in the *Zoo TV* video confessional. Hey, this is the information age. We're on the brink of a tele-visual revolution. Let's put it all up there.

It was frightening. Fascinating. So much potential. So much potential for disaster. Not a time to lie down and leave it to the buccaneers and the pirates. Time to engage. Time to help to make the future according to your own vision.

"We were opening this kind of *Bladerunner*-type world," Bono says. "It starts with this neon winking and blinking and these two characters come out of it. There's this image of the 'overground'. It was a time when

ZOOROPA
Written: U2
Length: 6' 30"
Album: *Zooropa*,
July 1993

everyone was all indie and grey and dull – the 'underground'. The overground was like coming out into the bright light of the modern city. It's an amazing place to be, walking around these modern cities like Houston or Tokyo. And the idea was coming out into that, embracing it."

But first there was the small matter of re-appropriating the language on which *Zooropa* was being founded. Steve Turner, who wrote the book accompanying the *Rattle and Hum* album and film, had begun sending Bono a digest of articles from all around the world. "I kind of stopped reading books and novels so much, and I started reading more magazines," Bono recalls. "I wanted to get away from the weight of where I was going. I wanted to fly. There was enough melancholy around."

'Zooropa' begins with the Audi slogan "Vorsprung durch Technik", and in the first three verses there are references to advertising copylines from Daz, Fairy Liquid, Colgate and Zanussi, among others. "And I have no religion," the protagonist proclaims, "and I don't know what's what." But far from seeing that as a weakness, the thrust of 'Zooropa' was that uncertainty could be a positive point of departure.

There was certainly a touch of anarchy about how 'Zooropa' was put together. Joe O'Herlihy had captured a couple of good sound check jams at the beginning of the *Zoo TV* tour. The Edge took the best bits as the basis for a backing track, fed them into a digital editor and created a song structure. The band did a separate jam for the sombre, ethereal opening. "I found sections of this jam," Flood recalls, "did a weird atmospheric mix of it and then when we were starting to piece the album together, I tried to cross-fade that into the beginning of 'Zooropa' as it stood then."

Everybody felt that Flood's intro worked. "The whole mad guitar stuff that happens on the second half was Eno treating a lot of guitars," Flood adds. That worked too. Then, at the last minute, everyone had misgivings about the original jam that formed the backing track for the first half. Now that there was a shape to the song, the band could play it through. Bono even tossed in an odd lyrical reference to 'Acrobat' as a coda. "In the end," Flood explains, "for the first half we just used what had been replayed and on the second half we used what was the jam, with some elements of the replay on it."

You can just imagine the producer at the console, as the band depart back into Europe for another date. "Don't worry, baby," he says. "It's gonna be alright."

'Zooropa'. Better by design team.

BABYFACE

ABYFACE
Vritten: U2
ength: 4' 00"
lbum: *Zooropa*,
ıly 1993

During the Zoo TV tour, U2 had entered another kind of celebrity zone. *Achtung Baby* had been their hippest album to date, claiming a place for them at (what was perceived to be) the contemporary cutting edge of rock.

The successful Paul Oakenfold remixes of 'Even Better Than the Real Thing' and 'Mysterious Ways' had won U2 a new cult respectability in clubs. They'd begun to understand the appeal of glamour, of fantasy. Glamour had begun to understand the appeal of U2 too. Adam had hooked up with Naomi Campbell. Kate Moss and Christy Turlington had become friends of the band, visiting Dublin frequently. Bono was on the cover of *Vogue* in his Fly gear in the company of Christy Turlington.

In some ways it was a natural drift. When you're operating at high altitude, you tend to make friends with other people who are operating in the same rarified sphere. But, on Bono's part at least, it was also a conscious decision. You can embrace this stuff or be ashamed of it. What was there to be ashamed of? Why not live the contradiction and report back on it?

109

'Babyface' – "cover girl with natural grace" – could have been written with any of the band's new model friends in mind, The Edge explains. But it was done with a twist. Bono had always been intrigued by the way in which the media turn consumers into voyeurs. It had been highlighted by the CNN coverage of the Gulf War, which had reduced a terrible human catastrophe to the level of a video game.

ım Clayton and
ımi Campbell.

By comparison, pornography – beamed into your home by satellite television – could seem like a benign calling. In the narrative of *Zooropa*, the camera moves up away from the couple in the opening song and goes in through a window in one of the high-rise buildings in the imaginary city of the future. There's a guy inside, watching a television. He has a remote control and he's slowing down the images. He's turning up the contrast and playing with it. "It's a song about watching and not being in the picture," Bono says. "About how people play with images, believing you know somebody through an image – and thinking that by manipulating a machine that in fact controls you, you can have some kind of power. It's about the illusion of being in control."

The irony is that 'Babyface' is delivered with all the tenderness of a love song. And, in its own way, maybe that's what it is.

NUMB

The band took a mid-tour break at the beginning of 1993. Yet The Edge needed to keep going. His marriage had split up. It drove him back into the studio, where he began to demo new material.

He came across a song called 'Down All the Days' that had been intended for *Achtung Baby*, but didn't make the cut. He liked the backing track, with its loop taken from the passage in Leni Riefenstahl's Nazi propaganda film, *Triumph of the Will*, where an 11-year-old boy is shown playing the drum at the 1936 Olympic Games. There was a hard, dirty, industrial feel to the instrumentation, making it a prime candidate for some kind of rap. They had considered the possibility of Bono reading 'In Cold Blood', his poem on the dehumanising effect of media coverage of violence and war, over it. But when that didn't work out, The Edge took over.

Sorry, Edge is a littl tied up at the moment.

He had become more involved in the lyric-writing, acting at times as Bono's editor, suggesting cuts and bouncing couplets off him. 'Numb', however, was entirely his own, and the chorus probably reflected his emotional frailty at the time, with Bono adopting his fat lady voice to testify "I feel numb" in a soulful falsetto that contrasted oddly with The Edge's flat delivery of the main vocal. Yet it also suggested that he was on the road to recovery because 'Numb' was an exercise in surreal humour, capturing the jaded rock star frozen into physical and emotional immobility by the self-imposed strictures of his position.

"It's arcade music," Bono said, "but at base it's a kind of dark energy that we're tapping into. It's us trying to get inside somebody's head. So you hear a football crowd, a line of don'ts, kitsch soul singing and Larry singing for the first time in that context. What we're trying to do is recreate that feeling of sensory overload."

The video for 'Numb', produced by Kevin Godley, was equally over-the-top, an absurd send-up of bondage games with The Edge being subjected to all kinds of arbitrary humiliations. But the song achieved its apotheosis when the band performed it in the Olympic Stadium in Berlin, where the Riefenstahl film loops had originally been recorded.

"That was a trip," Bono reflects. "There was uproar. There were people at the gig who could be – and probably were – the sons and daughters of the people in the film. But we wanted to point out, before anyone else did, the similarities between rock gigs and Nazi rallies."

NUMB
Written: U2
Length: 4' 18"
Album: *Zooropa*, July 1993

LEMON

You wouldn't have any inkling that 'Lemon' was about Bono's mother unless you were told. "Here's one for you," Gavin Friday had said conspiratorially. "The lyrical idea for that developed out of an old home movie that Bono saw."

It happened by chance. Someone had approached one of Bono's family at the airport and told him about the existence of this ancient footage in which Bob and Iris Hewson featured. Turned out it had been packaged by one of those companies that put kitsch music on top. It was eerie watching it. The image of his mother, on-screen, haunted Bono. "She was wearing lemon," Gavin recalled. "That's where the title came from."

From that starting point, the song became something else entirely: a meditation about film itself and the pleasure of looking. "The cinema is where we get to be nosy," Bono reflects. "Where we go to look into people's lives, without them minding. People like to stare at other people up close. But because of my position, I don't get to stare at people so much, so film is important for me, in that it allows me to do that."

'Lemon' is a complex song that flickers with different meanings depending on how you view it. But it is about seeing yourself more clearly through seeing someone else. "Through the light projected/He can see himself up close," Bono sings, and it doesn't involve a huge leap of the imagination to picture him seeing his own reflection in the poignant image of his mother in her youth.

He borrows a line from John Boorman about the film-making process when he talks about "turning money into light/To look for her". And in that phrase, it becomes a song about imagination itself, about the muse, about the female spirit with which U2 have always associated creativity.

There are hints of voyeurism too. "It's about the experience of looking rather than touching," Bono says. "I think my favourite image is the image of glass, where he melts the sand so he can see the world outside." The end product may sound fluent but it came together in fits and starts. "It began as a crude form of thing," Flood recalls. "Eno decided that there was one bassline he didn't like, so he just took it out. He treated a couple of guitars and those big string things, he just put on the track."

With the band flitting back and forth between various European cities in which they were gigging, and the studio, that was the way they had to work. They'd play for four or five hours in the middle of the night and Eno and Flood would divide up the end product between them. They'd work

[LE]MON

[Wr]itten: U2
[Len]gth: 6' 56"
[Al]bum: *Zooropa*,
[Ma]y 1993

separately, pushing the songs forward, tinkering with stuff, adding whatever they saw fit and getting down rough mixes. The band would come back in, repeat the process and hope they were going somewhere.

The Edge added a piano part at the bridge. Then he and Eno contributed the Talking Heads-style block vocals. They were getting down to some serious mixing when Bono finished the lyrics and did a vocal. Then, finally, Flood decided that they'd have to replace the drum machine with a real drum track and Larry obliged.

It was the last track to be finished. There was a deadline alright, but the days when they'd had to stick down '40' inside an hour were long gone. Sometimes they wondered if the greater latitude had actually made things harder for them.

John Boorman: turning money into light.

"They were on tour and flying back after each gig," Flood recalls. "They'd come in to the studio about midnight. I'd have been mixing. They'd listen and make suggestions, maybe do some music. They'd go home to bed. I'd carry on till about 4 or 5 in the morning. Then they'd come in at midday, make some suggestions on the mixing or do some more music. There was a whole two-week period where it was like that, which was absolute lunacy.

"With 'Lemon', I was mixing all night and I knew, by 9.30, 10 in the morning, that all the madness had come to a point where this is it. This really worked. Then I left. They heard what I'd done and really liked it. That was my last day on the album because I had other commitments. After I was gone, they spent another three days trying to perfect the balance, but ended up going back to the one that I had.

"It was a very strange sensation because for me it had been the ultimate feeling of everything coming together. You're digging through the dirt. You have all the frustration, all the lunacy that was going on. And finally you reach a moment where you know that that's it."

The Edge had doubts about it all along, the way it drew so many disparate elements together. When it was finished, however, he too knew it was a U2 song.

Whatever that is.

STAY (FARAWAY SO CLOSE)

During the mid-'80s, Bono had read one of Wim Wenders' books, *Emotion Pictures*. Wenders wrote about the way in which the USA had colonised the unconscious of the rest of the world through popular culture.

Bono was also reading Sam Shepard's plays at the time. Shepard had worked on the screenplay of *Paris, Texas* with Wenders and when it came to making *The Joshua Tree*, U2 had in mind a landscape similar to that depicted in that extraordinary film. When Bono met Wenders, he mentioned this. A bizarre synchronicity was revealed.

"He told me that when he was driving across America," Bono relates, "and preparing for *Paris, Texas*, he was listening to *Boy*. He had just one cassette in the car and that was it."

Wenders and Bono established a firm friendship, so it was no surprise when the director asked the band to do the title track for his *Stay (Faraway, So Close!)* movie.

The band watched the film and used it as a jumping off point for their own take on the theme. "The film was about angels who want to be human and who want to be on Earth," Bono explains. "But to do so they have to become mortal. That was a great image to play with – the impossibility of wanting something like this, and then the cost of having it."

In Bono's lyrics, it isn't clear where the lines can be drawn between fantasy and reality – if indeed they can be at all in the world of *Zooropa*. It isn't clear whether the girl who stumbles out of a nightclub – "Out of a hole in the ground" – into the grey morning is a stranger, a friend, a wife or a lover. Or if she's just another image on a screen, a chimera with whom the narrator presumes an intimacy that doesn't exist.

The action happens in a curious dreamscape in which nothing seems certain except uncertainty itself. And yet the performance is full of languorous beauty, a gentle understated kind of emotion that seems at odds with the disorientation in the lyrics.

It ends with a start, Larry Mullen emphasizing the downbeat on the cymbal as the dreamer suddenly sits up, staring into the black night, the image of a fallen angel burning in his imagination.

And a curious bang and clatter ringing in his ears.

113

STAY (FARAWAY SO CLOSE)
Written: U2
Length: 4' 58"
Album: *Zooropa*, July 1993
UK singles chart position: 4
US singles chart position: 61

DADDY'S GONNA PAY FOR YOUR CRASHED CAR

Is it a bird? Is it a plane? No, it's a super-Trabant.

There's a suspicion that *Zooropa* is largely about nightlife, and the obscure and often empty liaisons that fertilise in that artificial universe. 'Daddy's Gonna Pay For Your Crashed Car' is about a woman who's protected from the consequences of her own actions by an indulgent sugar daddy.

Bono originally conceived it as a blues. "John Lee Hooker is the person I'd love to sing that," he says and launches into a slower, rootsier version of the song. "You're out on your own/You know everyone in the world/But you feel alone/Daddy's gonna pay/for your crashed car/Daddy's gonna pay…" You can hear Hooker hollerin' it out alright.

"God is a sugar daddy, as well," Bono muses. "Is it God or is it the Devil? Who's gonna get you out of the mess? It's a song about being strung out. You can be strung out on a lot of things, not just smack. The thing you need is the thing you're a slave to. How much do you need this? How much do I need to be in a band? How much do you need anything?"

The fanfare which introduces the song is taken from the album *Lenin's Favourite Songs*, on what was formerly the state-owned Soviet label, Melodia. There's a sample in there too from the song 'The City Sleeps' by MC 900ft Jesus. But hey, why this sudden interested in crashed cars, Bono?

"They're Berlin images," he explains. "There's a piece of waste ground outside Hansa that's inhabited – or was inhabited – by a bunch of gypsies and crusties. They'd collected bits of F11s and tanks from Russia and wrecked cars. There's dogs and ducks flying around there. It was the Trafalgar Square of Berlin, and these travellers were living there almost in holes in the ground. Of course, now that Berlin has been reunited, they want to rebuild the centre but these gypsies had been given this place to live. That's where the crashed car imagery came from."

DADDY'S GONNA PAY FOR YOUR CRASHED CAR
Written: U2
Length: 5' 19"
Album: *Zooropa*, July 1993

SOME DAYS ARE BETTER THAN OTHERS

Zooropa is probably U2's least emotional record. It's something that Bono observes unprompted about 'Babyface', about 'Daddy's Gonna Pay For Your Crashed Car', about 'Numb'. And 'Some Days Are Better Than Others'? "They sure are," he says mischievously. "I think that's just one of those songs. It's like a summer song. It's just fun."

In fact Bono sends himself up royally in a track that reflects some of the turmoil that surrounded the making of the album. "It was mad," Bono laughs. "You can't imagine what it was like. We would fly out to Rome, play to 60,000 people and I'd still be dressed as MacPhisto with the make-up running, and we'd get into the cars, out to the airport, onto Zoo Airlines and all that. We'd get back to Dublin at 4 o'clock in the morning, work till 8, sleep till noon and then go back on tour. So a few things suffered, but the record has a nice kinetic energy to it, I think."

Between Bono, MacPhisto and The Fly, the main man was becoming an increasingly split personality. Bono felt that he needed some privacy, a way of keeping something for himself.

"Depending on the person I wake up as, one day I can be verbose, the next quite shy," he says. "But with this thing, it was great. Whether it was The Fly or MacPhisto, it was like put the batteries in and off he goes! I got through the whole tour like that. Also people thought we were just mocking rock 'n' roll stardom and all that, but I was actually owning up to it. It was owning up to the side of yourself that is an egomaniac.

"So then we put out a whole bunch of characters from the preachers in the travelling show, through MacPhisto to The Fly. Suddenly there was a lot of versions of the singer in the band. Now which one is for real? And of course they're all for real."

There's a bit of owning up on 'Some Songs Are Better Than Others' too. "Some days I feel like a bit of a baby," Bono confesses, and you can imagine Ali nodding in agreement. And then there's the line about bouncers that won't let you in. "I think The Kitchen might have to take credit for that," he laughs. "But it's just throwaway."

And I thought it was a profound statement about the human condition… "One of the things I have to deal with every day is the fact that I'm very moody, so I'm just having fun with that."

SOME DAYS ARE
BETTER THAN
OTHERS
Written: U2
Length: 4' 15"
Album: *Zooropa*,
July 1993

THE FIRST TIME

This was one that Bono heard in his head first. He'd been listening a lot to Al Green and it had influenced his singing: the Fat Lady was his version of Green's sweet high-pitched tone pushed a notch further.

Sometimes the inspiration sneaks up on you like that: you hear the chorus in someone else's voice. It can be easier to write if you come at a song in that way. The self-editing, the self-censorship that frequently comes into play when you imagine the words coming out of your own mouth, doesn't happen. You're free of baggage. People aren't going to be listening to Al Green and thinking that it's some kind of confession on your part, some kind of soul-baring.

It was intended to be an "up" song. Bono gives a demonstration of how the chorus might have sounded, and you can hear the soul backbeat and the swirl of imaginary strings.

Always someone looking at you.

It's hard to avoid the impression that the song was written in two separate bursts. It almost certainly began as a straightforward testifying song, but became something quite different in the third verse. Here, 'The First Time' abandons its symmetry and offers a new twist on an old parable.

"We decided to keep it for ourselves," Bono says. "Brian really loved it. But instead of doing an 'up' version, we just emptied it out, deconstructed the song and ended on this line about throwing away the key, and the prodigal son doesn't go back. He sees all this stuff there for him and he doesn't want it and he goes off again. That's a really interesting take on that story.

"There are many rooms to see/But I left by the back door/And threw away the key." It's a line that captures Bono's own wanderlust, the urge that's always there to light out, leaving all the obligations and responsibilities of his role behind.

"It's about losing your faith," Bono adds. "I haven't lost my faith. I've a great deal of faith. But that song expresses that moment a lot of people feel."

THE FIRST TIME
Written: U2
Length: 3' 45"
Album: *Zooropa*,
July 1993

DIRTY DAY

In some ways *Zooropa* was taking U2 right back. The imaginary city of the future had long been abandoned as a theme. Now, it was down to finishing an album that hadn't been planned, in the middle of the most demanding tour the band had ever undertaken.

'Dirty Day' was born out of a band improvisation. It was one of those murky numbers, with the band reflecting the tiredness they felt and the pressure they were under in a sulky, brooding performance. Bono felt a crushing sense of sadness in the music. Every time he went to improvise, an idea kept flashing up in front of him of a father giving surreal advice to his son.

On the mic, it was back to the influence of Iggy Pop and the way he'd make up songs in performance. He kept seeing Charles Bukowski in his head, and remembering the kind of advice he'd give, like "Always give a false name." He had the sense that there was some blackness at the heart of all this. Maybe the father had disappeared and left the son and the mother behind. That idea was preying on his mind. It was like a guilt thing about having been away from his own children so much when the band were on the road. It had become a bit of an obsession.

Things gel in funny ways. Sean Penn had come out to the house one night and they were talking bullshit about poetry and God knows what else until 6 in the morning. Bono told him he was a fan of Charles Bukowski and Penn said hang on a minute. Dialled Los Angeles on the spot and got the author on the line. Bukowski was in good form, laughing and joking. "I've got someone here wants to talk to you," he quipped. "It's my wife, Linda. And, by the way, she really wants to fuck you." It turned out she was a U2 fan who'd been to every concert the band had played in LA. She was also the backbone of this great writer.

The next time the band were in town, Bukowski came down to the gig and had a great time. Larry got up to sing 'Dirty Old Town', which was dedicated to him. It meant a lot, even to a hard-ass like Charles Bukowski.

Co-written by The Edge, it's also a song about passing the torch. About taking on responsibilities you don't know if you're cut out for. The days run away like horses over the hills, it ends, borrowing a phrase from Bukowski. Bono had a feeling it was out of control.

117

DIRTY DAY
Written: U2
Length: 5' 24"
Album: *Zooropa*,
July 1993

THE WANDERER

Zooropa was a trip. It took you into this strange terrain where nothing seemed quite to add up. Perspectives were constantly changing. Voices kept shifting. Gradually you realized that there was nothing you could rely on. Nothing you could believe in. Not even fantasy itself.

U2 had plunged you into this moonscape. Now they had to get you out. Bono thought he'd found the way. He'd made Johnny Cash's acquaintance a few years previously. They'd been promising to write a song together and had worked on something tentatively entitled 'Ellis Island'. It would be familiar Cash country, when it happened. If it happened.

In the meantime, Bono had another scam in mind. At first Eno and Flood opposed the idea, but he pushed it through. In the middle of recording *Zooropa*, Bono spotted that Cash would be arriving in Dublin for a gig. This is how it would work with Willie Nelson later: hook up with him in the studio while he's in town. No harm in seeing if the Man in Black could spare a few hours.

"If you imagine the album being set in this place, *Zooropa*," Flood reflects, "just when you're expecting the norm to finish the album, you get somebody who's outside the whole thing, wandering through, discussing it. It's like the perfect full stop."

The working title was 'Johnny Cash on the Moon'. But Bono was thinking of The Book of Ecclesiastes, which translates as The Preacher. That was the first real title. The Edge suggested that it would connect better with the rest of the album to call it 'The Wanderer'. Bono had no problem with that. Wanderlust was still on his mind.

The band wanted to end the album on a musical joke. They took on the identity of the ultimate Holiday Inn band from hell and produced an anachronistic noise to match. The Edge had the musical ideas. Eno made a few suggestions along the way to help it flow. But the track is dominated by Adam's wonderfully absurd arcade-game bass that sounds like some mutant cordovox programme on a cheap Casio. It is diabolically effective.

It might sound potentially like a thin joke – until Johnny Cash opens his mouth, that is. The result is awesome and eerie at once, the contrast between the cheap throwaway backing and Cash's monumental delivery lending the whole a thoroughly skewed power that's entirely appropriate.

It's the story of a preacher who embarks on an epic journey and experiments on himself at every level: knowledge, sex, gold, whatever's going, he's taking it. The setting is a kind of surreal, post-nuclear *Paris,*

THE WANDERER
Written: U2
Length: 4' 44"
Album: *Zooropa,*
July 1993

Texas world in which loyalty, faith and honour have become virtually extinct. Bono had Flannery O'Connor in mind – the way she writes about the strangest American characters and their do-it-yourself religion with humour, sympathy and love.

"I suppose, in our picture, I want to have that kind of crackpot in there," Bono told John Waters, "who's off to save the world and, at the same time, he's just up for the ride."

Bono knows when he says that kind of thing that he could be describing a song about himself. But Johnny Cash had reservations. He wouldn't have appreciated The Fly's phone-call on the run to his poor neglected partner at home on *Achtung Baby*. He wouldn't have been too keen either on the shyster falling off the sidewalk at 6 in the morning in 'Trying to Throw Your Arms Around the World'. Or the guy in 'Ultraviolet (Light My Way)' who sometimes feels like checking out, who wants to get it wrong – the bastard! Not at this stage of his life. And he never liked singing the line in 'The Wanderer', "I went out for the papers/told her I'd be back by noon." The jokey line: it was Bono through and through. The same old restlessness. The desire to cut and run. The need to be irresponsible.

"He used to leave that verse out because he liked it much heavier," Bono recounts. "I always liked that, you know, bottle of milk, newspapers and he's off. He's got God's work to do. He's looking for knowledge as well, and experience. He's on tour [laughs]."

There's a kind of freak energy that follows a band home after a spell on the road. It can take weeks to come down from it, months even. During the break in the *Zoo TV* expedition, U2 hadn't wanted to come down. "We have all this energy," they'd agreed. "Why not use it? Why not go into the studio and see what happens?" Now they knew.

POP

Backstage at some celebrity charity bash, a plum-accented classical conductor is talking at Bono. "You're involved in a pop group," he says, one eyebrow arched like an accusation. It isn't what he says, it's the way that he says it. There's a pause and then it comes out like... pop group. His contempt for the very thought of it is palpable. A lower form: pop music.

The encounter plays on Bono's mind. The condescension rankles. Who the fuck do these guys think they are? The implicit assumption seems to be that there's something unworthy in being in a rock 'n' roll band.

Pop music. A term of abuse.

It crystallises something for the U2 singer. Pop. Your man thinks it's an insult. Well, fuck him. It's time to reclaim the word. Turn it into a badge of honour.

They had thought of calling the album *Pop For Men* or *Pop Pour Hommes*. In the end they simply called it *Pop*. You can interpret it as defiant or ironic – or simply as a statement of fact. But it's not a bad title for an album destined to chart at No.1 in 21 territories around the world in the week of its release. Not a bad title at all. *Pop*.

So let's talk about – pop music...

U2 launch *Pop* in New York

DISCOTHÈQUE

If Howie B had known how it would end, he might never have started it. 'Discothèque' originated in a jam between himself and Edge, 15 minutes of rhythmic surfing that would provide a launching-pad for the opening single from *Pop*; the first, cleverly-pitched trailer to what was to become U2's most widely acclaimed album ever.

With 'Discothèque', U2 took the art of disguise to a new level of sophistication. It's a conjuror's trick. If it is tactically desirable to use an idiom, use it. While you're using it, learn how to use it well. Use it well and you'll enjoy it. Enjoy it, but don't let it absorb you. Stamp your own authority on it. And, in case all else fails, make sure that your tongue is somewhere in the vicinity of your collective cheek. Now, have fun!

And so they did. Howie had programmed up a selection of beats on his deck and at the end of a long evening he began to mess around with one of his favourites. Edge was hanging nearby and on impulse picked up the bass and began to riff along. Never one to be left out, Bono joined in on improvised vocals. "Virtually nothing remains from that original jam," producer Flood says, "but it was the inspiration."

To get the vibe right while they were recording, they dressed the studio up in mirror balls and disco lights – and gave it loads. Long before the final shape of the album had been decided, everyone knew 'Discothèque' was going to be the first single. That made it harder to finish. "It was going to be the first public statement, the first track that people were going to hear," Adam Clayton says, "so there was a lot of double-checking yourself to be certain that it was going to stand up as such."

'Discothèque' is an earnest little riddle about love, disguised as trash. "You know you're chewing bubblegum," Bono sings, "You know what that is but you still want some." Yes, there is an addictive quality about living for the moment. Yes, there is an undeniable pleasure in surrendering to the hedonistic buzz of the dancefloor. Yes, yes, yes!

Musically, the trick was to acknowledge those parts of your record collection you wouldn't normally own up to: "KC and the Sunshine Band, Boyz 2 Men, Donna Summer, Los Sex Pistoles," Bono lists them off. Village fucking People! The boys got to dress up like tarts for the video – and, mmm, they enjoyed that too. There's a *soupçon* of camp in all of us, girls.

'Discothèque' doesn't quite know what its chorus is. It mixes metal and dance in a cheesy hybrid. It is self-consciously kitsch. But it also undeniably rocks like a monster, particularly with the volume turned up to 11 on the

DISCOTHÈQUE
Written: U2
Length: 5' 19"
Album: *Pop*,
March 1997
UK singles chart
position: 1
US singles chart
position: 10

Bono: shampoo, haircut and a rave.

Howie B or Steve Osborne mix, when a club is jumping at 2 or 3 o'clock in the morning. Boom Cha Boom CHA DISCOTHÈQUE. The implicit message to humourless U2 fans was "You didn't think you'd like this, now did ya?" Meantime, the style counsellors were goin' "Well, hello! U2 are far cuter than we thought. U2 are far fucking hipper than we thought."

If it was going to be the first single, it had to be the first track on the album. The whole shebang in the bag, the entire entourage of band and producers set out for New York, further behind schedule than ever, to finally master the album. Even then, the job wasn't done. Even then, Bono couldn't let Howie be...

"It was outrageous," Howie says. "It had gotten to the stage where I couldn't speak, I was that ill. I was run down, my chest was caving in, everything was caving in. It was Saoirse's birthday and she was in New York as well and I had to meet her and then at about 10.30 Bono turns around and goes 'Listen, it'd be magic if you could get a new intro together for 'Discothèque'. And it was just like... (groans).

"I got into a cab, went up the road to the Hit Factory. I was kicking things like you wouldn't believe, going 'Fuck! Fuck!' Like, we were in the middle of mastering an album and they wanted to change the intro! It was like, 'any ideas?' And swirl was the idea. That was what they came up with, a 'swirl' sound. For fuck's sake!"

Howie had a bash, thought he'd cracked it, phoned Flood at Master Disc and played it down the phone to him. Flood said nothing and Howie got the message. Fuck! Fuck! He threw down the phone, turned up the speakers, pushed all the faders up – and BAM! Blew the fuck out of them: two £30,000 speakers gone for a burton.

"After I'd got all that aggression out of me, I got what is now the intro to 'Discothèque' about ten minutes later. So I phoned them up and I went 'Come on 'round, ye fuckers, I'm ready'. So they all trooped around and I couldn't play it to them properly 'cos I'd blown the fucking speakers! I'm still annoyed about that evening but I got a good piece of work out of it."

There were rumours that 'Discothèque' was about drugs. Well, no one's going to deny that but actually it's about something much simpler, and much more complicated too. It's about the pleasures of the flesh. And it's about the heart's yearning. In a way you could say it's as earnest as you can get. "U2 are just better at disguising it now," Bono says.

And he laughs.

DO YOU FEEL LOVED

How does a monstrously successful rock band, around for the best part of 20 years, get to grips with a whole new area of musical expression? U2 were facing that dilemma so they did the smart thing, not just immersing themselves in the new music, but getting a couple of its most livewire exponents involved. In particular there was Howie B, who'd worked on the Passengers record with them.

Part of his role was to act as a catalyst. He'd take records into the studio and play them for the band to see if they sparked any ideas. 'Do You Feel Loved' was a case in point, growing out of a Naked Funk track that Howie opened his set with one night in The Kitchen when the band were on the town. Everyone got off on 'Groove Sensation' because it was a blast, so they got Howie to do his DJ thang with the track in the studio and the band jammed along. Howie spent a lot of time working with Adam on getting an extraordinary bass sound that, in the jargon of the studio at the time, seemed to vibe everyone up.

It was one of the first cuts to get close to its final shape, but there was still work to be done. Steve Osborne, who made his name producing Happy Mondays' *Pills, Thrills And Bellyaches* album, and who'd been involved with Paul Oakenfold in remixing a few U2 tracks, came in for the final push.

When he got his hands on 'Do You Feel Loved' he felt that it needed a new groove and Larry came in to get that down. "Then I got Edge over, and we worked on the guitar line that comes in over the chorus," Steve says. "The core of the tune was there but we added a fair bit."

Bono talks about the lyrics as if they're playful and in a way they may be. But to someone coming at it fresh, they sound remarkably confessional. 'Do You Feel Loved' is nothing more or less than a love song, that strays into the erotic boudoir first mentioned by Bono in 'Your Blue Room', with its references to conversations and prayers amid the tangle of the senses.

'Do You Feel Loved' may be a smart thing to say to a lover – but it's an even smarter one to put to 50,000 people in an open-air arena.

"It's quite a question," Bono says, "but there's no question mark on it. We took the question mark out because we thought it was a bit heavy with it." Clearly a case for the grammar police to get working on...

123

DO YOU
FEEL LOVED
Written: U2
Length: 5' 07"
Album: *Pop*,
March 1997

MOFO

It began as a conversation with Simon Carmody. Bono picked Simon up on his use of "motherfucker" and a philosophical debate ensued about the origins of the word in black slang and the way it went from a term of abuse into one of praise. "It's such a dumb cliché, you wanna have a good reason to use it," Bono smiles. And so they set about finding one, settling on 'Mofo' as a likely title and building from there.

Edge and Bono were in Nice on a song-writing expedition. They got a structure down. It had a blues feel until they took it into the studio and Adam added a Motown-style bass part. It was shaping up but as the lyrical ideas began to crystallise, they felt that it needed to become tougher. "We spent months farting around with it," Adam confesses, "and then we said to Flood 'Let's hip-hop it, let's strip it back, let's get a beat together, let's see where it goes'. And it rose from those ashes."

> Salmon Rushdie: knows a God-shaped hole when he sees one.

It became the hardest cut on the record, a techno assault reminiscent of The Prodigy, powered by a towering double-tracked drum attack from Larry Mullen. It's the track Flood singles out as the one he had most influence on. Steve Osborne did his bit by throwing in a blaring Moog line. Meanwhile, with Howie B acting as critic and catalyst, Bono had gone for broke lyrically, throwing references to Salman Rushdie ("Lookin' for to fill that God-shaped hole") and William Butler Yeats ("Still lookin' for the face I had before the world was made") into a song that otherwise trades in rock jargon.

"I was reading in a book on Jack Kerouac," he says, "about him smoking a bag of grass and praying, literally, for a vision of a language, or a way of writing that would be both precious and trashy. That's what I'm aiming for," Bono reveals. "'Mofo' is one of my favourite tracks," says Gavin Friday. "To me it sounds like Led Zeppelin after taking an E (laughs). But it's got real heart to it. I just love Bono's plea to his mother in it."

It's a song of which Bono is proud, oscillating as it does between the throwaway and the profound with consummate craft, and amounting, in the end, to his best shot yet at capturing the demon spirit that drives him. "In the middle of it, when you go into that conversation piece, it's like WHAT?," he says. "It was as if my whole life was in that song. I think it was the first thing mixed on the album and when we were finished, we couldn't get over ourselves. I had a deck in the car and we were playing it, going on a kind of club-crawl – but we wouldn't go into the club because we just had to hear it one more time."

> MOFO
> Written: U2
> Length: 5' 49"
> Album: Pop, March 1997

IF GOD WILL SEND HIS ANGELS

'If God Will Send His Angels' had existed as a title at the time of the making of *Zooropa*. 'Stay (Faraway So Close)', on that album, had been inspired by a Wim Wenders film, which was about angels who wanted to be human and to live on Earth. The seed of an idea had been sown, and it lurked until the songwriting sessions for *Pop* began in earnest.

It was one that was written on an acoustic guitar, with Bono and Edge strumming away like latter-day Simon and Garfunkels. The tune reminded Bono of Fugees, or even Boyzone, and he became fiercely excited about its potential. "I thought – this is like pure pop. Now drop acid onto that."

What emerged is a classic U2 ballad, a song with a very subtle emotional tug that's brilliantly highlighted by the superb arrangement. Rhythmically, Adam Clayton and Larry Mullen supplied a light, lazy skank groove and then Howie B got to work. "He came on board about halfway through," Flood recalls, "and I think it's one of the tracks that's closest to his heart."

Howie B's imprint is there throughout but there is one sublime and quintessentially Howie moment. Having taken a sample of Larry's hi-hat, and lowered it a couple of octaves, he unleashed the resulting whoosh to magnificent dramatic effect.

Most U2 albums had been conceived with an imaginative location in mind. *Pop* was different. "The record doesn't seem to have any physical place that it's centred in," Bono explains. "Instead, to me the songs feel like conversations. Overheard conversations. It's like a movie that opens in the middle of a scene. You're brought immediately into the action and there's lot of little arguments going on."

That's certainly what's going on in 'If God Will Send His Angels', but there's an essential bleakness in the pictures being painted: loosely about a guy beating up his girlfriend. Bono describes it as being a sour song, "But you can still hear her somewhere in there, through the music," he adds. "You can feel there's light there."

Asked what the themes of the album are, Edge says: "Love, desire and the crisis of faith. The usual stuff." On 'If God Will Send His Angels', the crisis reaches epidemic proportions. In a world where love has taken a train heading south, the blind are leading the blond and God has got his phone off the hook, there isn't much left to hang on to. "So where is the hope and the faith and the love?" Bono asks. The eternal questions.

IF GOD WILL SEND HIS ANGELS
Written: U2
Length: 5' 22"
Album: *Pop*, March 1997
UK singles chart position: 12

125

STARING AT THE SUN

The band were working on another song entirely but they got stuck in an unproductive groove. A couple of bizarre loops were introduced, Larry got a really sweet pattern going against them and Edge made a significant call, out of the blue. It was familiar territory for U2: "Oh, I know another song that will work over this." It was a completely different speed and a completely different feel but the potential was immediately apparent.

"I had a great time with Edge on 'Staring At The Sun'. I got a mad wee sound out of his guitar," Howie recalls. "After we broke our first deadline, Edge and I spent a week playing around with the tune. We put his guitar through a Leslie and it was a nice little thing. What you think is an organ on 'Staring At The Sun' is actually Edge playing the guitar."

There's a Zen-like aspect to the lyrics, a sense of being immersed in the moment that's perfectly articulated through the euphoric music. Even after Howie was finished, however, there was work to do. Steve Osborne and Mark Grant got involved in the mixing and they did a lot of searching through tapes looking for different guitar parts. When Edge gets going he produces a lot of ideas and they found some discarded stuff that worked, enhancing the arrangement considerably.

The Something Happens album *Stuck Together With God's Glue* had been left lying around – it went into the song. Howie B had an abscess in his ear – it went into the song. The television was running in the background, newspaper headlines had been pinned on the walls, the marching season was in full swing – it all went into the song. The British presence in Northern Ireland is alluded to, as is the European Cup. And there's a modicum of self-mockery, too, in the line "Those who can't do often have to preach."

"If you're going to have a dig at someone, it might as well be yourself," Bono laughs. "But there are other things in there too. All these references are quite personal but they wouldn't be there if they were *just* personal."

Ali Hewson had a tremendous influences on the lyrics of *Pop*, and not just because of the fact that she's the focus for Bono's ongoing affair of the heart. She is also a woman of great courage, who has been placed directly at risk, through her involvement in the Children Of Chernobyl charity. There is a sense in which 'Staring At The Sun' may be a reference to Ali's experiences. An attempt to reassure in the face of all the odds, it's a blast of defiant optimism, underscored inevitably by a sense of creeping paranoia.

But what a blast!

STARING AT THE SUN
Written: U2
Length: 4' 36"
Album: *Pop*, March 1997
UK singles chart position: 3
US singles chart position: 26

LAST NIGHT ON EARTH

LAST NIGHT
ON EARTH
Written: U2
Length: 4' 45"
Album: *Pop*,
March 1997
UK singles chart
position: 10
US singles chart
position: 57

The song had been in gestation since early on in the recording of *Pop*. The backing tracks done, the search was on for riffs and moods and Howie slid in a couple of Don Cherry pieces. The guitar parts were revved up and sampled and slotted into different places in the song. "But we just couldn't crack it fully," Bono says. "The chorus only came into my head at about 4 o'clock in the morning on the final night, and the bit where it goes 'You've got to give it away/You've got to give it away/You've got to give it away'. I sang a vocal at 7 o'clock in the morning. Literally, we had people mixing that who hadn't been to bed in a week, while our roadies and Paul were waiting outside in the cars for us to go to New York to master the record. My voice was completely shot, which is why we put so much echo on it and Edge sang along with me to cover it up. 'Last Night On Earth' is right."

It's the kind of experience that you get to laugh about – later. By this stage, shuffling back and forth between the Dublin separate studios, Hanover Quay and Windmill, had become time-consuming, and so Bono had acquired a speed-boat for the purpose. On the final push, the ferry service, of necessity, had become particularly frantic. "It got so busy that we had to pull in Paul McGuinness to drive the boat," Gavin Friday recalls. "I don't drive, everybody else was either busy or tired, so McGuinness ended up bringing people from Windmill to Hanover and back."

There were some serious disagreements about the lyrics too, which didn't make matters any easier. "I had a row with Bono and Edge," Howie B confesses. "Right up till the last night we were still arguing about that one. But that's what's so great about music. You feel like expressing yourself. And with these guys anyway, they weren't looking for yes-men. They actually want to know what you think. But I had really strong opinions about that – and I still do (laughs)."

"I know that that track's based around a certain kind of woman that we've all met," Gavin Friday adds. "You're at a party or a club and you just don't know where this 23-year-old is getting her energy from. And we're not talking drugs or alcohol here. It's just a vibe, a wild woman who gives you a charge of energy."

Maybe Howie felt so strongly about it because he saw a reflection of someone close to him in the lyrics. Someone for whom freedom is not just a by-word but a name, perhaps?

George Harrison: The Beatles influence back in with the line "and the sun sun, here it comes".

GONE

It's one of the things that makes Bono most visibly angry. The basic premise seems to be that once you're successful, you've sold out. Automatically.

"Right through the '80s this is what we had to put up with," he remarked, early on in the recording of *Pop*, "the idea that there was something morally superior in being an indie band. I've written a song now that's like a two-finger salute to the people who tried to foist a sense of guilt on us because we were successful. The thing is, we always wanted to be one of the biggest bands in the world."

U2: real, real gone.

'Gone' was one of the first tracks that the crew knew would make it to the album, but it went through many personalities before it finally made the cut. "At one stage," Gavin Friday says, "it was a hard rock thing, then a punk thing, then a hard rock thing again." But they still couldn't seem to get to the core of it.

The indecision may have had something to do with the death of Bill Graham, the *Hot Press* writer who'd been a friend and inspiration to the band from their earliest days. It was towards the end of May and they'd just been working on the song in Miami, where they'd gone to do a photo shoot or two and to record, when they heard the news of his death. The connection sounded an eerie resonance that fed back into the sinews of the song. Rather than being the fuck-you to the begrudgers whom it had originally been intended for, it became instead a meditation on the superficiality and transience of success itself, over which the spectre of death hangs like a stark premonition. "Closer to you every day," Bono sings, "I didn't want it that much anyway" – and the echo is unmistakably of the hymn 'Nearer My God To Thee'.

"The background is so atmospheric and disturbing," Gavin Friday reflects. "It's weird. The track conjures up all the things that make U2 what they are. You can't properly put your finger on it. A vocal line here, a riff there, a lyric – it just gets you."

Bono puts it in context. "The bridge, which was put in to make it more of a pop song for me – and for Edge too – ended up having this incredible emotional weight," he says. "It's almost like Gavin's 'The Last Song I'll Ever Sing'. That's what it felt like to me. It felt like the last song I'd ever sing."

GONE
Written: U2
Length: 4' 26"
Album: *Pop*,
March 1997

MIAMI

Recording for *Pop* had started in November 1996. The Christmas break was followed by a period of down-time as Larry Mullen struggled with a bad back. Howie B took up some of the rhythm duties and by March they were on full alert again. But they still lacked any real sense of what was going to give the record the sense of continuity they'd always striven for in the past. It needed a location – or so they thought.

For a while they toyed with the idea of heading for Cuba and inviting the spirit of Havana to infiltrate the grooves, but the cynicism they'd almost certainly have been confronted with as a result dissuaded them. As April turned into May, they upped camp and split for Miami instead.

There were a dozen reasons why it might have made a good location for the record. It's a crossroads between North and South. It has a glamorous side, a humorous side, a dark side – and the strangest underbelly. But in the end, the idea was more enthralling than the experience. Instead of leading them to the heart of the record, their sojourn there produced a small movie of a song that Edge wryly describes as a kind of "creative tourism".

It's an experience that no-one regrets.

"We'd been in the studio, slugging it out with the direction of the record," Adam explains. "It's a nice place to be for six months or so, but I think we all needed a bit of fresh air. So we went to Miami and we had a very good time! We met a lot of very serious people and some very superficial people and enjoyed both. We were introduced to the art of smoking cigars. We went to this kind of Mafia late-night place – none of your old spit 'n' sawdust here, this was shag-pile carpet all the way. We came, we saw, we conquered – it's in the lyric. It was all there and our eyes were wide open. Some of the time (laughs)."

Lyrically, 'Miami' exhibits a kind of holiday snap-book gaudiness, coming on like a handy-cam diary that slips into the themes of consumerism and violence with remarkable ease. Bono's sense of humour comes across on the oedipal pun of the chorus: "Miami! My mammy!" But the whole thing hangs together because it was a labour of love for Howie B. "That was very much Howie's bag," Flood explains. "After it had been recorded, he locked himself into a room for three days and he arranged everything."

129

MIAMI
Written: U2
Length: 4' 52"
Album: *Pop*,
March 1997

THE PLAYBOY MANSION

Roy Orbison was a master of form. He never felt constrained by conventional song structures, instead producing mini-symphonies in two or three movements. Having befriended him before his death, and written 'She's A Mystery To Me' for his 1989 album *Mystery Girl*, Bono and Edge had learned something from the master. "He was always way ahead of the pack," Bono reflects, acknowledging the musical lineage into which 'The Playboy Mansion' taps.

THE PLAYBOY
MANSION
Written: U2
Length: 4' 40"
Album: *Pop*,
March 1997

It started life as 'Hymn to Mr Universe', beginning with a jam, back in the early stages of making the record. It popped out and everyone felt confident about it – so much so that it was one of the last tracks completed. Over a looped trip-hop backdrop Bono was back on familiar turf, playing with clichés, truisms and advertising slogans. Having been alluded to in 'Miami', plastic surgery gets another mention here; Michael Jackson is also on the guest-list in an opening verse that recalls 'Even Better Than the Real Thing' before moving on: "If coke is a mystery/And Michael Jackson... history/If beauty is truth/And surgery the fountain of youth/What am I do to/Have I got the gifts to get me through/The gates of that mansion."

"I think surgery with Michael Jackson might have something to do with editing," Bono muses. "If you're in the studio and you're in control of what you hear – you can up the bass, down the snare – I think Michael Jackson started to do that to himself in some way. It's the critical eye that makes him such a genius being turned on himself – the knife turned around."

Its wry humour notwithstanding, 'The Playboy Mansion' is not intended to be smart. For all the warped values in evidence, the song is infused with a real sense of spiritual yearning, as if at some deep level the covetous protagonist knows that it's all fake, that far from being even better than the real thing, his desires are but a pale shadow of the heart's need for a more fulfilling kind of truth.

"People in America say 'if you don't have cash it's hard to believe in yourself'," Bono explains. "It's almost like prosperity as a religion." That's the territory we're in here. 'The Playboy Mansion' is a gospel song for American white trash but it ends in a sublime slice of gospel-verité, a la Al Green, which enables us to see the grace that is to be found in even the more mundane things – if you look hard enough.

It's a bunny old worl Hugh Hefner forget to put on his playgir uniform.

IF YOU WEAR THAT VELVET DRESS

When the news first emerged that U2 were in the studio, the word was that they were making a trip-hop album. The assumption was based not just on the soundings they'd taken about Howie B's availability. After all, the first producer on board was Nellie Hooper, one of the lynchpins of the thriving Bristol scene and a man with a proven feel for a good groove.

They got together with him in London and stuck a number of backing tracks down. Among them was 'If You Wear That Velvet Dress', a song that comes from the same place as 'Your Blue Room', but which also dips into territory mapped out by Massive Attack and Tricky.

If there was any disagreement between U2 and Hooper, it doesn't show now. Though he isn't listed in the credits on the album, his involvement is openly discussed. "He started things off on 'Velvet Dress' but because of time constraints he couldn't stick with it," Flood says.

"Actually what happened," Hooper adds, "is that I sat down for a day and did my usual sort of fascist number: 'I don't like this, this or this. Now, how about trying this? And then Howie came in and did the same kind of thing, and the track began to take its final shape."

Bono reflects ruefully on the need for such strong-arm tactics. "We gave Flood a spiky helmet at one stage," he laughs, "because he had to become quite the gaffer. Flood was amazing at pushing things through. I don't know how anyone can be so anarchistic and yet so organised. Howie on the other hand is like music itself. There's no difference between him and the music he makes."

Which may explain what he brought to the song. "For me my main input was sexual," he says. "There was a lot of sex put into that one. Again, it was like a little bit of a throwdown from the band to me. 'OK, Howie, we want this to be on the album. Make this be on the album'. So I put a lot of jazz into it. Jazz and sex." A familiar combination.

"It's great to be able to get away with it," Bono says. "We can write sexy songs and spiritual songs – and songs that are both. This is the place we've made for ourselves after 15 years of making albums."

And Adam always thought the song was addressed to him!

IF YOU WEAR
THAT VELVET
DRESS
Written: U2
Length: 5' 15"
Album: Pop,
March 1997

PLEASE

Anyone who thought that *Pop* was going to be a dance album was entirely wrong. "I'm sceptical about these reference points," Larry Mullen states. "I just like the idea of taking what's out there and fucking with it."

And so that's what U2 did, using techno, trip-hop and hip-hop as jumping off points for the different tracks. Ultimately they had to pass the Mullen test: if what the band produced was unmistakably a U2 song it could go on the record. Larry had been concerned about elements of *Zooropa*, which had been rushed. And he had been downright disgusted with what he saw as the self-indulgence of parts of the Passengers album. 'Please' was an example of how the synergy could work.

Gerry Adams of Sinn Féin: the political stuff bleeds through

Howie B had been playing stuff to the band. Over one shimmering rhythm, Bono came up with an idea for a melody and everything flowed from there. "Once Bono got it – boom!" Howie reflects. "Once the band got it – boom! The actual backing track is the first take."

On the face of it, 'Please' sounds like a bitter song of personal disillusionment, set against an unsettling wider backdrop, where things are falling apart and the centre cannot hold. Bono acknowledges that it is hard, almost spiteful. It was written with someone specific in mind but there was much more at stake than the satisfaction of a well-crafted put-down.

It is a song about victimhood, self-indulgence and hypocrisy. Written against a backdrop of the collapse of the ceasefire in Northern Ireland and the summer of conflict that ensued, with the siege of Drumcree as its tribal nadir, it could be addressed, in different verses, to people on either side of the sectarian divide. "It's a mad prayer of a tune," Bono attests.

The lyric device that gives the song its form – a series of lines beginning 'You never' – was Edge's, linking back to the 'Numb' lyric and its use of lists. And the guitarist must also take considerable credit for the song's astonishing arrangement which builds from a relatively contained opening into one of U2's most molten – and moving – statements ever.

'Please' may be steeped in ambiguity but the finished painting is magnificent.

PLEASE
Written: U2
Length: 5' 02"
Album: *Pop*,
March 1997
**UK singles chart
position:** 7

WAKE UP DEAD MAN

Pop begins on a high. 'Discotheque' is bright, contemporary and in your face. At least on the surface, it is a hedonistic celebration of the ephemeral. But from that acknowledgement of worldly addictions on, the record journeys down – from dance to despair.

As a lyricist, Bono emerges as a kind of Everyman desperately searching for something to hang onto amid the escalating din we're surrounded with: a hellish combination of political mayhem, consumerism gone crazy and the culture of the soundbite.

"Jesus, Jesus help me," the final song on *Pop* begins, "I'm alone in this world and a fucked-up world it is too." Bono has never sounded quite so hopeless. If Pop begins with dance, it ends with a slow *danse macabre*.

The song was started during the *Zooropa* sessions under the title 'The Dead Man'. It had been a big rock song with distinct gothic leanings, but no one was too enthusiastic about that anymore. They did some work on it with Nellie Hooper in London and came up with what you might call a trip-hop version – but it still wasn't right.

It took shape during a jam, with Howie on the decks. "I think that was the first time I saw the band go 'Wait a minute, something interesting can happen here with these decks!'," Howie laughs. " 'How come he's playing a record on top of our record and it sounds OK? Not only does it sound alright, it sounds ho-ho!' So that was an interesting adventure for them."

It came together quickly. In the end it was unanimous. It made sense to tie the album up with an end of the millennium psychosis blues-song.

Neither Protestant nor Catholic, neither working-class nor middle-class, U2 had started out as a band who would have to forge an identity without much of the familiar ballast of Irish cultural life. As a result, they could wrap rock'n'roll and religion up together in a way very few other bands would even have contemplated. It was inconceivable that an album as ambitious and searching as *Pop* would go out on any other note.

'Wake Up Dead Man' comes on like a call to arms, a plea for Jesus or God to reveal himself. But the strength of Bono's faith notwithstanding, there is something eerie and forlorn about the call, even amid the epic beauty of the music.

"People want to believe but they're angry," Bono says. "If God is not dead, there's some questions we want to ask him."

'Wake Up Dead Man' doesn't attempt to offer any answers.

133

WAKE UP DEAD MAN
Written: U2
Length: 4' 52"
Album: *Pop*,
March 1997

ALL THAT YOU CAN'T LEAVE BEHIND

After *Rattle and Hum*, U2 started playing their own kind of mind games. Dressing up. Wearing masks. Wrapping their songs up in hip threads. Throwing shapes. From *Achtung Baby* through to *Pop*, subversion was the order of the day.

You could say that this strategy worked too well: they succeeded in confounding legions of their own fans too, while failing to pick up enough hip young gunslingers to compensate. U2 were still huge. But ticket sales for their live shows were disappointing. Album sales were down.

You could take the pessimistic view and conclude that U2 was a brand – and a band – in decline, and that it would be better to bow out gracefully. Or you could go for the big one again.

U2 decided to go for it. On *All That You Can't Leave Behind*, they ditched the dance gurus and went back to their roots. The trip-hop techniques of *Pop* were abandoned. Instead, they called in Eno and Daniel Lanois, with whom they'd made their biggest-selling record, *The Joshua Tree*. This was a time for big hearts. This was a time for soul.

Daniel Lanois picks ◀ U2's Grammy Award for 'Beautiful Day'.

According to Lanois, it was a hell of a record to make – almost as black as *Achtung Baby* at times. With Bono's voice badly frayed around the edges, the approach had to be different: the conductor could no longer afford to bawl his heart out in the studio. Lacking this, the collective were plunged into uncharted territory and the strain was palpable. Making *The Million Dollar Hotel* exacerbated it. And, noble as it may have been, Jubilee 2000 turned the screw even further.

But U2 are made of stern stuff. It was fraught – and, hey, when has it not been? – but they battled through and made it to the finishing line. And released a wonderful, exhilarating, triumphant and, above all, accessible record. Like as if it couldn't have happened any other way.

BEAUTIFUL DAY

BEAUTIFUL DAY
Written: U2
Length: 4' 08"
Album:
All That You Can't Leave Behind,
October 2000
UK singles chart position: 1
US singles chart position: 21

When Jimmy Iovine landed in Dublin, he was given a preview of what was going down in the studio. It wasn't finished but he was still overwhelmed by the power of 'Beautiful Day' in its formative stages. This was where U2 had come in all those years ago, on a silvery glistening guitar ride that spoke of exhilaration and of rapture. "It's a beautiful day a-a-a-a-a-a"! There wasn't an iota of doubt in Iovine's mind. "You've landed a big bass," he told them. Now all they had to do was to reel it in.

Brian Eno had come up with the beat. Edge found a guitar sequence that went with it. And in a moment of spontaneous invention, Bono yelled out the declaration that would take the song into another dimension. "It's a beautiful dayeeeeeee", he ejaculated, because the feeling was good.

Daniel Lanois also had that feeling. "The track at that point was really pumping," he remembers, "and the mix that we did had the power of shattered metal. And I had this image of Bono, singing about beauty in the midst of flying pieces of metal and mayhem." Lanois pushed Bono to consider what had been a throwaway interjection as the chorus and constructed the melody line. Edge came up with a harmony line and when they put them together and processed it they sounded almost like angels.

The Jubilee 2000 campaign that Bono got involved in was a distraction from making *All That You Can't Leave Behind*. This typical Bono crusade followed the indulgence of making *The Million Dollar Hotel* movie. Yet he experienced a surge of optimism. He'd sat down with arch-conservative Congressman Jesse Helmes in Washington and hit some kind of emotional nerve. Now the US had come on board, to the extent of $435m in cancelled debts. Maybe the world wasn't such a bad place after all. There was hope. It's a beautiful day! Edge reached for the Explorer – the Gibson guitar he'd used during U2's formative years – and the sound was complete.

When Steve Lillywhite arrived in at the death and polished it up even more with a sparkling final mix, they had the opening track, the lead single – and a monumental U2 anthem that would run and run, delivering them back to the top spot in singles charts all over the world. It would eventually be awarded a Grammy for Single of the Year.

There it was. A shimmering triumph.

135

STUCK IN A MOMENT YOU CAN'T GET OUT OF

Bono first bumped into Paula Yates when she was just 17. She was an extravagant doll at the time, hanging out with Bob Geldof during the prime of the Boomtown Rats and making like a particularly chintzy rock moll. Bono was chalk to her cheese. "I ducked her for years," he says, "'cos I just thought 'Whoa, where's she coming from?' And then years later, I really discovered this thing that people who've had a lot of pain in their lives are not in pubs talking about it."

Smart and feisty, Yates spent her whole life trying to come across as a dizzy blonde. But there was substance there, and as Paula's life moved on through her own brand of celebrity, her path crossed Bono's with increasing frequency. Both the breakdown of her marriage to Bob Geldof and the ensuing battle for custody of their children were played out in the full glare of the tabloid spotlight. So was her romance with Michael Hutchence, the glamorous and flawed INXS frontman.

Excess was the defining quality in their lives. Drink and drugs were about the place and they indulged. Yet it still came as a shock, even to those closest to him, when Hutchence was found dead in his bedroom in the Ritz Carlton Hotel in Double Bay, Sydney, in his home country of Australia. Paula clung desperately to the belief that he had died accidentally in the course of an auto-erotic experience of some kind.

Bono read it differently. He had spoken to Hutchence along the way about suicide, and they had agreed how pathetic it was. Now Bono felt angry at the probability that Hutchence had chosen an easy way out. In the heat of his anger, not long after he heard the news, he wrote the guts of 'Stuck In a Moment You Can't Get Out Of', a song he describes as being a row between mates. "The greatest respect I could pay him," Bono reflects, "was not to write some stupid, sentimental, soppy fucking song."

And so he wrote instead what he describes as a tough, nasty, little number which, in Bono's account, slaps his old, lost friend around the head. "It's like somebody's in a stupor and you're trying to wake them up," he says, "cause the cops are coming and they're sitting at the wheel and you're trying to get them out of the car 'cause they're gonna crash it."

But the song doesn't quite bear out that explanation all the way, sounding at times more like a plea written from the vantage point of Paula Yates, as she attempts to wrestle with the loss of her lover.

STUCK IN A MOMENT YOU CAN'T GET OUT OF
Written: U2
Length: 4' 32"
Album:
All That You Can't Leave Behind,
October 2000
UK singles chart position: 2
US singles chart position: 52

ELEVATION

ELEVATION
Written: U2
Length: 3' 47"
Album:
All That You Can't
Leave Behind,
October 2000
UK singles chart
position: 3

Bob Dylan once said that he never heard a good song that had a middle eight. Which just goes to show that even Bob Dylan can be wrong. It was also where Eno and Lanois parted company with 'Elevation'. The song had started out with a sound from Edge, fashioned on an effects pedal that Lanois describes as his secret weapon. "It's like a distortion pedal that has a warp, or a tone control, built on," he explains. "As you push the pedal down, you get the high frequency. It's a great little pedal. It has a lovely, specific personality to it."

Eno conjured up an electronic beat as an undertow and Adam and Larry played on top of it. Edge came through with a riff and they were halfway there. But the song still needed a bit of contrast to open it up – or so the band thought. When Eno and Lanois were slow to play ball, reinforcements were called in. The masters were taken across the river from U2's Hanover St. HQ to Windmill Lane studios. There the boys joined forces with ace pop producer Richard 'Biff' Stannard and his cohort Julian Gallagher to conjure up a kind of science-fiction middle-eight that provides a tender interlude, amid the onslaught of 'Elevation'.

A distant cousin of Sly and the Family Stone's 'Higher and Higher' and the Pixies' 'Levitate Me', 'Elevation' is scarcely the album's most original moment. The mole livin' in a hole diggin' up his soul in the fourth verse is reminiscent of the central character in 'The Fly' from *Achtung Baby* and there's a hint of the climax to 'Mysterious Ways' in here too. But from Adam Clayton's engorged opening bass figure onwards, the song captures well the murky terrain inhabited by a writer struggling with the attempt to make

Brian Eno: not a big fan of middle eights?

art of his or her experience. "Adam really came into his own on 'Elevation'," Edge reflects. "He's the hip hop man in the band, and there's a hip hop attitude in the rhythm section on that one."

'Elevation' achieves a quality that's reminiscent of the Rolling Stones, and their capacity to create epic muck. But there is an exhilaration to it that is uniquely U2 – a combination of primordial lasciviousness, ecstatic spirituality and soulful need – that renders analysis virtually redundant.

WALK ON

In March 2000, U2 were given the freedom of Dublin

Among the previous recipients to be thus honoured by City Hall, in their home town, was Nelson Mandela. And there was another recipient of this somewhat arcane honour, on the same day that the achievements of Bono, Adam, Larry, Edge and Paul McGuinness were being acknowledged and celebrated in a civic ceremony in Smithfield Square, just north of the River Liffey that runs through the heart of the capital. In all probability, her name meant little to the vast majority of the 5,000 citizens who gathered in the square that day, but Bono had taken the trouble to find out as much as he could about her and knew that, like the black South African leader, she was a hero.

A Burmese academic based at Oxford University, Aung San Suu Kyi took her courage in her hands and returned to Burma. She knew that she was going back to a country controlled by a brutal and oppressive regime and that inevitably her life and her freedom would be under threat. But inspired by the belief that only by fighting – and defeating – fear can you be truly free, she became leader of the National League for Democracy and spearheaded the campaign against the corrupt controlling military junta. "It was just one of the great acts of courage of the twentieth century," Bono reflects, "and it continues into the twenty-first."

Aung San Suu Kyi was placed under house arrest in 1989. She was unable to receive visitors or communicate freely. But neither her spirit nor her convictions could be broken and she has struggled on, and in the process has become a powerful and enduring symbol of the fight for democratic rights in the face of totalitarianism. Following international pressure, democratic elections were held in Burma in 1990, and over 80% of those eligible voted for the National League for Democracy. In the wake of that rebuke, the military tightened their grip, imprisoning newly-elected MPs and forcing others into exile. Awarded the Nobel Peace Prize in 1991, Aung San Suu Kyi remained under house arrest until 1995, and her movements have subsequently been severely restricted.

It was the human dimension of the story that captured Bono's imagination. As someone who has demonstrated his own sense of outrage at inequality and injustice, and taken some flak for it along the way, the empathy that he felt was in part at least political. But Aung San Suu Kyi's experience had a particular poignancy, leaving as she did not just the comfort and security of academic life in Oxford but also her husband, her

WALK ON
Written: U2
Length: 4' 56"
Album:
All That You Can't Leave Behind,
October 2000
UK singles chart position: 5

son and the home they had built together to go back to the place that she grew up in, the place she truly thought of as home.

At first Bono tried to write the song from the point of view of the husband and son left behind – dreaming of what might have been and living through the pain of not knowing how Aung San Suu Kyi was, or even if she was still alive. But it seemed presumptuous. "So I kept it a little abstract," he explains, "and just let it be a love song about somebody having to leave a relationship for all the right reasons."

But of course it becomes much more than that, as Bono explores some of his own obsessions on what is clearly perceived by the band as one of the major songs on the record, giving *All That You Can't Leave Behind* its title and inspiring the sleeve artwork of a band in transit, apparently travelling light through an otherwise sparsely populated Charles de Gaulle Airport in Paris. You can sense a touch of envy on Bono's part in the shifting refrain, especially the second time around. "Walk on, walk on," he proclaims, "What you've got they can't deny it/Walk on, walk on/Can't sell it, can't buy it" – and you know that he knows that the same can never quite be said of his own contribution to making the world a better place, heartfelt and immense as it might be.

And Aung San Suu Kyi's journey becomes a point of departure in itself, a springboard towards the realisation that in the end we're all going to have to leave the baggage that we create or accumulate behind, as we undertake the final journey to whatever home awaits us in the beyond.

The obsession with the meaning of the word home, and the way it impacts on our lives, is a familiar one for U2. It's also understandable in a man who has spent a substantial part of the last 25 years living in hotels. But Bono finds a new twist here with a freshly-minted aphorism of the kind that has been engaging him since *Achtung Baby*. "Home," he sings, "Hard to know if you've never had one/Home… I can't say where it is but I know I'm going home/That's where the hurt is."

That's what they say, isn't it – that home is where the hurt is?

KITE

It happens to most of us at some stage in our lives. The cards fall in a certain order, and suddenly people around us seem to be dropping like flies. And others are threatening to. That's the way it was during the recording of *All That You Can't Leave Behind*.

Death was in the air and Bono was confronted afresh with a visceral sense of his own mortality. Death had shaped him since his teens, when his mother was lost in tragic circumstances. Now, having himself passed the big four-oh, he saw his father in serious decline for the first time.

Tributes to his mother litter U2's repertoire. Bono's relationship with his father is more sparingly evoked but now that there was cause for serious concern, it was a subject that could no longer be circumvented. It gnawed away at him, demanding that a song be written. But it needed something to give it lift-off, to get it airborne. It needed a metaphor to make it fly.

The rock star's life is a dislocated, disorientated one. Locked in the studio for months on end, and then – gone. For Bono's children – now he's here, now he disappears. And the minstrel feels guilty, he wants to do all the daddy-like things that he remembers from when he was a kid. And so he troops down to the beach at Killiney with Jordan and Eve to fly a kite.

The expedition could hardly have been deemed a successful one. The kite went up, and it came down with a *phhht*, embedding itself in the strand. "Daddy, can we go home and play with the Playstation?" one of the kids asked. But when the kite hit the sand, a seed was sown.

'Kite' begins with a portent of doom. "Something is about to give," Bono ruminates. "I can feel it coming… I'm not afraid to die."He's seeing the world through the eyes of his father, and imagining how he himself will assess his own life, his own contribution, from the edge of the abyss. He's looking at his children and thinking about his father – who could be spirited away at any time.The voice could be his or his dad's: "In summer I can taste the salt in the sea/There's a kite blowing out of control on a breeze/I wonder what's gonna happen to you/You wonder what has happened to me."

It's a big subject: writing about it didn't come easy. Bono struggled with the verses. Edge got stuck in and gave him a hand, pushing the vehicle across the finishing line. "It seemed I knew what he was writing about and he didn't," Edge laughs. "It was one of those weird scenes. I was throwing in lines and he didn't like them at the time, but we went through this circular process where he was thinking, 'Oh yeah, that was a good line,' and so they went back in."

KITE
Written: U2
Length: 4' 26"
Album:
All That You Can't Leave Behind,
October 2000

IN A LITTLE WHILE

IN A LITTLE
WHILE
Written: U2
Length: 3' 39"
Album:
All That You Can't
Leave Behind,
October 2000

'In a Little While' was an Eno line, one that he'd been playing with for some time. It's the measure of a hook with potential – it nags at you, and refuses to go away, till you just know that you have to do something with it.

It's part of the pattern when U2 record; the Thursday night drink. Bono may insist he's abstaining for Lent, but come St Patrick's Day, or someone's birthday or even any old Thursday night, he'll be slamming 'em down till 5 in the morning, better than the best.

It was one of those Thursday nights and the age-old ritual was being enacted. The gang were there, but Bono bumped into someone he hadn't seen in 15 years, maybe even 20. The conversation was an awakening, ricocheting into the morning. It was a long night, and the next day Bono arrived in the studio and blurted out most of the lyrics of 'In a Little While' – a spiritual song that draws on the legacy of Al Green, mating it with a high, lonesome keening figure that gives the track its special haunting power.

In fact, a few things came together in the song. Around the turn of the year, Bono had been thinking Millennium thoughts, watching old clips of the Apollo moon landing on TV and experiencing again the sense of awe that he'd felt when he saw those pictures for the first time as a kid, the ecstatic realisation of how tiny and insignificant we are as individuals. It was a mood that fed into 'Beautiful Day' with its vision of Bedouin fires, the Great Wall of China, the Grand Canyon and other earthly phenomena, as seen from above. It slipped in here too, in a metaphor for the restless spirit that's so often denied but that nestles dangerously even in the warmest embrace of the most committed relationships. "A man dreams one day to fly," Bono sings and you can tell that it's the Wanderer in him talking.

141

Bono: always
in transit

'In A Little While' drew a great vocal performance from Bono, aching, tender and full of longing and guilt. "In a little while/I won't be blown by every breeze," he promises. And he's got so much soul, you almost believe him.

WILD HONEY

There's a sub-text to any album – the story of what might have been.

There were two or three big rock songs that everyone was committed to getting onto the album. A lot of work went in. But there's something in the dynamic of making a U2 record that defies logic. You're operating on instinct. "We reckoned people aren't buying rock records any more," Bono explains, "because of this progressive rock lurgy, where the single has been forgotten. In our heads we've written eleven singles for this record."

At the same time, there was another key complementary impulse: a desire to take a step sideways from the kind of dance-stances that U2 had experimented with on *Pop*. So they asked themselves the question that they have tried, consistently, to ask themselves each time it comes to making a new U2 record: what is it that you want to hear? And if you can get four people to answer that question in the same way, you're onto something.

The din of dance and the indulgence of progressive rock were to be avoided. And there was another foil that they identified, in the music that has dominated charts the world over these past five years and more. Pop!

It's one of the oddest moments on the record, the neat little acoustic guitar intro to 'Wild Honey'. The technology is so sophisticated now that the temptation is there to use it all the time. 'Wild Honey' was captured in its raw state. "It was never monkeyed with," Lanois says. "That's why it sounds like that."

There's so much melancholy elsewhere on the album that it's a vital tangent, slipped in at the last minute to enable people to lift their heads up from the sheer weight of the surrounding sonic and lyrical material. It isn't just the rudimentary sound that makes you think of the '60s: there's a Beatle-ish flavour to the melody and the harmony lines. And it's impossible not to hear Van Morrison, not just in Bono's voice but also in the pantheistic flavour of the sentiments. "Well, Van sings in major keys a lot," Daniel Lanois speculates. And Bono sounds like Van now and again. They grew up in the same backyard, so he has a licence!"

"We thought it would be fun to include it," Lanois adds, "a nice, simple, clear song with a lovely sentiment. It does have a lightness to it but it's a song of appreciation. I think it's like taking time out to say a little prayer. That's what it is." A song of praise, indeed.

Bono, Van Morrison and Bob Geldof at Morrison's induction into the Irish Music Hall of Fame.

WILD HONEY
Written: U2
Length: 3' 46"
Album:
All That You Can't Leave Behind,
October 2000

PEACE ON EARTH

It was hardly a surprise that U2 responded positively to the call they received on the run-in to the referendum on the Good Friday Agreement – a historic document which set out a way forward for Northern Ireland which held the promise that paramilitary guns might, in the nuanced language of this most intricate of political processes, be placed permanently beyond use. As polling day approached, the referendum seemed to be in trouble: would they lend their support to the campaign for a 'yes' vote? And so U2 from Dublin travelled North, to join forces with Ash from Downpatrick in Northern Ireland, playing together at a historic rally in Belfast. The 'yes' campaign prevailed. Peace, for so long an impossible dream in Northern Ireland, seemed finally to have a context in which it might flourish.

That illusion was shattered in the most appalling, heart-breaking and gruesome way when a bomb went off at 2.30 in the afternoon, on 15 August 1998, in the town of Omagh in County Tyrone. The resulting carnage was the worst in the bloody history of the Northern troubles with 29 killed and dozens more scarred, maimed and wounded. The bomb had been planted by a new paramilitary grouping styling itself the Real IRA. 'Peace on Earth', an angry and bitter response, was written in the shuddering aftermath of the mass murder of innocent citizens.

"It was written literally on the day the Omagh bomb went off," Bono recounts. "Nobody could actually believe it. In Ireland, when they read out the names of all the people who died on the six o'clock news, the city just came to a complete standstill.... People were just weeping – in cars, on O'Connell Street, all over the place. It was really a trauma for most people – because not only was it the destruction of lives, it was the destruction of the peace process, which had been put together with sticky tape and glue and tacks and a lot of faith. I couldn't believe that people could do that."

'Peace on Earth' is Bono's most agnostic song – "Jesus, can you spare the time/To throw a drowning man a line?" he asks, knowing that the answer must be no. In 'Wake Up Dead Man' he had paraphrased Seamus Heaney, beseeching Jesus to listen as hope and peace try to rhyme. He returns to the same theme: "Jesus, this song you wrote/The words are sticking in my throat/Peace on earth/Hear it every Christmas time/But hope and history won't rhyme/So what's it worth/This peace on earth."

"That Christmas, the whole 'peace on earth, goodwill to all men' struck a sour note," Bono observes. "It was very hard to be a believer that Christmas."

PEACE ON EARTH
Written: U2
Length: 4' 48"
Album:
All That You Can't
Leave Behind,
October 2000

143

WHEN I LOOK AT THE WORLD

Bono (as MacPhisto with Salman Rushd[

At the start of the '90s, U2 had decided that in order to reach people and touch people during a new decade, they had to come in a different guise.It was time to don some mad glad rags and to top it off with a pair of shades. Or three. "We played it cool for about ten years," Bono reflects. "And we got quite good at it. I was surprised! Yet we always saw it for what it was. We always knew it was a bit silly."

Now, at the turn of the millennium, a new strategy was called for. They wanted an album of big songs that would be strong enough lyrically and subtle enough melodically to reach into millions of hearts. "We're going up against 'Bridge Over Troubled Water'," Bono jokes, "and we have our work cut out." This was a time for empathy, for tenderness – for love. It was a time for homage to the muse. It was a time for humility.

Bono's partner Ali has done extraordinary work on the Children from Chernobyl project that assists the children of a region that will remain infamous as the location of the worst ever peacetime nuclear catastrophe. At great risk to her own health, Ali and her co-workers have gone to Chernobyl and Belarus and spent time there working with people who are still being affected by disaster, and with their children, in an attempt to alleviate the suffering, isolation and neglect.

Written by Bono and Edge, 'When I Look at the World' acknowledges the special qualities that this kind of commitment takes. It isn't just the capacity that Bono's muse has to light up any room that she enters – it's the empathy of which she's capable, the composure that she shows, and the example that she gives to someone who by comparison feels flawed and impatient.

WHEN I LOOK AT THE WORLD
Written: U2
Length: 4' 17"
Album:
All That You Can't Leave Behind,
October 2000

NEW YORK

Friday is meeting day. The boys in the band sit down and wait for the bad news. We've been asked to do this. Yes. We've been asked to do that. No. We've got to find a way around this. Oh! It was a phenomenon throughout the making of *All That You Can't Leave Behind* that became a right royal pain in the ass for anyone outside the most inner of inner circles. It wasn't just Fridays anymore, it was every second fucking day.

Passionately as they might have felt like railing against it, Eno and Lanois had to live with it. The Friday meeting is on? Fine, we'll work away. Can we dig up that Larry rhythm thing? We might get something out of that.

Frequently, Eno does his best work when he gets the hell out of the studio. "We're always glad when he goes away," Larry smiles, "because we know that when he comes back, he'll be back with some more goodies! Danny just stays in there and brings a different touch to it. So we're pushing one way, they're pushing others – and the results are always interesting."

On other occasions, it happens in the room, where the smell of the conflict and the frustration is fresh in everyone's nostrils. "Brian brings a very different thing to U2," Larry adds. "He gets onto those keyboards and he just takes songs in directions you wouldn't expect."

The meeting was a long one, but in the meantime Brian was in inspired form. He got a kind of a foghorn sound going over Larry's drumbeat. He conjured another chordal thing out of his bag of tricks and Lanois snuck in on guitar and they had a groove happening. The band came down from the meeting feeling itchy and scratchy. They grabbed their instruments and whaled into it. The chemistry worked. Eureka! "It all happened very, very quickly," Lanois remembers. "Bono thought 'This is going to be the home for my New York idea'!" A song was born.

Hearing it, it's impossible not to think of Lou Reed, of Frank Sinatra, of Ian Curtis and of P.J. Harvey, whose *Stories from the City, Stories from the Sea* is in part at least a paean to the city that never sleeps. Originally the song ended with a free-form conversation about Frank Sinatra, with whom Bono had the privilege of sharing a duet on 'I've Got You Under My Skin' before he died. Old BlueEyes! Bono says: "I was at dinner once with Frank and he took a blue paper napkin from the table and he was just staring at it and he said, to no-one in particular, 'I remember when my eyes were this blue'. He put it, and kept it, in an inside pocket. It was very cool."

For the most part 'New York' is just that, the cool pulsing groove acting as a backdrop as the narrator confesses quietly to the terms of the mid-life

NEW YORK
Written: U2
Length: 5' 30"
Album:
All That You Can't Leave Behind,
October 2000

U2 scoop the honou
at the 43rd annual
Grammy Awards, 21
February, 2001.

crisis afflicting him, while all around nine million other, fascinating stories are being written. New York! New York! But halfway through it explodes in a grungy mess that's impressively appropriate to the theme of the song. That sonic thunderstorm was there in the track's infant state but Edge got to work on it and bent it into a different shape. "That's an overdub. It's very effective," Lanois comments. "He was right."

But was Bono? There's a line in it that's sounds almost boastful: "I just got a place in New York," Bono declares. "I was gonna change the line to something less consumerist," he admits, "but... I had just got a place in New York! And it made me smile. Even though the song is not autobiographical. Now you're thinking 'the bastard's got a nice place on Central Park' – but for the character in the song it could be a shoebox."

Obviously there are a bits of Bono in there. But only bits, he insists. No mid-life crisis here. "If anything I'm at the other end of that," he says. "I'm trying to calm down. I had a mid-life crisis much earlier, about age 27, for all the classic reasons. I just went downtown in Los Angeles, drank a lot of whiskey and made up for all the years pushing a rock up a hill. Or a rock band up the hill! I got quite good at being silly and that, in a way, prepared us for the silliness of the '90s – which I've thoroughly enjoyed."

Oddly, it ends on a glancing reference to 'The Stolen Child', a poem by William Butler Yeats. "In the stillness of the evening/When the sun has had its day/I heard your voice a-whispering/Come away child/New York, New York." Unconscious? Maybe.

GRACE

The mood starting out had been relaxed and positive. They went into the studio without a fixed agenda. The plan was to jam, to see what would come out of it without the pressure of actually making an album. It had worked well for U2, and for Eno and Lanois as their producers, in particular with *The Joshua Tree*. So they tried it again. It was kind of a fun time, but a fruitful one.

Grace was minted in that first loose flush of creativity. It was put on the shelf in embryonic form: one to come back to later. They did about mid-way through, but nothing gave. Bono hadn't linked it with any lyrical cue yet, and they had a frustrating time trying to move it along. It went into cold storage.

On one of his retreats to London, Eno took it with him. He was looking for a melody to open it out and help it take flight. Nothing. It went into storage for a third time. They were on the final countdown, with paranoia playing havoc all around, when the lightbulb went on. "Pretty much at the end of the record," Lanois recalls, "we pulled it out and Bono wrote something very beautiful for it. I came up with the guitar part and that sparked another keyboard part from Brian and Larry put some drums on it – it was kind of layered. And Bono just had this idea that we should approach the subject matter of 'grace'. It was lovely."

It's a tribute to womankind. You can sense the spirit of Ali informing it, but 'Grace' is not just about an individual, or about women – it's about a way of dealing with the world that offers intimations of a better place.

An album that exploded into life on a wave of barely-founded optimism – the sky is falling but hey, it's a beautiful day! – ends on a deeper note. 'Grace' finds beauty in everything. It's a state we can aspire to. Not easily attained when you're trying to finish a U2 album, and the world is collapsing all around you. But worth chasing nonetheless.

GRACE
Written: U2
Length: 5' 30"
Album:
All That You Can't Leave Behind,
October 2000

HOW TO DISMANTLE AN ATOMIC BOMB

The band came off the *Elevation* tour on a high. They were back at the top of their game, with over ten million sales of *All That You Want To Leave Behind* racked up, and the coveted title of Biggest Rock Band in the World successfully defended against all-comers. And they had a whole batch of new songs brewing, or at least that was the way it felt. Bring 'em on!

They began a new phase of recording in the South of France and got enough stuff down to feel that they were on the way. Then it was into the longer haul. With a ballsy rock'n'roll record in mind, they picked Chris Thomas to produce the album and the band ensconced themselves in their Dublin HQ to get the job finished. Well, started…

The best U2 record ever was on the way, we were told. It was a return to the band's rock'n'roll roots that would blow everyone away – a guitar album, with Edge leading the way. But those in the know sensed that all was not right down in Hanover Quay. The record – as yet untitled – had been scheduled to hit the racks in time for the Christmas rush, 2003, but the deadline for the delivery of the finished masters came… and went.

The band decamped to the South of France again, and there was the by now almost de rigeur security scare when a CD of rough mixes was lost or stolen. Chris Thomas departed in ambiguous circumstances, the band later acknowledging that they had probably driven him mad. Steve Lillywhite was drafted in, and was still there as the finishing tape came into view, but by the time the album was fully done and dusted, no less than eight producers in all had been involved.

Sometimes it's necessary to do things the hard way. Over 25 years on, no one knows this better than U2. After a colossal and at times painful two years in the studios, the record was finished and put to bed. Someone joked that next time maybe someone should put a bomb under them.

VERTIGO

It began with a riff, concocted at Edge's house in Malibu. He played it to Bono – Da da da da da da da da dahn – and it registered. When you get a good one, it plays itself back to you when you're least expecting it, slipping in and out of your consciousness, until it claims its place in a song. Da da da da da da da da dahn. This felt like a classic, one that might have been purloined from the Stones, the Pistols or even Led Zeppelin, but it was where Edge was leaning in the early stages of making what was to become *How To Dismantle An Atomic Bomb*.

It's only rock'n'roll but I like it. The Vines, the Hives, the Strokes and outfits like Black Rebel Motorcycle Club had thrust the guitar back to the centre of things. U2, ever aware of the zeitgeist, wanted to see any new pretenders off by coming up with an even bigger riff, a harder one – something that would blast out of the radio like a calling card. Edge thought of the working title 'Full Metal Jacket' and that was how it started to take shape. There'd be blood on this track alright. Blood and guts.

Bono got enthused, thinking MC5 and the Stooges and deciding that the riff alone, and the rock'n'roll energy that blazed through it, was reason enough to make a new album before Larry and Adam had even heard it.

The Vines: guitars were back in fashion.

149

He came up with an agit-prop set of lyrics about the plight of the native American Leonard Peltier, wrongly jailed for aiding and abetting in the killing of two FBI agents. He called it 'Native Son' and the song took shape in that guise. Thinking that a blazing punky record was on the cards, they'd hired Chris Thomas to produce. Not only had Thomas worked with Roxy Music – an unacknowledged influence on U2 throughout their career – but he was the man at the control desk for the recording of the Sex Pistols' landmark album *Never Mind The Bollocks*, a record notable for its snarling guitars. With Thomas in the production seat, they recorded 'Native Son', and the band loved it so much they sent it to their American label Interscope to get them equally fired up. It worked and everyone was buzzing about it, thinking they had a winner on their hands.

It was a fling that was destined to come to an end. The recording went into a slump and the band decided to bring in Steve Lillywhite to act as, in footballing parlance, the fresh pair of legs that was needed to get them through the second half. He immediately decided to change things around, to set the band a different kind of challenge. To take them out of the comfort zone, he turned the studio inside out, pushing them into the bigger of the Hanover Quay rooms to play. He found a more ambient room for Larry, to get closer to the early U2 sound and in the process to bring something fresh to the rhythm department. The track was still called 'Native Son' when they whacked down some great new parts in the re-organised set-up. Lillywhite asked Bono for a guide vocal and the frontman started to sing it – and something odd happened. "After 30 seconds he stopped," Steve Lillywhite recalls. "All of a sudden I realised 'he's imagining this as a stage and he's up there in front of 20,000 people singing this – and he doesn't want to'."

Leonard Peltier: falsely accused and placed in jail.

It's an ever-present consideration now for U2, and for Bono in particular. He writes a U2 song, especially one with a big stonking riff that's potentially an album opener and the first single, knowing that he's going to have to go out and play it live. 'Native Son', he had just figured out, wasn't one that he would feel comfortable doing that with.

Going back to the drawing board was hard. Larry talks about the fact that the song had to be deconstructed and put together again – and that's what they did. They changed the chords around, tried a variety of different lyrics and titles. It became 'Shark Soup' and then 'Viva La Ramone', a tribute to the great Joey Ramone. There was even a Spanish version that gave the track the mathematically challenged intro – "Unos, dos, tres, catorces" (One, two three, fourteen!) – bellowed by Bono at the start of the record. Eventually it transmuted into 'Vertigo', and even then they struggled to choose between a number of different potential choruses. They weren't sure which was the one, until a few outsiders had heard it and support for the "Hello, hello…" variation gathered momentum. "It's a club and you're supposed to be having the time of your life," Bono said in an interview on the U2achtung.com website, "but you want to kill yourself. Vertigo is a dizzy feeling, when you get to the top of something and there's only one way to go.

VERTIGO
Written: U2
Length: 3' 14"
Album: *How To
Dismantle An
Atomic Bomb*,
November 2004
UK singles chart
position: 1
US singles chart
position: 31

"In my head I created a club called Vertigo with all these people in it," he added (though there's a Club Vertigo in Boston and rumours of a place in Germany called Vertigo too), "and the music is not the music you want to hear and the people are not the people you want to be with and then you see somebody and she's got a cross around her neck, and you focus on it. Because you can't focus on anything else. You find a tiny little fragment of salvation there."

Whatever the origin of the imaginary club, they had found the fragment of salvation necessary to realize the full potential of the track. Steve Lillywhite took the unusual initiative of double-tracking Bono's voice on the chorus, which gave it added impact. Finally, after more heartache, indecision and grief than Edge could possibly have imagined when he came up with that first killer riff, they knew that this was the one. And the riff had survived. Da da da da da da da dahn.

"'Vertigo' refers back to their past," according to Neil McCormick, who conducted interviews for the album's accompanying DVD. "Bono sings at one point, 'Hello, hello' and I said, 'You've used that line before' and he said, 'Have I? Where?' and I said, 'Well you used to use it all the time, basically when you ran out of words!' And it's on 'Stories For Boys'. And that's on their first single, on *U23*.

"So 'Vertigo', the first single off the new album refers back to their first. It's like the early U2 pumped up in the 21st century, a really exciting record. It actually includes my name in it, so I definitely voted for that as the first single! At the end, Bono's singing 'Your love is teaching me how to kneel'. And then he goes: 'Kneee-heel!' He and Edge were playing this in the studio and at that exact moment they both looked up and saw me standing there and Bono went, 'Hey Neil!'"

But the break in the song also directly references the guitar part in 'I Will Follow'. Thus 'Vertigo' takes them back and forward at the same time, reclaiming their heritage and putting it in a modern rock context. According to producer Trevor Horn, the first overdub on the record doesn't appear until over two minutes into the song, making it essentially a live recording by the band – an incredible thought given that they were a full two years in the studio making *How To Dismantle An Atomic Bomb*.

"Adam is fantastic on that song," Steve Lillywhite says, "because on the verse there's nothing but bass and drums and vocals. Edge just does a couple of clicks, so Adam and Larry have to carry it. It's a really big song, as big as any of their songs actually."

The ideal electric shock treatment, you might say, with which to open the record.

MIRACLE DRUG

When the first glow of the pounding rock'n'roll of the Chris Thomas sessions had dimmed and the hard labour they'd put in subsequently had worn thin, there was a feeling of uncertainty, bordering on depression, in the air.

There was a lot of stuff there, a lot of sweat in the tracks, but nothing was getting finished, no one was coming up trumps. Larry, who'd had his foot off the gas, listened to the material, and decided that what had been done didn't add up to the record he wanted to make. Exhaustion was beginning to take its toll, the band were feeling down, individually and collectively, and there was no guaranteeing that they'd get back up off the floor. There never is: the way U2 work, they're a catastrophe waiting to happen. The band had a

Adam performing in San Diego on the firs night of U2's 2005 world tour.

creeping feeling now, that they might have been barking up the wrong tree all along. Originally scheduled to hit the shops late in 2003, the release of the record had to be put back. When Steve Lillywhite was drafted in, he had a good listen and tended to share the downbeat assessment: this gig wasn't going to be about mixing and fixing. A radical change of tack was needed.

Too often, what was there didn't have the spark; it was like, Lillywhite mused to himself, not-great versions of things U2 had done before. He girded his loins and said what nobody wanted to hear. "I think you need a few new songs," he announced, to the dismay of all concerned. But in a way it was liberating. Adam, for one, recognised that he was right. Having been so down, the only way was up. So they went away and wrote. 'Miracle Drug' was one of the first pieces under the new dispensation and it felt like another big song in the making.

The chord sequence was one Adam came up with, the band improvising their way to a song shape from there. Bono'd long had an idea in his head to write a song about Christopher Nolan, who went to Mount Temple, the school in north Dublin, at which the band originally formed. The working assumption had been that Christopher, in a wheelchair as a result of cerebral palsy, and unable to communicate, was just a spectator. But with the support of his mother, a woman of great dedication and love, and the help of a new drug – a miracle drug – he was able to move his head. At the

MIRACLE DRUG
Written: U2
Length: 3' 59"
Album: *How To Dismantle An Atomic Bomb*,
November 2004

age of 13 he began to write, using a unicorn on a band around his head to type. And when he did, hard as the tortuous process made it, the words began to flow. In 1981, his first book of poetry was published, and he called it *Damburst Of Dreams*, capturing with beautiful eloquence the sensation of finally being able to express the thoughts and feelings that had forever been racing through his mind. At 21, Nolan produced a powerful autobiographical novel, *Under The Eye Of The Clock*, that won the Whitbread Prize. Hard to believe! Such an unprecedented outpouring of intelligence and emotion from someone who hadn't been able to speak or walk or even move independently. Yes, there was a song in it, alright.

"I want to trip inside your head," Bono wrote, the image of Christopher Nolan in his mind's eye, "Spend the day there/To hear the things you haven't said/And see what you might see…"

Without the familiar presence of either Brian Eno or Daniel Lanois in the studio for any extended period, the band felt that they would benefit from having another musician involved in the production and brought in Garrett 'Jacknife' Lee to fill the role. A keyboard player, and a former member of Dublin bands Thee Amazing Colossal Men and Compulsion, as a producer Lee had hit paydirt with Snow Patrol's *Final Straw*, and the feeling was that he might now bring a bit of left-field sonic experimentation to the high table. He got involved, helping to push 'Miracle Drug' along. But, as it evolved, in Bono's mind it wasn't just going to be about Christopher Nolan. There was something else working its way through, something to do with AIDS and the drugs that have been developed to contain it.

There was a line he wanted to use, and it fitted. He'd had a conversation with Sean Lennon about Tibet, in which the younger Lennon asked him what freedom smelled like. "Like the top of a new-born baby's head," he'd said at the time. And he'd carried that around with him since. He'd tried it in a different context, but now, definitively, he'd found a home for it. "Freedom has a scent/Like the top of a new born baby's head…" he sang. And the melody and the mood took on an anthemic purpose, allowing the track to grow until it became a kind of prayer of hope about the miracles that can be wrought through science and medicine.

"Some people think it's a great lyric and some people think it's terrible," Steve Lillywhite reflects. "I think it's great. I think Bono does the things that make people question themselves and their responses. In a strange way, though, it works. It's a special song.

153

SOMETIMES YOU CAN'T MAKE IT ON YOUR OWN

Daniel Lanois.

Bono had known for a while that his father was dying of cancer. It was a tough time for him, the hardest since his mother had died. And so he wrote a song for Bob, and called it 'Tough' because that was what his father had always seemed to him. "A tough old boot of a guy," in Bono's own words, "Irish, Dub, north side Dubliner, very cynical about the world and the people in it, but very charming and funny with it."

They worked on the song for *All That You Can't Leave Behind*, and it turned into 'Sometimes You Can't Make It On Your Own' during those sessions – but it wasn't ready. Bob died the week before the band's Slane Castle appearance. Bono sang the song at the funeral, a portrait of the artist as an old man – a working class guy who loved opera, and who had bequeathed something of his beautiful tenor voice to his son.

"He never talked about [our] music," Bono said. "Oh, I do remember he liked the song 'The Unforgettable Fire'. He thought we were getting quite good around the time of *Rattle And Hum* but he didn't know where we were going in the '90s!"

They came back to the song for *How To Dismantle An Atomic Bomb* and it felt good. Everyone felt that they had it nailed. Except Steve Lillywhite. When he came in, he gave it a critical appraisal that was to prove, well, critical.

"My contribution to that song is that I was listening to it with Edge – and Bono was there as well – and I said 'Edge, this song doesn't have a chorus'. And they said 'What do you mean?' And I said, well, it just finishes the verse and then goes 'Sometimes you can't make it on your own'. And Bono immediately went 'Give me a guitar'. So he picked up a guitar and went 'And it's you when I look na na na na' – he didn't have the lyrics yet – 'And it's you du du du du du du du/ Sometimes you can't make it on your own'. And all of a sudden the song was finished. That song had been around for the best part of five years and no one had ever said to them that it didn't have a chorus."

SOMETIMES YOU CAN'T MAKE IT ON YOUR OWN
Written: U2
Length: 5' 08"
Album: *How To Dismantle An Atomic Bomb*, November 2004
UK singles chart position: 1
US singles chart position: 97

LOVE AND PEACE OR ELSE

How To Dismantle An Atomic Bomb was made against the backdrop of the invasion of Iraq There was a song hanging over from *All That You Can't Leave Behind*. Now, every time they listened to the out-takes from those earlier sessions, it clamoured for attention.

Lyrically, inspired by Eno's end-of-the-world, subterranean guitar sound, Bono had in mind a preacher-type character, cracked but making sense. "It's like The Fly went to the seminary and became a priest," he revealed to u2achtung.com. Around the time of the album launch Bono enjoyed quoting couplets that he was especially pleased with to anyone who was writing about the record. In 'Love and Peace Or Else' it was this one; "When you enter this life I pray you depart/With a wrinkled face and a brand new heart." Bono had set out to write a political record, in part at least with Iraq as a backdrop, but you can only write the songs that flow through you.

"I very much sat down to address it, hence the title of the album," Bono reflects. "It's worth reminding ourselves of those days after 9/11, and what they felt like. At no other point in history had there been a sense that people would commit that sort of mass murder as a terrorist act. That's no excuse for prosecuting a war in Iraq, but it puts it all into context.

"I told Thom Yorke two years ago, 'I know what the album's about and what it's going to be called, which is *How To Build An Atomic Bomb*'. That was the original title because the toothpaste was out of the tube. There was an article in the *Guardian* newspaper with two college students discussing how easy it is to get your hands on this kind of weaponry.

"A private arms company in the US has developed this GPS-guided system made out of papier-mache and plastic, which for less than a $1m can fly 2,500 miles with anything you want attached to it. Somebody asked their CEO, 'Are you not worried about these getting into terrorist hands?' to which he replied, 'We've offered them to the Pentagon if they're prepared to buy in bulk, but the knowledge to make these things exists everywhere. We're just packaging it commercially'

"Someone who's paranoid, in my opinion, is a person in full possession of the facts," he says. "These are nervous times. After Bikini Atoll, after Mexico, after indeed Enola Gay was dropped in Japan, everything has changed – and the idea that the human race can destroy everything and remove all traces of itself is now in the air. What does it mean? Two things – you party hard, and you hold on to your loved ones a little tighter. I kind of enjoy forgetting I'm in a band."

155

LOVE AND PEACE OR ELSE
Written: U2
Length: 4' 50"
Album: *How To Dismantle An Atomic Bomb*, November 2004

CITY OF BLINDING LIGHTS

There are love affairs that never end. When U2 first went to the US, they were wide-eyed kids, open to what the world had to offer them. A lot of the other British and Irish bands of the time were deeply cynical and condescending about America. U2 crossed the Atlantic knowing that they had a lot to learn, conscious that they needed to establish a foundation there in order to further their ambition to become the biggest rock band in the world. Their first trip to New York was a magical experience, and one they'd never forget. 'City Of Blinding Lights' is just the latest manifestation of an enduring crush. It's one of Steve Lillywhite's favourite tracks on the album.

More shades of Scott Walker in 'City Of Blinding Lights'.

They came up with the idea as far back as the recording of *Pop*. The way they work is at once sprawling and instinctive. If something feels right for the time, it gets done. If it doesn't, it's filed away. The skeleton of 'City Of Blinding Lights' didn't have the necessary flesh put on it for *Pop* and it wasn't revived successfully for *All That You Can't Leave Behind* either. But it was one in reserve that they could turn to when the hits failed to do whatever they do to the fans. They plugged back into it for *How To Dismantle An Atomic Bomb*, and listening to it now, it's hard to believe that it could have waited so long to come good.

Talking about it, Bono name-checks Scott Walker but there's a hint of Blue Nile in here too, in the restrained visual evocation of the world, and the spirituality that's to be found in every sparkle of light. "You can hear that in our music," Bono attests, "that painterly side of the lyrics, that kind of melodrama." But it is an Ali song too, a love song to Bono's muse, that's shot through with a sense of the ravages of time.

"I've seen you walk unafraid," he sings, "I've seen you in the clothes you've made/Can you see the beauty inside of me?/What happened to the beauty I had inside of me?"

"It's a New York song," Bono said. "About going there for the first time. We were the first band to play Madison Square Gardens after 9/11. During 'Where The Streets Have No Name', the house lights came up, and there were 20,000 people in tears. It was beautiful."

'City Of Blinding Lights' indeed.

CITY OF
BURNING LIGHTS
Written: U2
Length: 5' 47"
Album: *How To Dismantle An Atomic Bomb*, November 2004

ALL BECAUSE OF YOU

At times, it seems that momentum is the key. The *Elevation* tour was a triumph for U2, not least because in the dark days after 9/11 they decided to keep the show on the road. It would have been natural to retreat into their shells. Instead, U2 upped their collective game. What America, in particular, needed was a return to some semblance of normality.

The adrenalin from the tour was irresistible. They felt good about what they were doing, so good that they pressed ahead almost immediately into recording. They were on a high, and blasting into the sessions in the south of France they believed they were really onto something. They wrote 'Electrical Storm', a new track recorded for *Best Of 1990-2000*, and 'The Hands That Built America' for *Gangs of New York* there, and lashed some other stuff down too, full of punky energy, that gave them a lift at the time. It seemed like maybe they were on their way to a new album already, but the initial buzz tailed off. In a way, in retrospect, that was inevitable. "That tour, playing indoors, doing the material from *All That You Can't Leave Behind*, we really seemed to connect with people'" Adam Clayton recalled. "But the one survivor from that session was 'All Because Of You'."

It survived, but had to be revived. Steve Lillywhite took over the production. Jacknife Lee tossed in some keyboards. They changed the melody in the chorus, did some tinkering with the lyrics, changing a verse, and gave the lot to Flood to mix. They were in business.

One of the things that delayed the making of *How To Dismantle An Atomic Bomb* was Bono's involvement in issues relating to the Drop The Debt campaign and AIDS in Africa. In that milieu, the singer brings a sense of organisation and purpose to his work that is sometimes missing from his rock'n'roll adventures. "He is, as he says of himself in 'All Because Of You', an intellectual tortoise," Adam reflects. "He is a unique character. He is organised intellectually, but he wouldn't know where his car keys are. And to say he is disorganised is kind of derogatory. That stuff isn't important to him and it never was."

ALL BECAUSE OF YOU
Written: U2
Length: 3' 39"
Album: *How To Dismantle An Atomic Bomb*, November 2004

'All Because Of You' is another mother song, in a line from 'I Will Follow' and 'Tomorrow' through 'Mofo'. It could be addressed to his mother Iris, it could be to Ali, it could even be to God the Mother. But it is, without doubt, about the debt that man owes to woman, one that can never be dropped. "I'm alive/I'm being born /I just arrived/ I'm at the door/Of the place I started from/And I want back inside."

Don't we all.

A MAN AND A WOMAN

It's a couple of weeks before the album is due to hit the shops and Bono is conducting another gathering of notables through *How To Dismantle An Atomic Bomb*. As the playback progresses, he's like a man possessed. .

We're on 'A Man And A Woman' and he makes like a magician about to pull off his

An influence on 'A Man And A Woman the late Phil Lynott.

ultimate party piece, a conjuring trick to end all conjuring tricks. "Wait till you hear this," he yells again. "No one would know it, but I'm about to show you where this song came from – where it was stolen from. I'm going to sing it in a Phil Lynott voice and you'll get it. This is Thin Lizzy. Listen."

The languorous guitar strum and Latinised feel of 'A Man And A Woman' pour from the speakers, redolent of Burt Bacherach in its romantic pop-ishness. Bono starts singing. Through his nose, just a little bit, and in a Dublin accent. And you recognise the antecedents of the song, you see them perfectly. Caramba!

He goes back into character, in a way that is both funny and lovely and moving. The original Dublin rocker's presence fills the room. And a wonderfully beautiful song about "The mysterious distance between a man and a woman" – how come no one ever expressed that idea so perfectly before? – becomes even more mysterious and beautiful in the re-telling.

As far back as 2000, Bono was asked if he ever felt constricted in his writing and his interviews by the knowledge that Ali was going to be listening. "Ali doesn't read newspapers." Bono had answered with a laugh. "Or listen to the radio. (Laughs). There's a mysterious distance between us. And that's all I can say. I don't feel in any way constricted, though at times I have. Yeah. I'm as honest as I can be in talking about songs but I'm really honest when I'm singing them. That's just the way it goes. It's a song for adults, for people who have been together for a long time and who are still together."

You know what he means when he sings: "I could never take a chance/ Of losing love to find romance/In the mysterious distance/Between a man and a woman."

A MAN AND A WOMAN
Written: U2
Length: 4' 30"
Album: *How To Dismantle An Atomic Bomb*, November 2004

CRUMBS FROM YOUR TABLE

Bono's initial intentions notwithstanding, *How To Dismantle An Atomic Bomb* isn't a political record. The more personal it got, the more often Bono would refer to it as 'How To Dismantle An Atomic Bob', the reference to his father reflecting the band's growing understanding that – more than anything else – it was a record about the ties that bind us to what we are.

But Bono's personal politics seep through it. There may be nothing on the record as virulently hostile to US hegemony as 'Bullet The Blue Sky'. But Bono insisted that this was not down to having to do business with George Bush and his aides in the cause of Drop The Debt.

"It's a real question and one that I can honestly answer with a 'No'," he said. "I don't really have much control over it – and if there are lyrics that offend some of the people I work with, so be it. 'Crumbs From Your Table' is one of the most vicious songs ever. It's full of spleen about the church and its refusal to hear God's voice on the AIDS emergency."

He describes the recording, the band in full flow in the studio, when a call comes through from a friend. She's full of good humour and heart. Hard to believe that she's in a hospital in Africa, taking care of AIDS patients. It's Sister Annie, an Irish nun, and she's looking for a favour. "You're going into the song," he tells her. And so she does.

"I went to speak to Christian groups in America to convince them to give money to fight AIDS in Africa. It was like getting blood from a stone," he recalled. "I told them about a hospice in Uganda, where so many people were dying they had to sleep three to a bed."

The last thing U2 need is a return to the self-consciousness of the *Joshua Tree* era. But there are different ways to skin this particular cat.

"Whenever U2 gets specifically agitprop,' Bono says, "the band here starts nodding off and Brian Eno or Daniel Lanois or Steve Lillywhite will start making people dance. 'Bullet The Blue Sky' is like U2 doing The Bad Seeds, it's biblical much more so than it's a polemic. We didn't make those kind of anti-personnel type songs to suddenly stop. There are moments when I keep my opinions out of the press – but not out of songs."

159

CRUMBS FROM YOUR TABLE
Written: U2
Length: 5' 03"
Album: *How To Dismantle An Atomic Bomb*, November 2004

ONE STEP CLOSER

Edge had been doing the prep work, burrowing away in the kitchen in Zen mode, coming up with some melodic structures, getting the possible recipe for a song down. There comes a time when you have to put it into the pan and see what the others think. He produced the chord sequence with everyone in the studio and the band began to jam it. It's the most distinctive element in the creative process for U2, the stage where they all get to toss in different ingredients and see if they can come up with a signature dish. It's why the song credits run: "Music: U2".

The Edge cooked up the basics of 'One Step Closer'.

This one smelled good. Early on, it felt like a Velvet Underground song, with Bono delivering a melody that Edge loved, and the rest of the band responding in kind. Everyone knew that it had potential, but they still had to unlock it fully.

"The U2 working process is utterly unique to them and quite frustrating for everyone else," Steve Lillywhite observed. "It involves working tracks over and over and over again, dismissing every possible thing they don't like and ultimately ending up with the thing they like."

The theme was a big one. 'One Step Closer' ponders the meaning of death: shades of The Blue Nile in the picture of the tail lights glowing and the imminence of our inevitable demise captured in a plaintive question – 'Can you hear the drummer slowing?' – that sounds like it might have been tossed in first as a studio in-joke, but rises way above that:.

They almost nailed this with Chris Thomas in the driving seat, aided first by Daniel Lanois, who put some extra guitars into the mix. Jacknife Lee added synthesizers, giving a stately backdrop to the throbbing heartbeat evoked by the band. But it is the beautiful simplicity of the idea around which the song is built that gives it its special resonance. Bono had been talking to Noel Gallagher of Oasis about the fact that his father, dying at the time, seemed to have lost his faith – that he no longer believed he knew where he was going in the after-life, if indeed there was one. "Well, he's one step closer to knowing," Gallagher had drawled.

"He's on a pint of Guinness and a packet of crisps for coming up with the title," Bono laughs.

ONE STEP CLOSER
Written: U2
Length: 3' 51"
Album: *How To Dismantle An Atomic Bomb*, November 2004

ORIGINAL OF THE SPECIES

Adam Clayton talks about the thematic threads that run through *How To Dismantle An Atomic Bomb*.

It deals with questions about how you fit into the world, about the power and strength of family relationships. Larry Mullen makes similar observations. That the world U2 are in now is one in which people recognize the value of family. That it's a dangerous world out there. That we are, to one degree or another, collectively living in a state of fear.

Sometimes what we have to fear most are the ghosts inside, the things that haunt us about who we are, about what we should do and be – and about how we fit into and around the images of ourselves that have been ingrained into us.

Bono was thinking about Edge's daughter Holly when 'Original Of The Species' took shape first, during the making of *All That You Can't Leave Behind*. Bono is her Godfather, and so he feels a special, different kind of closeness. Edge loved the lyrics when he heard them: it was a song that made him cry. "It started about Holly," he told *Q* magazine. "He's her Godfather. The lyric became more universal, about being young and full of doubt about yourself." Edge speculates that there is, in the song, an element of Bono looking back to when he was 20, and remembering his own insecurities: you have to have been there to know what it feels like, to identify with the confusion over self and worth.

Bono sees it as a melodic journey. There is something of Roy Orbison's mini-operas here, with Edge's piano adding to the orchestral flavour. "It's about seeing some people who are ashamed about their bodies," Bono explained, "in particular teenagers with eating disorders, not feeling comfortable with themselves and their sexuality. I'm just saying to them 'you are one of a kind, you're an original of the species'. So it's a 'Be who you are' song. I can't wait to play it live."

ORIGINAL OF
THE SPECIES
Written: U2
Length: 4' 41"
Album: *How To Dismantle An Atomic Bomb*,
November 2004

YAHWEH

"It just formed in my mouth, as a lot of U2 songs do," Bono explains. "There's the sound, and then trying to figure out what that sound is – and it was this word, 'Yahweh'."

It's one of the biggest songs on *How To Dismantle An Atomic Bomb*. "I had this idea that no one can own Jerusalem," Bono said, "but everybody wants to put flags on it."

"Yahweh is the name for the Most High," Edge elaborates, "which Jewish people do not utter. It is written, not spoken. It's a sacred name for God, and in this song it's a prayer."

Bono ponders the fate of Jerusalem.

"It's not meant to be spoken," Bono confirms, "but I got around it by singing it. I hope I don't offend anyone."

They recorded it with Chris Thomas, Daniel Lanois came in and added mandolin and they kicked it around with Steve Lillywhite – but eventually went back to the original.

"I played it to Jimmy Iovine of Interscope," Bono recalls, "who loved it up until the point where I told him it's the unspeakable word for God. And he said: 'Call it 'Mozza Balls'. Call it 'Ali'. Call it anything but that!'"

"It's the record company guy," Steve Lillywhite laughs. "It's like the guy who said 'Can you take the bloody out of 'Sunday Bloody Sunday', so that we can get it played on the radio?' That's a true story."

"A delegation came to see me from the Middle East to talk about the fact that there's no peace movement there," Bono reveals, "They asked would I give them a hand, and I said, 'Look, I'm at the point where the world will find it projectile vomit-inducing if I attach my name to another worthy cause.

"The only idea I had," he continues, "is a Festival Of Abraham, which will celebrate the three traditions that call Abraham their father. Out of that conversation there's another project – to build a sort of cathedral of understanding in Europe, called the Eye Of Abraham, where Jews, Muslims and Christians can watch each other worship. The two very inspirational people who are heading up the initiative were opposing negotiators during the Oslo Peace Accord, but are now friends."

It's an initiative for which the widescreen beauty of 'Yahweh' might yet make an appropriate anthem.

YAHWEH
Written: U2
Length: 4' 21"
Album: *How To Dismantle An Atomic Bomb*, November 2004

FAST CARS

They needed an extra track in Japan. It's to do with release dates and the dangers of imported copies – and so it's a tradition with U2 to give their Japanese fans something extra as a kind of bonus for waiting. The UK and Ireland generally get the benefit – in this instance with the inclusion of 'Fast Cars' on the album release.

They had a track, 'Xanax and Wine', that everyone had agreed should be on the album. They spent weeks on it that turned into months.

It gave them the title of the album. "I'm going nowhere," the lyrics ran, "Where I am it is a lot of fun/They're in the desert to dismantle an atomic bomb." That much established, there was a sense of 'fuck it, it has to make the cut' – so they spent some more time on it. And then a little bit more.

They had taken it to a stage where it was ready for release – or not – but in the end the band came to the hard conclusion that, like the narrator of the song itself, it was going nowhere. Reluctantly, they decided to ditch it, though it would be used as part of the Apple iTunes Digital Box Set release of every U2 track.

"U2 albums at the end are always mad times," Steve Lillywhite says, "So there we were on the last night, thinking, 'There, we've done it, we've got away with it, we've finished the album and there's no madness' and of course Bono walks in and goes let's re-record 'Xanax and Wine'."

Except now he had a new set of lyrics to work with. "Bono can sometimes use the same lines in different songs," Lillywhite adds. "Like, if it doesn't work in one, it might work in another. He likes the couplet, so he'll try to see how it fits into a few songs. So he had this line that had been the chorus of 'Vertigo' at one stage, when it had a different melody: 'I know these fast cars will do me no good'. So that came in handy. It was a bit weird calling a song 'Xanax and Wine' anyway, so we re-arranged it at midnight, that final night, as 'Fast Cars'."

The studio lay-out had been dismantled and so the band all set up around Lillywhite. They began recording at 2am and by 3.30am it was done. They came in the next day, did the vocals and mixed it – and ended up with one of the (extended) album's small gems.

"They're in the desert to dismantle an atomic bomb." Chunks were junked, including the Xanax and wine line, but the atomic reference stayed in. The album title rescued! A good job, well done. Thank you very much, ladies and gentlemen. Have a good night.

Nobody even mentioned love.

FAST CARS
Written: U2
Length: 3' 43"
Album: *How To Dismantle An Atomic Bomb*, November 2004

NO LINE ON
THE HORIZON

The original plan had been to work with Rick Rubin. Edge went to LA and got stuck into some one-on-one sessions with the legendary producer. They picked up the thread with the rest of the band in Abbey Road Studios in London and made 'Window In The Skies', a new track to put on the *U218 Singles* album, which brilliantly crossed the Beatles, the Stones and David Bowie in a heady pop brew. They also worked up 'The Saints Are Coming', which was to become a collaboration with Green Day for a New Orleans charity, Music Rising. But they weren't sure if this was the direction they needed to take for the follow-up to *How To Dismantle An Atomic Bomb*.

Somewhere in there, from all of the sessions, they had uncovered the bones of an otherworldly music that hinted at the Arabic. Bono had been invited for a few years running to the festival of sacred music in Fez, in Morocco. The thought occurred that he should go. Maybe, he said to Edge, they could all take a trip to get out of their comfort zone? "To our surprise, Adam and Larry showed huge enthusiasm for the idea," Edge recalls.

There was a feeling in the camp that this album needed to attempt something audacious, that they should write what Bono had taken to calling 'future hymns'. If there was a reference point it was *Achtung Baby*: masks and characters were back. They'd have to change the rules again, reinvent themselves, make a record that would chart new territory creatively, and sound like nothing they had ever done before. If Berlin had been the catalyst for what many people consider the band's greatest record, then perhaps Morocco could provide the magic spark for their next meisterwork.

They asked long-time producer collaborators Brian Eno and Daniel Lanois to join the expedition, only this time to sit in as part of the songwriting team. The group of six formed a circle in a riad right by the walls of the ancient city, the clear Moroccan skies overhead, and set to work, recording everything. Inspired by the setting, Brian Eno in particular came into his own. There was an atmosphere, an ambience, a spice to what they did that felt like the start of something special, if only they could bottle it! As ever, that would be the hard part…

NO LINE ON THE HORIZON

NO LINE ON THE HORIZON
Written: U2/ Eno/Lanois
Length: 4' 12"
Album: *No Line On The Horizon*, March 2009

It began with Larry. This time his drums served as the notice board, the rhythm he was toying with his statement of intent. It was a kind of Bo Diddley groove and he was nailing it down good. Eno, who was positioned in the station beside him in the studio, sampled it. Now they had a bedrock. The Edge began to improvise over that. It was coming together, but what did it sound like? Space age rock 'n' roll, Lanois said. Edge, who had become acquainted with Benjamin Curtis, ex- of Secret Machines and now with School Of Seven Bells – the man who got him into Death By Audio's latest fuzz pedal – knew exactly what Danny meant and went for it. When he heard the track later, Curtis couldn't believe what the U2 guitarist had done with the pedal on 'No Line…' churning out a grinding rhythm guitar part that Edge himself conceptualised as 21st Century distortion. Eno, in his element, added Germanic Krautrock touches.

The vocal happened early: Bono had lyrics sketched out that seemed to suit. "In my head it happens over 24 hours," he told *Q* magazine. When he gets up at six in the morning to work in his Killiney home, Bono looks out the window across Dublin Bay, over the Irish sea. It's a privileged view and an inspiring one. At times the sea and the sky blend in an otherworldly way that seems to erase the horizon, leaving a vision of infinity, a sense of the immense possibilities of life. But its Zen like qualities notwithstanding, more than anything else 'No Line On The Horizon' is a love song to Ali, for whom the sea becomes a metaphor. "One day she's still, the next she swells/ You can hear the universe in her sea shells." Oh oh oh oh oh oh oh oh-o…

no: always close The Edge.

MAGNIFICENT

Listening to the playback, Bono is excited. The intro sounds like it could be a show-opener. Then the guitar sweeps you back to 1979 and the sound of the fledgling U2. The vocals, too. "Ooooooh/Oooooh/Oooh": a return to *Boy*. Over the exhilarating clamour of Edge's repeat echo, arms pumping as he listens, the singer namechecks The Magnificat – a passage from the Gospel of Saint Luke that was put to music by Bach. "This is our take on that idea," he says, "It's devotional disco. This is a gospel song that transforms into the carnal, then into a song for family, for children."

But that wasn't how it started. Steve Lillywhite came to the album late. "There's a lot of Brian Eno on the album," Lillywhite told PBS radio in the US. "He's an incredible man. His job is to sort of destroy U2. He'll take one of their songs and go off and work on it and erase everything they've done. But then it'll be handed over to me. They bring me in towards the end. What's that baseball person? The closer. That's how they see me. It's like a relay race. I'll come in and add back in some things that were there before and try to make it into some sort of cohesive thing."

The track had originally been called 'French Disco'. It was slower. Not as visceral. Lillywhite encouraged them to work it up a bit. Adam Clayton conjured some Motown-inspired bass, Larry pitched in a sustained drum roll on the extended pause that becomes one of the song's most ingenious hooks, and Edge and Lanois evoked the spirit of Ennio Morricone with the reverb drenched guitars. Then Edge added a beautifully mellifluous slide solo. "It's new U2 because of the wonderful sounds on it," Lillywhite says. "But it also reminds you of old U2."

MAGNIFICENT
Written: U2/ Eno/Lanois
Length: 5' 24"
Album: *No Line On The Horizon*, March 2009
US singles chart position: 79

Time for your close-ups... the band at the Dublin Film Festival.

MOMENT OF SURRENDER

**MOMENT OF
SURRENDER**
Written: U2/
Eno/Lanois
Length: 7' 24"
Album: *No Line
On The Horizon*,
March 2009

Bono began the album with two words in his head: reverie and revelry. 'Moment of Surrender' was connected to the first part of the equation. The title borrows a term from Alcoholics Anonymous for the moment an addict admits his or her helplessness. For inspiration, Bono could look at Adam, who has been over 10 years on the dry. But the U2 bassist is just one of the many who have had to deal with their demons the hard way. "I've been surrounded a lot in my personal life by addiction," Bono says. The song turns the idea into something broader, however, that simultaneously suggests love, sex, war and religion. It is at once unapologetically modern and dreamily mystical. Bono had played with the phrase "vision over visibility" before; now, he'd found a home for it in a song that is suffused in a kind of meditative, Sufi yearning for selflessness, subtly embroidered with Middle Eastern grace-notes in the melody. Healing music.

It started with a rolling hand-drum pattern courtesy of Eno and Larry Mullen. The song started to emerge in earnest as the final chord sequence, constructed by Eno with appropriate nudges from Edge, took shape. Adam snatched a leaf out of Grandmaster Flash's 'White Lines', before switching to a trancey bass part. In a moment of collective inspiration, the six-piece U2 improvised the entire structure of the song in real time, effectively a first-take backing track that stood proudly, unbelievably intact at the end of the session. "They're supposed to be spiritual," Eno told *Rolling Stone* about the recording of 'Moment of Surrender'. "They don't spot a miracle when it hits them in the face. Nothing like that ever happened to me in my whole life." It is Lanois' favourite track on the album. "The original sketch had me in charge of the chorus," he says. "Bono would point to me: 'OK, Lanois: you sing the chorus'. It's very much a Canadian sound there, a tribute to The Band." Even more so, it recalls another great Canadian, Neil Young, in the aching use of the major seventh in the final line of the chorus. And at the heart of it, there's a wonderful George Harrison-esque guitar solo, courtesy of Edge.

"Eno was obsessed with 'Moment of Surrender'," Gavin Friday observes. "He wanted it to be the first single." An edited version that dispensed with a verse was hammered into shape and Eno was outraged. He argued passionately for the complete seven minute epic to be included and in the end it was: a soulful masterpiece that Friday describes as "Al Green on Irish steroids, so guttural and so true." A modern rock classic, it will stand forever as one of U2's most inspirational creations

UNKNOWN CALLER

The band was working on 'Unknown Caller' when the birds of Fez shat on Larry Mullen's drums. "It was just one of those great moments," Larry says. "This idyllic place – everything is perfect or close to it. The roof is open. The sun is shining. And suddenly the birds are shitting on you! That suddenly brought us down to reality." It was a moment of surreal humour amid the serious business of making great art. It's an essential part of what U2 do. They find a groove, work a potential song into shape, hammer a few different ideas together, to see if – like the birds – it'll fly. Then they do it again only differently. There were two versions of 'With Or Without You' and the band stayed up in the studio till five in the morning on the final *Joshua Tree* session, trying to figure out which one to go with. They got it right – but what if they had chosen the other one? Sometimes they'll have as many as three or four versions simmering.

The initial surge of creativity on 'Unknown Caller' had been impressive. "It came together in about four hours," Edge says. "It was a live performance and once we had hit the arrangement, we only ever played it once." Towards the end of the recording, when the process of selection was getting intense, Lillywhite came in – a pair of fresh ears. Free of the preciousness of having been involved in the improvisational stage, he saw what needed to be done to make 'Unknown Caller' brilliant. "I thought the drumming needed changing, and so we did that," he says. "And we redid some of the bass as well. I could say 'this is the chorus, but we're not expressing the chorus in the way it should be'." Listening back to a track that unfolds like a piece of choreographed Moroccan soul, Bono hints at echoes of Joy Division. There are elements of Talking Heads too – that Eno had a hand in it is clear. The song's narrator has lost his bearings: "3:33," he recounts, "when the numbers fell off the clock face" – a reference to Jeremiah 33:3 ("Call unto me and I will answer thee and show thee great and mighty things, which thou knowest not"). The song is a conversation, with the protagonist's phone taking on the role of deity, as it offers him instructions on the chorus. The language is borrowed from the world of computers. It is a song about alienation and identity, shot through with grains of optimism. "*Shout for joy/ If you get the chance,*" Bono sings and the massed voices gather on the chorus, in a very male display of togetherness, Greek chorus style: "*Oh oh oh oh/ Oh oh oh oh oh oh oh…*" The guitar solo delivers a heavy emotional payload. What Gavin Friday describes as "a new age 'Bad'" is, without doubt, another U2 classic.

UNKNOWN CALLER
Written: U2/ Eno/Lanois
Length: 6' 02"
Album: *No Line On The Horizon*, March 2009

et's go crazy!

I'LL GO CRAZY IF I DON'T GO CRAZY TONIGHT

The album had been leaning towards reverie. Everyone loved what had been done in Fez and beyond, but as the summer deadline approached it bacame clear that the album was missing something. Where was the revelry? "We needed patience," Edge says. "We went down a few blind alleys before we got songs like 'I'll Go Crazy'." The fifth track, it's the beginning of what Bono calls the *Rubber Soul* section of the record. The title had been just a line in a verse until Will.i.am of Black Eyed Peas got involved. "That line – that's a T-shirt," he told Bono. The singer thought about it. "OK, he said. "I'll make that the song!" He started to see it as this album's 'Beautiful Day' – one of the brighter, more upbeat, tracks that would make a good single (and accompanying T-shirt). The LA rapper helped with putting the original demo together, and was called in later to assist in putting the finishing touches to it, with Steve Lillywhite in charge of production. But ultimately, as the classic pop middle eight – "Baby, baby, baby/I know I'm not alone" – confirms, it is essentially a Bono and Ali love song boasting a title that makes you think: it's so right that it's hard to believe that no one ever wrote it before…

I'LL GO CRAZY IF I DON'T GO CRAZY TONIGHT
Written: U2
Length: 4' 13"
Album: *No Line On The Horizon*, March 2009

GET ON YOUR BOOTS

They'd gone so far out on the Sufi singing – the ecstatic music – that they had to rein it in. 'I'll Go Crazy' was one counterpoint. 'Get On Your Boots' was another, a shot of shamelessly hedonistic sexy, danceable, night-time electro rock, written by U2 *sans* Lanois and Eno. It began as a demo recorded on Garageband by Edge. "I put the original version together really fast, playing over a drum loop of Larry's, it sounded like punk Funkadelic," the guitarist says. "At first Brian and Danny hated it. The breakthrough in making it our own was finding the right guitar sound. The fun-fur synth treatment took us into new territory and the Eno hip hop loop gave it some hips."

For Bono there's a hint in there of the Damned, but you can hear the Rolling Stones, the Beatles, T.Rex and Primal Scream in the musical mix, too. It went through a phase with 'Four Letter Word' as the title, before metamorphosing into 'Sexy Boots'. In the end it became 'Get On Your Boots' – at 150bpm, the fastest U2 track ever.

The 'Let me in the sound' chant – delivered in a sort of Lee Dorsey 'Working In A Coalmine' rhythm (Gavin Friday describes it as Happy Mondays on acid) – came late in the process. "It was a chant we all loved," Lanois says and it makes a great additional hook. It's a moment of visceral, horny, carnival pop: yet strangely, according to Bono, it is another earnest love song in disguise, based on a family holiday in France at the start of the war in Iraq when, after a night at the fun fair, husband and wife were lying out under the stars worrying about the rumble of the air force high above them on the way to war. It was the first single release...

GET ON YOUR BOOTS

Written:	U2
Length:	3' 25"
Album:	*No Line On The Horizon*, March 2009
UK singles chart position:	12
US singles chart position:	37

STAND UP COMEDY

STAND UP COMEDY
Written: U2
Length: 3′ 49″
Album: *No Line On The Horizon*, March 2009

Some of the songs are in character. Not this one. It is Bono having a laugh at himself. "Stand up to rock stars," he sings. "Napoleon is in high heels/ Josephine be careful of small men with big ideas." It started as a very Moroccan-influenced rhythmic thing, but gradually took on a more rock 'n' roll character. Lanois remarks that it would be a great study in itself of the evolution of a U2 track – it was about six songs along the way. But it felt too crafted, and so they went in search of soul and found it in a groove where John Lennon meets Led Zeppelin meets David Bowie, with a touch of the Stone Roses thrown in. "What are you going to stand up for?" Bono asks. "What are you going to stand against? I love the idea of standing up to rock stars. Because they're a bunch of megalomaniacs." And what better weapon to use than a huge, barnstorming riff – probably the most powerful in U2's entire history – and, risking a double-entendre, the exhortation to "stand up for your love."

U2 open US President Obama's inauguration ceremony.

FEZ – BEING BORN

'The first time ever I saw your fez...'

The start of the album's third movement, it's a miniature symphony, in three parts. 'Fez – Being Born' (original working title 'Tripoli') opens like morning, through an exploratory eastern-inflected, painterly sonic squiggle. Edge had a symphonic guitar moment that was 'free time'. Lanois put one of Eno's library of beats to it; now they had something to go on! There was separate high-speed piece they'd been calling 'Being Born': it became the main body of the song, an inspired reworking of an Edge composition that led the band into one of the most original moments on the album. Marrying the two, 'Fez – Being Born' was a feat of genius. "I always look for outstanding transitional moments like that," Lanois says. "They can't be taken for granted. They have to be thought of scientifically."

The lyrics tell the story, in impressionistic strokes, of a Moroccan-French cop who's going AWOL: the lost soul of 'Stay (Faraway, So Close!) in another gender, time and space continuum. He drives through France and Spain, Bono explains, to Cadiz at the southern tip of Europe, from where you can see the fires of Africa burning. The track shifts a gear as the journey develops, Adam's bass hitting the high notes. With Eno providing Kraftwerkian keyboards, it resolves itself into a chanted unison vocal reminiscent of Talking Heads. As the lyrics recall the emergence of a child from the womb ("A speeding head, a speeding heart/I'm being born, a bleeding start/The engines roar, blood curling wail/Head first then foot/Then heart sets sail") musically it is quite staggeringly beautiful.

FEZ – BEING BORN
Written: U2/Eno/Lanois
Length: 5' 16"
Album: *No Line On The Horizon*, March 2009

WHITE AS SNOW

Daniel Lanois was working on a piece with the idea of 'future hymns' in mind. His friend Lori Anna Reid, a singer from Toronto, had begun digging up some spirituals for guidance. "One stood out to me," Lanois told *The National Post*, "It's an old church hymn called 'Oh Come, Oh Come, Emmanuel'." Dating from the 12th Century, and put to music in the 15th, coincidentally it was recorded by another Irish artist Enya on her *And Winter Came* album. Lanois put down a piano version and found a rhythm. It might have gone nowhere, but when Jim Sheridan asked for a song for his movie about the US war in Afghanistan, *Brothers*, Bono felt he had things to say on the theme. There was the war itself, the reality of invasion ("The road refuses strangers/The land the seeds we sow") and the sense of desolation it provokes in those unlucky enough to find themselves in the frontline. But the movie is also about the theme of brotherhood. Bono looked at a rough cut and was inspired: with the minor key air Lanois had unearthed in mind, he constructed the story from the perspective of a soldier in Afghanistan, and delved into his own childhood memories of life alongside his elder brother Norman for the lyrics, retaining an optimistic Christian thread ("Where might we find the lamb/As white as snow?") in a desolate story. Edge had been listening to Fleet Foxes, and their CSNY influences, with wonderful harmonies to the fore, crept into a song that harks back to the folk leanings of *Rattle and Hum*. Its inclusion meant that another ballad that Eno loved, entitled 'Winter' was left off: these are the trade-offs that are involved in shaping a U2 record.

173

WHITE AS SNOW

Written:	Traditional/U2/Eno/Lanois
Length:	4' 41"
Album:	*No Line On The Horizon*, March 2009

BREATHE

Musically, this was one that Edge cooked up. Based on the early demo, Eno proclaimed it one of his favourite U2 songs of all time. Chord-wise, it was effectively fully composed before being brought to the sessions. The waltz beat presented interesting problems, and after a few failed attempts at cutting the track, the final version was recorded without fanfare. Bono's scatter-gun vocal suggested a surreal stream-of-consciousness lyrical approach. Two completely different sets of lyrics were completed and Bono and Edge agonised over which to go with during the final recording sessions. One of the lyrics vying for inclusion was about Nelson Mandela. And the other? Bono had been reading Cormac McCarthy and came up with an impressionistic word painting, rooted in paranoia, and based on the idea of a runic encounter with an enigmatic early morning caller. It was in the mould of Dylan's 'Subterranean Homesick Blues' and REM's 'E-Bow The Letter', but the lineage goes even further back to the beat poets and Allan Ginsberg's seminal raps, the verses teeming forth in an urgent orgy of colour and detail, observing a world that's busy turning itself upside down. The song takes place on Bloomsday, 16 June – the day on which James Joyce set his Dublin masterpiece *Ulysses*. But the character at the heart of it – a Bono alter-ego if ever there was one ("Coming from a long line of travelling salespeople on my mother's side") – ultimately finds redemption. The band re-recorded it and Steve Lillywhite provided the finishing touches. "What have they done to the Fez version?" Eno asked. Turned it into a monster, that's what!

BREATHE
Written: U2/
Eno/Lanois
Length: 5' 00"
Album: *No Line
On The Horizon*,
March 2009

Chewing the cud with David Letterman.

CEDARS OF LEBANON

**CEDARS OF
LEBANON**
Written: U2/
Eno/Lanois
Length: 4′ 16″
Album: *No Line
On The Horizon*,
March 2009

Of all the characters on *No Line On The Horizon*, the journalistic narrator of 'Cedars of Lebanon' is the most clearly drawn. "I'd just kind of got worn out with my own biography," Bono says. "The last two albums were very personal. The irony, of course, as Oscar Wilde taught us, is that the mask reveals the man."

From Sarajevo to El Salvador to Addis Ababa, Bono has spent time with the men and women who deliver the news from the frontline, and so he feels an unusual empathy with them. Danny Lanois got the musical inspiration for the mood of the song from a piece he and Eno had done back in the 1980s with an artist by the name of Harold Budd. "It's really thick with ambience," he says. But the track fully kicked into life when Larry came in with a killer drum part. "I've a deep conviction that were I not doing what I'm doing now, I'd be doing what you are," Bono told Olaf Tyaransen of *Hot Press*. "I'd probably be writing about music and art and all my other interests, but I can imagine I'd also find myself in very unsafe places because that's my tendency."

It is a powerful song, rich in observation and detail that reminds us of what rock stars and war correspondents might have in common ("I'm here 'cos I don't want to go home.") There is a lot of Bono and U2 in the portrait of the journalist, not least – as Bono has acknowledged – in the closing verse: "Choose your enemies carefully 'cos they will define you/Make them interesting 'cos in some ways they will mind you/They're not there in the beginning but when your story ends/ Gonna last longer with you than your friends."

But 'Cedars of Lebanon' is a less than veiled criticism too of the war in Iraq. "I think of all the energy that went into that," he told *Rolling Stone*'s Brian Hiatt, "and the bravery of the men and women who served, and I think of what those resources could have achieved, if only the lives of the poorest of the poor were as valuable as the idea of bringing democracy to the desert." Amen to that.

verleaf: Where The
Streets Have Their
ame: a NY street
ecomes U2 Way.

SINGLES, B-SIDES AND EXTRA-CURRICULAR ACTIVITIES

PASSENGERS

Released in November 1995, *Passengers: Original Soundtracks 1* was a one-album side-project for U2, recorded by the band as the Passengers, together with Brian Eno, as a tribute to their favourite cinema soundtracks. The loose idea was that Eno would call the creative shots and U2 would obey…

United Colours of Plutonium

U2 recorded this track thinking of the bullet train in Japan. "We wanted that sense of speed," says Bono. "We wanted it to sound like being aboard the bullet train." Originally U2 and Eno recorded an extended improvisation piece. It was cut down to seven minutes, then Howie B played around with it and it was snipped down to five-and-a-half. "It's a helluva sound as an opening track," says Bono. "But probably still a bit too long."

Slug

'Slug' was an attempt to paint a picture of the lights coming on in a city like Tokyo. "It's like a Christmas tree," explains Bono of the sweet musical tinkling that opens the track. It was originally called 'Seibu', after a Japanese department store. "It's a portrait, like '…Arms Around The World', of somebody a little the worse for wear," says Bono, "which we all were in Tokyo, because it was the end of the tour."

Your Blue Room

Musically, on this track, U2 were thinking of Serge Gainsbourg, yet Bono's voice has the deep, reassuring quality adopted by Leonard Cohen on his songs of seduction. "It's my favourite song on the record," says Bono. "If we weren't keeping a low profile – we have to, because people get sick of us if we're always putting stuff out – we'd have really pushed it." It also features Adam Clayton's first lead vocal as the bassist's voice comes in at the end, quietly chatting in the background as if in a late-night conversation post-sex.

Always Forever Now

While U2 were recording as Passengers, somebody scrawled a slogan on a blackboard in their new Dublin studio: MAKE THE MUSIC OF THE FUTURE YOU WANT TO LIVE IN. The album was to reflect a positive vision of where Earth was heading, and 'Always Forever Now' fits the bill. The title was based on a picture by artist Damien Hirst. "It's just an affirmation," says Bono. "The words are self-explanatory."

A Different Kind of Blue

Some reviewers claimed U2 were nowhere to be heard on 'A Different Kind of Blue'. At best, they were only partially right. Bono came up with the title and the beginnings of a jazz song to go with it, Edge did a version of it and then Eno sneaked into the studio overnight. "In a sense, it's a hybrid," says Bono. "I'd say the perfect hour to listen to the record is either at dawn or in the half-hour of twilight, when the sun is going down. What it suggests to me – 'Twilight breaking through' – is getting up out of bed for the night."

Beach Sequence

"That was me playing one-finge piano," says Bono. "In fact, it w called 'One Finger Piano' at one point." Which only goes to show that it doesn't really take an instrumental genius to produce beautiful notes. Like 'Your Blue Room', 'Beach Sequence' was used in the Michelangelo Antonioni and Wim Wenders collaboration *Par-Dela Les Nuag* (*Beyond The Clouds*).

Miss Sarajevo

After MacPhisto phoned Pavaro live from the stage in Bologna during the Italian leg of the *Zooropa* tour, Pavarotti began phoning U2 demanding to reco a song together. Bono became obsessed with the idea of findin the right track and U2 came up with a track that ended up on t Passengers album. 'We came up with the libretto by impersonati my father singing in the bath, impersonating Pavarotti,' admit Bono. The song was about the Serbian siege of Bosnians in Sarajevo, a city that U2 had ma a satellite connection to on the night they also phoned Pavarot Bono was to finance and produ a film on the underground resistance in the city. The song was premiered at the annual Pavarotti and Friends concert in Modena, Italy on September 12 1995. It was released as a singl in aid of the War Child charity two months later and only prevented from being a UK

ristmas No 1 by Michael
ckson's 'Earth Song'.

o Okashi
ian Eno contacted a Japanese
nger, Holi, who had moved to
ndon. She met U2 in the studio
th nothing planned, but Bono
as impressed nonetheless: "She
pt using this phrase over and
er – ito okashi." The term
eans 'something beautiful' and
oli used that simple idea to
eate a short, evocative, almost
iku-style lyric in Japanese in a
flective piece evoking the sun
ing in the East.

ne Minute Warning
2 often played along to
panese animation movies being
own on a studio TV as they
corded *Original Soundtracks 1*.
ey were greatly influenced by
an Luc Godard's *Alphaville* and
en got a request to produce a
ece for *Ghost in the Shell*, an
imation feature directed by
amoru Oshia. The
provisations inspired by
phaville seemed to fit – and
en Howie B got to work on it.
When Howie came in, he left out
ge elements that we had
ought were very important,"
ys Edge. "Suddenly that was
ry refreshing."

rpse
orpse' saw U2 twist a blues
ical convention to have the
ng's protagonist moan that the
ains binding him were too long.
e Edge adopted the persona of
character on Death Row and
ng it as a dirge-like
knowledgement of what can
ppen to someone who doesn't
cognise any limits to human

behaviour. It is, you could say, a
different kind of blues.

Elvis Ate America
This song began life as 'Elvis:
American David', a beat poem
written by Bono as the preface to
an art exhibition book named *2 x
Immortal: Elvis + Marilyn*. "It's just
like a list," explains Bono. "Some
people don't get that concept but
the American David idea is
interesting. I've always conceived
of David in the Bible as the first
blues singer." The list became a
rap and Howie B made it into a
song. "He's the guy who's
chanting 'Elvis' throughout it,"
confirms Bono.

Plot 180
In *A Year With Swollen
Appendices*, his diary of 1995,
Brian Eno unveiled some of the
rationale behind the *Original
Soundtracks 1* concept – namely,
that an awareness that music is
being composed for a film
stimulates the imagination to
think pictorially and scenically. It
also opened up opportunities for
humour, and 'Plot 180' sounded
like a send-up of some standard
stereotypical piece of Hollywood
flim-flam.

Theme from The Swan
Eno would go into the studio
before anyone else and find a loop
to operate as the basis of a track.
The band would then come in and
build on top of it. Eno's signature
was supposed to be clearly
discernable and it was on 'Theme
from The Swan', a slow, haunting
piece where he plays the cello.

Theme from Let's Go Native
There were times when U2 had

sounded like Talking Heads – and
there is, of course, a lot of Brian
Eno in Talking Heads. "He'd
always talked about doing an
experimental record with us,
along the lines of *Bush of Ghosts*
that he'd done with David Byrne,"
says Edge. With that in mind, this
impressive African-influenced
rhythm piece, with heavy bass
and lolloping drums, was a fitting
wrap-up for Passengers.

THE MILLION DOLLAR HOTEL
U2 and Daniel Lanois contributed
five songs to the soundtrack of
this 2000 Wim Wenders movie
based on a drama story by Bono
and Nicholas Klein and starring
Milla Jovovich and Mel Gibson.
Bono was inspired to sketch out
the movie's storyline when the
band did a photo shoot at LA's
Million Dollar Hotel in 1987. "I
think it is sad," laughs Bono, "but
I know a lot about hotels."

Stateless
'Stateless' came out of a
soundcheck jam before a U2
show in Australia which they
returned to during the recording
of *All That You Can't Leave
Behind*. "It's mostly Bono," says
Daniel Lanois. "He picked up
Edge's guitar, with those huge
sounds, and came up with this on
the spot." "It's like a Robert
Johnson blues," avers Bono.
"Kind of a sci-fi blues."

Dancin' Shoes
Producer Daniel Lanois confirms
that Bono being involved in *The
Million Dollar Hotel* at the same
time as the recording of *All That
You Can't Leave Behind* was not
regarded as good timing. "Bono
asked me to do the soundtrack

with him and I largely did it so we could finish the U2 record," he says. The pair created 'Dancin' Shoes' from a chord sequence that Lanois had lying around.'

The Ground Beneath Her Feet

Before he wrote his *The Ground Beneath Her Feet* novel, author Salman Rushdie – then lying low after being the victim of a religious fatwa after the publication of *The Satanic Verses* – stayed at Bono's place in Killiney. Rushdie wrote lyrics for a song of the same name, which Bono shaped a song around. The singer put it forward for *All That You Can't Leave Behind* but found the band unenthusiastic and so used it on *The Million Dollar Hotel*. Wim Wenders described it as "… the song that really defines the movie. When I heard it, I thought he had so perfectly grasped the spirit of the film."

Falling At Your Feet

This beautiful Bob Dylan-like litany song found Bono back in familiar terrain, echoing the adoration –

abasement, even – of 'Mysterious Ways'. Written for the movie, it was constructed around a chord sequence that Lanois had already sketched out. "I like love songs that are bittersweet," explains Bono. "I don't want to hear a song that reddens my face when I hear it on the radio."

Never Let Me Go

Trumpeter John Hassell got a writing credit on 'Never Let Me Go', a song that began with a jam over which Bono improvised a lyric that was later refined. "This is the first U2 song that sounds specifically influenced by Gavin Friday," said *Hot Press* writer Peter Murphy. "I wouldn't rule it out," says Bono. "He's influenced pretty much everything else. He certainly lent me the big shoes."

OTHERS
Boy-Girl

The third track on *U23*, the band's legendary Ireland-only debut recording, 'Boy-Girl' was born when U2 and the Virgin Prunes

took the title and wrote two separate songs. "Ours was dealing with bisexuality," recalls Gavin Friday. "They were talking about a more conventional form of love, with quite a strong boyhood-to-manhood theme going down."

Another Day

'Another day' was recorded at t same time as *U23* and released February 1980. The theme was one of adolescent angst, with Bono struggling to be optimistic despite waking up to 'the toll of another dull day'.

11 O'clock Tick Tock

Late one evening, a teenage Gavin Friday stuck a note on his friend Bono's bedroom door: "1 o'clock, tick tock. Gav called." Ever the magpie, Bono stole the phrase for a song that criticised the style self-consciousness that dominated the UK's music scene at the end of the 1970s. "I've n time for cynicism with no direction," commented Bono at

e time. "I've no time for casual
els." Produced by Martin
mnett, '11 O'Clock Tick Tock'
came U2's second single.

uch
iginally called 'Trevor', possibly
er the Virgin Prunes' Trevor
ongman, the Martin Hamnett-
oduced 'Touch' was the b-side
'11 O'Clock Tick Tock'.

ings To Make And Do
s whimsical instrumental
peared on the B-side of 'A Day
thout Me' in August 1980. "No
e else was in town and we
eded a B-side," recalls Edge. "So
st did it on the 4-track cassette –
t me in the rehearsal room."

Swallow
needed a song for the b-side of
e". "It was done in a mad
nic," says Edge. "It was a case
two hours to go, let's do it.
nny Swallow was one of our
tes, called Reggie Manual."

Celebration
corded as a single between
tober and War, 'A Celebration'
s intended to fill a gap caused
the relative lack of singles on
e former. Like much of October,
eflected U2's Christian
mmitment, although the Dublin
erences to Christ Church and
untjoy give the hint of a social
text. Bono remembers the
eo. "We had itinerant boys as
e four horsemen of the
ocalypse and me in ridiculous
d pants in Kilmainham jail. I
nk I had a badger on my head,
well. Some pieces of music are
scured by the haircuts, I think
fair to say."

Trash Trampoline And The Party Girl

Written, according to one rumour, about the Edge's wife-to-be, Aislinn O'Sullivan, this B-side to 'A Celebration' was trashy, throwaway and fun. But who was Trash Trampoline? The smart money was on Adam Clayton, who played the field in a way the rest of U2 never did.

Treasure (Whatever Happened To Pete The Chop)?

Written about Pete the Chop, a friend of early U2 management associate Andrew Whiteway, 'Pete The Chop' was so poppy that Paul McGuinness wanted to release it as a single. "It was very melodic," says The Edge, "but not really very good." It eventually surfaced as 'Treasure', the B-side of 'New Year's Day'.

Endless Deep

Adam Clayton focussed on the business side of U2 in the early days but by War he was coming into his own as a bass player. This was evident on this track, the B-side of 'Two Hearts Beat As One'.

Boomerang I and Boomerang II

U2 had always liked Talking Heads so it was almost inevitable that the influence would show when they began to work with the band's producer, Brian Eno. 'Boomerang' came in two mixes, which accompanied different releases of 'Pride (In The Name Of Love)' as a single. "I think African influences were important there," says The Edge. "That was when the first wave of African music was hitting the West: Fela Kuti, King Sunny Ade and all those people."

The Three Sunrises

U2, Eno and Lanois concluded that 'The Three Sunrises' would not have worked on The Unforgettable Fire but its Beatles-style pop harmonies and stabbing, almost hard-rock guitar made it an interesting departure. Neil McCormick of Hot Press called it "One of U2's finest out-takes."

Love Comes Tumbling

This was relatively unfamiliar company for U2 – a simple, gentle, rhythmic love song with a distinctly romantic feel. It was released first with the 'The Unforgettable Fire' single, with the 'Pride (In The Name Of Love)' double 7" pack and on Wide Awake In America.

Bass Trap

Produced by Eno and Lanois, 'Bass Trap' was a bonus track on the 12" single of 'The Unforgettable Fire'. "Brian [Eno] used a really cheap electronic device to trap a bass figure that Adam had played," says Edge. "It was sort of like what Philip Glass does with his work."

Sixty Seconds In Kingdom Come

This was an extra track on the double 7" single of 'The Unforgettable Fire' but – despite its great title – Edge dismisses it as a piece of music that never went anywhere.

Luminous Times (Hold Onto Love)

The piano-driven 'Luminous Times' didn't make the cut for The Joshua Tree but surfaced on the 'With Or Without You' single.

It sounds improvised but has a quality of emotional honesty running through it that is hugely impressive as Bono struggles to come to terms with love's contradictions and complexities.

Walk To The Water
This also didn't make *The Joshua Tree* but Philip Lynott's influence is discernable in the gentle evocation of some past, more romantic Dublin – and might Bono have been trying to describe the courtship between his own father and mother on Dublin's north side? Either way, it was an impressive first flirtation with rap.

Spanish Eyes
'Spanish Eyes', released as a B-side to 'I Still Haven't Found What I'm Looking For', ranked alongside 'Desire' and 'Hawkmoon 269' as a statement of intense, primal lust. "I think it is Ali, to be honest," says Edge. "I think that's what Bono was on about."

Deep In The Heart
With love and sex not heavily represented on *The Joshua Tree*, it was left to B-sides and bonus tracks such as this to do so. Like 'Spanish Eyes', 'Deep In The Heart' does so powerfully, depicting a Lolita-style scene with an almost disquieting sense of detachment.

The Sweetest Thing
Bono was not totally convinced about 'The Sweetest Thing'. It would have made a powerful, radio-friendly single – but might it have tilted the perception of the band in a way that might ultimately prove unhelpful? It was

consequently omitted from *The Joshua Tree* and turned up on the B-side of 'Where The Streets Have No Name', where Adam supplied a massive, rumbling bass attack to give musical root to Bono's intense, besotted ode to Ali.

Race Against Time
Like 'The Sweetest Thing', 'Race Against Time' – which also appeared on the 'Where The Streets Have No Name' 12" – is interesting as an indicator of the album U2 might have made instead of *The Joshua Tree*. "It was a kind of Afro-centric piece I put together," says Edge. "We realised it wasn't going to make the album so left it to one side."

Hallelujah (Here She Comes)
The B-side to 'Desire', this was a piece of upful gospel rock that was written by Edge and Bono in John Heather's house in Connemara.

A Room At The Heartbreak Hotel
This song saw Bono explore his fascination with Elvis Presley to reflect on the themes of love, lust, fidelity and betrayal without achieving the condensed poetic power that *Achtung Baby* was to reveal. The Edge calls it "Gospel meets Suicide" and it appeared on the 12" of 'Angel of Harlem'.

Alex Descends Into Hell For A Bottle Of Milk
Director Ron Daniels approached U2 to write an original score for the Royal Shakespeare Company's theatrical production of Anthony Burgess's *A Clockwork Orange* in 1990. "He wanted a hit musical," says Edge. "We warned him we

weren't very good at hits." Burgess was reportedly disdainful towards U2's efforts but, says Edge, "I've a feeling it was just a reaction against the fact that it wasn't Beethoven, so I'm not too upset." A few of the snatches of music U2 prepared were combined for this track, a B-side to 'The Fly'.

Lady With The Spinning Head
The original demo backing track that spawned both 'The Fly' and 'Light My Way' on *Achtung Baby*, 'Lady With The Spinning Head' had a good groove courtesy of Larry's carefree drum part. U2 tracks that aren't laboured over tend to sound like someone else and Primal Scream and Happy Mondays lurked in the shadows here.

Where Did It All Go Wrong?
When George Best was at the height of his powers and fame, was staying in a suite at the Dorchester Hotel. As the famous and possibly apocryphal – story goes, as a grizzled old porter from his home town of Belfast brought the footballer up yet more champagne, he looked at Best lying on the bed, surrounded by beautiful women and wads of cash, and asked: "George, when did it all go wrong?" "It's a great story," says Edge. "We just wrote the song around that quote."

Salome
This was recorded at STS Studios in Dublin, which played a pivotal role in U2's development. It had dual existence: a blistering R&B version on the cassette single of 'Even Better Than The Real Thing' and a Zooromancer dance remix

the 'Who's Gonna Ride Your
ld Horses?' single.

ow Dancing

no wrote 'Slow Dancing' for
llie Nelson, sent it off and
ard nothing. Assuming the
untry star was not interested,
recorded it and put it on the
ay (Faraway So Close)' single
ly for Nelson to make contact
th the band next time he played
blin. Nelson recorded a vocal
d this appeared as an additional
ck on the 'If God Will Send His
gels' single.

ttoms

his was one of Brian [Eno]'s
zy mixes of 'Zoo Station',"
plains Edge. "He did different
ototype mixes which helped us
get to our final version."
ottoms' appeared as an extra
ck on the Japanese version of
iginal Soundtracks 1.

ld Me, Thrill Me, Kiss Me,
ll Me

no was initially dismissive of the
ea of U2 contributing a song to
e Batman Forever soundtrack
t Edge was keener: "I figured
d be good for us to be involved
something that's basically
owaway and light-hearted."
e band revisited a piece they
d been unable to finish for
oropa and the cartoon video
at accompanied it was
minated for Best Video from a
m at the MTV Awards, losing
t to Seal.

ssion Impossible

ictly speaking, this theme from
ssion Impossible isn't a U2 track
t Adam Clayton and Larry

Mullen Jnr, underlining something
that is too often ignored: they
make a great rhythm section, and
one which has been absolutely
central to U2's success.

North and South of the River

Written with Christy Moore in
1995, U2's version appeared on
the CD single of 'Staring At The
Sun'. At heart it's a political song
about the difficulties of
reconciling Nationalist and
Unionist traditions in Northern
Ireland and is a companion piece
to U2's other songs about the
national question, from 'Sunday
Bloody Sunday' to 'Please' and
'Peace On Earth'.

Two Shots of Happy One Shot
of Sad

Bono was proud of this song,
which in his head was being sung
by Frank Sinatra. He tried to get
Old Blue Eyes to sing it but Sinatra
didn't bite, which is a shame, as it
captures his persona superbly,
peppered with sparkling nuggets
that temper the braggadocio of
'My Way'. Produced by Nellee
Hooper, it was released on the 'If
God Will Send His Angels' single.

I'm Not Your Baby

'I'm Not Your Baby', an
instrumental piece that would not
be out of place on Passengers,
was U2 gone trip-hop. Produced
by Howie B and Flood, it's
engaging in its combination of
sonics and rhythm but is
essentially background music.

Summer Rain

Written at Larry's place in the
south of France, 'Summer Rain', a
B-side to 'Beautiful Day', is a

gentle acoustic track in a minor
key that resonates of the 1960s.
Bono muses on how he lost
himself to the summer rain: you
can almost see the clouds rolling
in over Provence. "I love that
tune," says Edge. "It just didn't
quite measure up against other
tunes on the record [All That You
Can't Leave Behind]."

Big Girls Are Best

From the Pop sessions, this didn't
surface until the release of the
'Stuck In A Moment' single. The
melody owes more than a bit to
John Lennon, as does the
sentiment of homage to a
departed mother. The title is
hardly politically correct, but Edge
says: "I think when Bono talks
about big girls, he means large
girls – not big-breasted. He's
talking about women who aren't
stick insects. It's pretty tongue-in-
cheek and throwaway."

Always

'Always' is the original band jam
that gave birth to 'Beautiful Day'.
"It really wasn't that unique or
special," says Edge. "So when we
finished 'Beautiful Day', we went
back and said, 'That's a B-side.' It
doesn't really stand up."

183

CHRONOLOGY

1960 March 13: Adam Clayton born in Chinnor, Oxfordshire. May 10: Paul Hewson born in the Rotunda Hospital, Dublin.

1961 August 8: Dave Evans born in Barking Maternity Hospital, east London. October 31: Larry Mullen born in Artane, Dublin.

1974 September: Iris Hewson dies of a brain haemorrhage four days after collapsing at her own father's funeral.

1976 Autumn: As Feedback, Paul Hewson, Dik and Dave Evans, Larry Mullen Jr and Adam Clayton play their debut gig at Dublin's Mount Temple Comprehensive School. The highlight of their 10-minute set is a cover of Peter Frampton's 'Show Me the Way'. They later become The Hype.

1978 March 17: On St. Patrick's Day The Hype win £500 and some studio time at a Limerick talent contest sponsored by Harp Lager. March 20: The Hype change their name to U2. Dik Evans leaves the band following a farewell gig at Howth Community Centre. May 25: Paul McGuinness sees U2 live for the first time at a gig in Dublin's Project Arts Centre and decides to become their manager. September 9: U2 support The Stranglers at a gig in the Top Hat ballroom. Playing to 2,500 people, it is their biggest gig to date. They receive a fee of £50. December: U2 support The Greedy Bastards, a band made up of members of the Sex Pistols and Thin Lizzy, at The Stardust nightclub in Dublin.

1979 May: U2 play the first of six now legendary afternoon gigs at the Dandelion Market in Dublin. September: Their debut record, an EP entitled *U23*, is released in Ireland only, on CBS Records. December 1: Having borrowed £3,000 from family and friends to finance a short English tour, U2 play their debut London gig as support for the Dolly Mixtures in the Moonlight Club in West Hampstead.

1980 January: U2 win five awards in the *Hot Press* readers' poll, beating both the Boomtown Rats and Thin Lizzy in most categories. February 26: Their second single 'Another Day' is released in Ireland on CBS and U2 play a sold-out show in Dublin's National Stadium. March 23: U2 sign a major international recording deal with Island Records. May 23: U2's first release for Island, a Martin Hannett-produced single called '11 O'Clock Tick Tock', is released in Ireland and the UK. October 20: U2's debut album, *Boy*, is released. December 6: U2 play their debut US gig at The Ritz in New York.

1981 March 3: *Boy* is released in America and U2 begin a support tour over there with a gig in the Bayou Club in Washington. October 12: U2's second album *October* is released. It enters the British charts at No. 11.

1982 March 3: U2 play the first of 14 support dates with the J. Geils Band in the Lee County Arena at Fort Meyers in Florida. August 8: U2 begin working

with Steve Lillywhite on their third album in Windmill Lane Studios, Dublin. August 21: Bono marries childhood sweetheart Alison Stewart in Raheny, Dublin.

1983 February 28: U2's third album, *War*, is released and goes to No. 1 in the UK. March 31: U2 perform 'Two Heart Beat as One' on *Top of the Pops*. June 5: U2 play the Red Rocks amphitheatre in Denver. Despite adverse weather conditions, more than 9,000 fans show up. The gig is recorded and later released on video. Some tracks also appear on the live mini-album *Under a Blood Red Sky*, released later in 1983. July: The Edge marries Aislinn O'Sullivan. November 22: U2 play their debut Japanese gig in Osaka. December: U2 are voted 'Band O' The Year' in the *Rolling Stone* writers' poll.

1984 May 7: U2 hole up in Slane Castle, Co. Meath, to record with new producers Brian Eno and Daniel Lanois. August 1: Mother Records is established by the band as an outlet for new Irish talent. July 8: Bono joins Bob Dylan on stage at Slane Castle. He sings along on 'Leopard Skin Pillbox Hat' and 'Blowing in the Wind'. October 1: *The Unforgettable Fir* is released worldwide.

1985 February: Sales of *The Unforgettable Fire* pass a million. April 1: U2 sell out Madison Square Garden in New York. May: *Wide Awake in America* is released.

July 13: Following an introduction by Jack Nicholson, U2 steal the show at Live Aid. Their album and concert ticket sales treble over the next few months.

986 May 17: U2 play their only European date of 1986 at the Self Aid festival in the RDS Showgrounds, Dublin.
June 4: U2 join Peter Gabriel, Sting and others for the first date of the *Conspiracy of Hope* tour in aid of Amnesty International.
July 3: U2 crew member Greg Carroll is killed in a motorcycle accident in Dublin.
August 1: Recording sessions for *The Joshua Tree* begin in Dublin.
Autumn: Bono visits El Salvador and Nicaragua on the invitation of Rene Castro. His experiences there will form the basis of many of the songs on *The Joshua Tree*.

987 March 9: *The Joshua Tree* is released and quickly goes to No. 1 worldwide.
March 27: U2 perform an impromptu gig on the roof of a liquor store in downtown Los Angeles to film a video for 'Where the Streets Have No Name'.
April 27: U2 become the third rock band to appear on the cover of *Time* magazine, after the Beatles and the Who.
May: Sales of *The Joshua Tree* pass even million.
June 27: U2 play a homecoming gig at Croke Park Stadium, Dublin.
November 8: An IRA bomb explodes in Enniskillen, Northern Ireland, killing 13 people. Onstage at the McNichols Arena in Denver, Bono launches an emotional attack on paramilitaries in Northern Ireland before the band

perform a highly-charged version of 'Sunday Bloody Sunday'. The scene winds up in the *Rattle and Hum* movie.
November 11: U2 play an impromptu free gig to 'Save the Yuppie' in front of 20,000 people at the Justin Herman Plaza in San Francisco. During the show Bono spray-paints 'ROCK & ROLL – STOP THE TRAFFIC' on the nearby Vaillancourt Fountain.

1988 February: U2 move to Los Angeles to begin on the *Rattle and Hum* movie.
March 2: They win 'Best Vocal of the Year' for 'I Still Haven't Found What I'm Looking For' and 'Album of the Year' for *The Joshua Tree* at the Grammy Awards.
October 10: The *Rattle and Hum* album is released.

1989 August 6: Adam Clayton is arrested in Dublin on minor drug charges. He is later ordered to pay £25,000 to The Women's Aid Refuge Centre by a District Judge.
September 21: The *Lovetown* tour kicks off in Australia.
December 31: After months of non-stop touring, U2 play the last of four packed nights in Dublin's Point Depot. At the end of the gig Bono announces their intention to go away and "dream it all up again".

1990 November: U2 begin recording their new album, with Daniel Lanois producing, in Berlin's Hansa Studios. Brian Eno later joins them to help with the production.

1991 March: U2 return to Dublin for further recording at STS and

Windmill Lane Studios.
November 18: U2's seventh album, *Achtung Baby*, is released to widespread critical acclaim.

1992 February 27: U2 record a live version of 'One' from a soundcheck in Florida for broadcast on *Top of the Pops*.
February 29: The *Zoo TV* tour kicks off with a gig at the Lakeland Arena in Florida. Support is by the Pixies.
March 27: Bono orders 10,000 pizzas for the audience at a gig in Detroit. Speedy Pizzas eventually manage to deliver 100.
May 7: The European leg of the *Zoo TV* tour opens with a gig in the Palais Omnisports De Bercy Centre in Paris. Support is by Fatima Mansions.
June 19: U2 play alongside Kraftwerk, Public Enemy and Big Audio Dynamite II at the 'Stop Sellafield' show in the G-Mex Centre in Manchester.
August 1: The Outside Broadcast leg of the Zoo TV tour opens with a gig in the Hersheypark Stadium in Hershey, Pennsylvania.
August 28: During a New York interview with Dave Herman for Rockline (a syndicated radio broadcast on some 300 local stations across America), US Presidential candidate Bill Clinton contacts U2 live on air.

1993 January 20: Larry and Adam team up with REM's Michael Stipe and Mike Mills in Washington for a performance of 'One' at the MTV 1993 Rock & Roll Inaugural Ball for newly elected American President Bill Clinton.
February: U2 begin to record new material in Dublin.

July 5: The *Zooropa* album is released worldwide.

August 11: Salman Rushdie joins U2 on stage in front of 70,000 people at Wembley Stadium.

September 3: The Edge makes his first ever solo appearance at the MTV Awards in Los Angeles, where he performs 'Numb' in front of a mini-version of the *Zoo TV* set.

October 1: U2 play a version of Thin Lizzy's 'The Boys Are Back in Town' at Gavin Friday's wedding reception in the Clarence Hotel in Dublin (which they'd recently purchased).

November: Bono records the vocal for his duet with Frank Sinatra, 'I've Got You Under My Skin', in a Dublin studio.

November 12: The final leg of the tour – dubbed *Zoomerang* – opens with a gig in the Melbourne Cricket Ground.

December 10: U2 play the final gig of the Zoo TV tour at the Tokyo Dome in Japan. Support is by Big Audio Dynamite II.

1994 January 19: Bono inducts Rita Marley into The Rock & Roll Hall of Fame in New York's Waldorf Astoria Hotel.

February: U2 issue a writ challenging the Performing Rights Society on their exclusive right to collect songwriting royalties for performances of songs.

March: *Zooropa* wins the 'Best Alternative Album' award at the Grammys.

April: Larry Mullen and Adam Clayton record four tracks with Nanci Griffith for her *Flyer* album.

April 5: The *Live In Sydney* video is released in Europe.

November: U2 and Brian Eno spend two weeks recording new material in a West London recording studio.

1995 February: Bono and The Edge team up with veteran Irish songwriter Christy Moore to record 'North and South of the River' in Dublin's Windmill Lane Studios. Produced by Steve Lillywhite, the track is available in Ireland only.

March 30: Bono joins Prince for some parts of 'The Cross' at his after-show performance in Dublin's PoD nightclub.

April: Bono introduces a reading by Beat poet Allen Ginsberg at the Cúirt Festival Of Literature in Galway.

Summer: U2, Eno, Howie B. and other Passengers spend five weeks recording in Dublin.

June 1: U2 release their first single of the year, 'Hold Me, Thrill Me, Kiss Me, Kill Me', a track that features in the *Batman Forever* soundtrack. It goes to No. 2 in the UK, No. 16 in America and No. 1 in Australia and Ireland.

June 18: U2 give their first major interview in two years to Liam Mackey of *The X-Press*, a rebel organ launched by journalists who had found themselves unemployed when The Irish Press Group closed down. It is later reprinted in *Hot Press*.

September 12: Bono, The Edge and Brian Eno premier 'Miss Sarajevo' at the annual Pavarotti And Friends concert in Modena, Italy.

November 6: Passengers' *Original Soundtracks 1* is released worldwide. On the same day, Tina Turner releases 'Goldeneye' – the theme to the new 007 movie, written by Bono and The Edge – on Capitol Records.

1996 January: U2 begin working on a new album in Dublin.

April: The band relocate to Miami for further work on the album.

May 1: Adam and Larry release their version of the *Mission Impossible* theme track. It goes Top 10 in the US, the UK and numerous other territories.

July: The first deadline to finish *Pop* is missed. Release date put back.

September: Second deadline missed. The decision not to release album till 1997 follows soon afterwards.

1997 January: Early snippets from *Pop* are leaked on the internet.

February: 'Discothèque' single is finally released and goes straight to No. 1 in 13 countries. Later on in the month, on Ash Wednesday, U2 launch the *Pop* album and the *Pop-Mart* tour in a K-Mart supermarket in Manhattan.

May: U2's *Pop-Mart* tour opens in Las Vegas.

August: Following objections from residents in the area, Ireland's Supreme Court finally clears the way for U2 to play back-to-back concerts at Lansdowne Road in Dublin.

October: Bono makes good his 1995 promise to the people of the city as U2 play to 45,000 in Sarajevo.

1998 April: The band bring the final leg of *Pop-Mart* to a close with a 67,000 sell-out show at the Johannesburg Stadium in South Africa.

May: U2 receive the ultimate accolade: an appearance in *The Simpsons*, during which Homer interrupts their concert in Springfield to tell the crowd – via the giant screen – that he should be the town's next sanitation commisioner.

October: U2, along with Ash, The Divine Comedy, Van Morrison, Boyzone, The Corrs, Sinead O'Connor, The Cranberries and others, are featured on a new album that will benefit victims of the Omagh bomb in Northern Ireland.

November: The newly released compilation *The Best of U2 1980–1990* yields a smash hit single in the form of the reworked 'The Sweetest Thing'.

1999 January: U2 begin work on new studio album in Dublin.
September: Bono, Bob Geldof and Quincy Jones meet the The Pope on behalf of Jubilee 2000.
October: Following the MTV Europe Awards show in Dublin, Bono joins Marilyn Manson and Iggy Pop onstage at the latter's gig across town in HQ.

2000 February: Recording of the band's new album is put on hold as Bono travels to the Berlin Film Festival for the world premiere of *The Million Dollar Hotel*, a movie written by the singer, directed by Wim Wenders and starring Mel Gibson.
March: Soundtrack to *Million Dollar Hotel* released. U2 are granted the Freedom of the City of Dublin in a ceremony in the city's new Smithfield Plaza.
August: *Propaganda*, the official U2 fanzine, gives away 50,000 copies of *Hasta La Vista*, a live album recorded in Mexico on the *Pop-Mart* tour.
September: As part of his on-going Jubilee 2000 campaign in support of Third World

countries, Bono delivers a 'Drop the Debt' petition to UN Secretary General Kofi Annan in New York.
October: U2 take to the roof of the Clarence Hotel in Dublin to play their new 'Beautiful Day' single for *Top of the Pops* and release new album *All That You Can't Leave Behind*.
December: *All That You Can't Leave Behind* is banned by the Burmese Government. The album contains a track, 'Walk On', which is dedicated to the imprisoned opposition leader Aung San Suu Kyi.

2001 February: The band pick up an Outstanding Contribution to Music gong at the Brits in London.
March: U2 open their *Elevation* tour in Miami.The band win three awards at the 43rd Grammy Awards in Los Angeles.
September: U2 and other big names of music and film take part in a show that raises $150m for victims of the 9/11 terrorist attacks on New York and Washington.

2002 February: U2 perform live during the haf-time interval at Superbowl XXXVI with 130 million people watching in America and 800 million globally.
March: Bono has an audience with President George W. Bush at the White House to discuss his campaign against world poverty.
November: A new greatest hits compilation is released: *U2: The Best of 1990-2000*.

2003 January: U2 begin work on their new album.
June: They win a Golden Globe for their contribution to Martin Scorsese's *The Gangs Of New York*.

2004 June: Bono addresses a summit of EU leaders in Dublin to present his views on aid development in Africa.
November: U2 are inducted into the UK Rock and Roll Hall of Fame. Their long-awaited 11th album, *How To Dismantle An Atomic Bomb*, hits the shelves and goes straight to No 1 in the UK.

2005 February: U2 win three Grammies for 'Vertigo', bringing their career total to 16.
March: They are inducted into the US Rock and Roll Hall of Fame in New York. The first leg of their world tour kicks off in San Diego.

2006 August: U2 are criticised for moving their publishing business to the Netherlands after the Irish government caps artists' exemption from tax.

2007 June: Having shelved earlier recording sessions with Rick Rubin, U2 begin work on their new album and take a trip to Fez, Morocco with Brian Eno and Daniel Lanois.

2008 March: U2 sign a 12-year deal with giant US entertainment corporation Live Nation worth an estimated £50m.
December: The band finish work on their new album, *No Line On The Horizon*.

2009 February: *No Line On The Horizon* is released. The band say they intend to release another album of material from the sessions before the end of the year.
June: They begin their *360* world tour.

SELECTIVE DISCOGRAPHY

ALBUMS

BOY
Release date: October 1980
Catalogue number: ILPS 9646
Producer: Steve Lillywhite
Track listing: I Will Follow/Twilight/
Into the Heart/Out of Control/
Stories for Boys/The Ocean/A Day
Without Me/Another Time,
Another Place/The Electric Co./
Shadows and Tall Trees.
Highest chart position: No. 52

OCTOBER
Release date: October 1981
Catalogue number: ILPS 9680
Producer: Steve Lillywhite
Track listing: Gloria/I Fall Down/I
Threw a Brick Through a Window/
Rejoice/Fire/Tomorrow/October/
With a Shout/Stranger in a
Strange Land/Scarlet/Is That All?
Highest chart position: No. 11

WAR
Release date: March 1983
Catalogue number: ILPS 9733
Producer: Steve Lillywhite
Track listing: Sunday Bloody
Sunday/ Seconds/New Year's Day/
Like a Song/Drowning Man/The
Refugee/Two Hearts Beat as One/
Red Light/Surrender/40.
Highest chart position: No. 1

THE UNFORGETTABLE FIRE
Release date: October 1984
Catalogue number: U25
Producer: Brian Eno/Daniel Lanois
Track listing: A Sort of
Homecoming/ Pride/Wire/The
Unforgettable Fire/Promenade/4th
of July/Bad/Indian Summer Sky/
Elvis Presley and America/MLK.
Highest Chart position: No. 1

THE JOSHUA TREE
Release date: March 1987
Catalogue number: U26
Producer: Daniel Lanois/Brian Eno
Track listing: Where the Streets
Have No Name/I Still Haven't Found
What I'm Looking For/With or
Without You/Bullet the Blue Sky/
Running to Stand Still/Red Hill
Mining Town/In God's Country/ Trip
Through Your Wires/One Tree Hill/
Exit/Mothers of the Disappeared.
Highest Chart position: No. 1

RATTLE AND HUM
Release date: October 1988
Catalogue number: U27
Producer: Jimmy Iovine
Track listing: Helter Skelter/Van
Diemen's Land/Desire/Hawkmoon
269/All Along the Watchtower/ I
Still Haven't Found What I'm
Looking For/Freedom for My
People/Silver and Gold/Pride (In
the Name of Love/Angel of
Harlem/Love Rescue Me/When
Love Comes to Town/Heartland/
God Part II/The Star Spangled
Banner/Bullet the Blue Sky/All I
Want Is You.
Highest Chart position: No. 1

ACHTUNG BABY
Release date: November 1991
Catalogue number: U28
Producer: Daniel Lanois, with
special thanks to Brian Eno
Track listing: Zoo Station/Even
Better than the Real Thing/One/
Until the End of the World/Who's
Gonna Ride Your Wild Horses?/
So Cruel/The Fly/Mysterious Ways/
Tryin' To Throw Your Arms Around
The World/Ultraviolet (Light My
Way)/Acrobat/Love Is Blindness.
Highest Chart position: No. 1

ZOOROPA
Release date: July 1993
Catalogue number: U29
Producer: Flood, Brian Eno & The
Edge
Track listing: Zooropa/Babyface/
Numb/Lemon/Stay (Faraway, So
Close)/Daddy's Gonna Pay for Your
Crashed Car/Some Days Are Better
than Others/The First Time/Dirty
Day/The Wanderer.
Highest Chart position: No. 1

MELON
Release date: Spring 1995
Catalogue number: MELONCD1
Producer: Various
Track listing: Lemon (The Perfecto
Mix)/Salome (Zooromancer Mix)/
Numb (Gimme Some More Dignity
Mix)/Mysterious Ways (The
Perfecto Mix)/Stay (Underdog
Mix)/Numb (The Soul Assassins
Mix)/Mysterious Ways (remixed by
Massive Attack)/Even Better Than
the Real Thing (The Perfecto Mix)/
Lemon (Bad Yard Club Mix).
Not a commercial release, *Melon* is

compilation of remixes only
available to members of
Propaganda fan club.

POP
Release date: 3rd March 1997.
Catalogue number:
IDU210/524334-2
Producer: Flood.
Additional Production: Steve
Osborne, Howie B.
Track listing: Discothèque/Do You
Feel Loved/Mofo/If God Will Send
His Angels/Staring At The Sun/
Last Night On Earth/Gone/Miami/
The Playboy Mansion/If You Wear
That Velvet Dress/Please/Wake Up
Dead Man.
Highest Chart position: No. 1

2: THE BEST OF 1980-1990
Release date: November 1998
Catalogue number: U211
Producer: Flood
Additional production: Howie B,
Steve Osborne
Track listing: Pride (In The Name of
Love)/ New Year's Day/With or
Without You/I Still Haven't Found
What I'm Looking For/Sunday
Bloody Sunday/Bad/Where the
Streets Have No Name/I Will
Follow/The Unforgettable Fire/
Sweetest Thing/Desire/When Love
Comes to Town/Angel of Harlem/
All I Want Is You
Highest Chart Pos: No.1

HASTA LA VISTA BABY!
U2 live from Mexico
Release date: Summer 2000
Catalogue number: HASTACD1
Sound Engineer: Joe O'Herlihy
Sound Supervisors: Flood and
Howie B
Track listing: Pop Muzik/MoFo/I
Will Follow/Gone/New Year's Day/
Staring at the Sun/Bullet the Blue

Sky/Please/Where the Streets Have
No Name/Lemon (Perfecto Mix)/
Discotheque/With or Without
You/Hold Me, Thrill Me, Kiss Me,
Kill Me/ One
Not a commercial release, Hasta La
Vista Baby is a live recording from
Foro Sol Autodromo, Mexico City
on 3 December 1997 during the
PopMart Tour. It is only available
to members of *Propaganda*.

ALL THAT YOU CAN'T LEAVE
BEHIND
Release date: October 2000
Catalogue number: U212
Producers: Daniel Lanois and
Brian Eno
Additional production: Steve
Lillywhite, Mike Hedges, Richard
Stannard and Julian Gallagher
Track listing: Beautiful Day/Stuck
in a Moment You Can't Get Out
Of/Elevation/Walk On/Kite/In a
Little While/Wild Honey/Peace on
Earth/When I Look at the World/
New York/Grace/The Ground
Beneath Her Feet
Highest Chart Position: No.1

U2: THE BEST OF 1990-2000
Release date: November 2002
Catalogue number: CIDU213
Track listing: Even Better Than The
Real Thing/Mysterious Ways/
Beautiful Day/Electrical Storm/Miss
Sarajevo/Stay (Faraway, So Close!)/
Stuck In A Moment You Can't Get
Out Of/Gone/Until The End Of The
World/The Hands That Built
America/Discotheque/Hold Me,
Thrill Me, Kiss Me, Kill Me/Staring
At The Sun/Numb/The First Time.
Highest Chart Position: No.2

HOW TO DISMANTLE AN
ATOMIC BOMB
Release date: November 2004

Catalogue number: CIDU214
Producer: Steve Lillywhite
Track listing: Vertigo/Miracle Drug/
Sometimes You Can't Make It On
Your Own/Love And Peace Or
Else/City Of Blinding Lights/All
Because Of You/A Man And A
Woman/Crumbs From Your Table/
One Step Closer/Original Of The
Species/Yahweh
Highest Chart Position: No.1

NO LINE ON THE HORIZON
Release date: March 2009
Producer: Lanois/Eno
Track listing: No Line On The
Horizon/Magnificent/Moment Of
Surrender/Unknown Caller/I'll Go
Crazy If I Don't Go Crazy Tonight/
Get On Your Boots/Stand Up
Comedy/Fez – Being Born/White
As Snow/Breathe/Cedars Of
Lebanon
Highest Chart Position: No.1

MINI-ALBUMS

UNDER A BLOOD RED SKY
Release date: November 1983
Catalogue number: IMA 3
Producer: Jimmy Iovine
Mixed by: Shelly Yakus
Track listing: Gloria/11 O'Clock
Tick Tock/I Will Follow/Party Girl/
Sunday Bloody Sunday/The Electric
Co./New Year's Day/40.
Highest Chart position: No. 1

WIDE AWAKE IN AMERICA
Release date: US May 1985
UK (CD only) October 1987
Catalogue number: US 90279 UK
CIDU22
Producers: U2, Brian Eno/Daniel
Lanois, Tony Visconti
Track listing: Bad (live)/A Sort of
Homecoming (live)/The Three
Sunrises/Love Comes Tumbling.

INDEX

AUTHOR'S ACKNOWLEDGEMENTS

A lot has been written about U2, some of it very good. Researching this book, the insights to be gleaned from John Waters' *Race of Angels - The Genesis of U2*, Bill Flanagan's *U2 At The End Of The World* and Brian Eno's *A Year With Swollen Appendices* were particularly valuable. I owe all three writers a vote of thanks. Carter Alan's *U2 Wide Awake In America* and Dave Bowler and Bryan Dray's *U2: A Conspiracy of Hope* cover a lot of ground and were also very useful sources of reference and information. Where covering ground is concerned, however, it would be impossible to equal Pimm Jal de la Parra's exhaustive *U2 Live: A Concert Documentary* – a remarkable labour of love!

Other sources of reference included: Pete Williams and Steve Turner's *U2: Rattle And Hum*; *U2: The Rolling Stone Files* edited by Elysa Gartner; *The Penguin Book of Rock 'n' Roll Writing*, edited by Clinton Heylin; *The Unforgettable Fire* by Eamon Dunphy; *Faraway, So Close*, by B.P. Fallon; *The Greenpeace Book of The Nuclear Age*, edited by John May; *Cultural Icons* by James Patza and numerous editions of *Propaganda* , the U2 fan magazine, and *U2 Collectormania*. I don't think I have taken any undue liberties with any of this material but if I have – sorry!

Inevitably, I plundered the *Hot Press* files and in particular the material gathered in *The U2 File* and *U2: Three Chords and The Truth*, both of which I had the dubious pleasure of editing all those years ago. (Editing is always a dubious pleasure). Finally, in terms of critical writing about U2, there is nothing out there to match Bill Graham's superb *The Complete Guide To The Music of U2*. I have to admit that its existence made my job difficult because so much Bill wrote hit the bullseye. It meant that I had to take a very different approach. This book is the result. I hope that you enjoy it.

It is now almost 30 years since I first met Bono, Adam, Larry and The Edge and they have never been less than utterly courteous and genuinely helpful and supportive in all our many encounters over that frightingly long period. This book might have happened without their co-operation but I certainly wouldn't want to have read it!

I would also like to offer a special thanks to Olaf Tyaransen who undertook so much of the preparatory hard labour for me. Others who helped enormously in different ways were Ali Hewson (for loaning me her husband!), Gavin Friday, Ossie Kilkenny, Anne-Louise Kelly, Candida Bottaci, Paul McGuinness and everyone at Principle Management, Joe O'Herlihy, Steve Iredale, Flood, David Herbert, Ian Jones, Neil Storey, Guggi, Dermot Stokes, Neil McCormick, Colm Henry, Steve Lillywhite, Howie B, Saoirse (of the hair-raising coffee) and Ian Cranna.

At *Hot Press*, Liam Mackey carried me over the hump and Mette Borgstrom and Chris Hackney were wonderful – thanks a million to them, to Paula Nolan, Miranda Moriarty, Maureen Buggy and all of the *Hot Press* crew. As MacPhisto might say, 'I'm baaaaaack'. My commissioning editor Lorraine Dickey was a model of composure throughout what must have been a difficult ride (stay calm, Lorraine).

And finally, the biggest thanks of all to Mairin Sheehy, Duan Stokes and Rowan Stokes without whom it wouldn't have been worth doing. They have supported me wonderfully throughout, without a single word of complaint. I love you.

Niall Stoke